DEAR JOSEPHINE
THE THEATRICAL CAREER OF JOSEPHINE HULL

JOSEPHINE HULL was associated with the theater for more than half a century. She knew everyone and acted in plays from the melodramas of Clyde Fitch and Rupert Hughes to the comedies of Kaufman and Hart, George Kelly, Joseph Kesselring, Mary Chase, and Howard Teichmann. Her story is the story of the American theater for the period from 1902 to 1957.

From a stage-struck Radcliffe college girl, Mrs. Hull developed into one of the most finished and beloved actresses of her time. Endowed with exceptional intelligence, she applied herself with resolution and persistence to the mastery of every phase of her art until finally, in her seventies, she achieved stardom.

The way was often hard, but her determination and courage never flagged. When she died, she left behind her the memory of such irresistible little ladies as Penny Sycamore in *You Can't Take It With You*, Aunt Abby in *Arsenic and Old Lace*, Veta Louise Simmons in *Harvey*, and Laura Partridge in *The Solid Gold Cadillac*.

Here is also the story of her great love for her husband, Shelley Hull, whose untimely death deprived the theater of one of its most promising actors. She outlived him thirty-eight years, but the love story did not end until she died, a very old lady, in 1957.

Dear Josephine

DEAR
JOSEPHINE

The Theatrical Career
of
Josephine Hull

BY WILLIAM G. B. CARSON

UNIVERSITY OF OKLAHOMA PRESS : NORMAN

BY WILLIAM G. B. CARSON

The Theater on the Frontier (Chicago, 1932)

The Letters of Mr. and Mrs. Charles Kean (ed.) (St. Louis, 1945)

St. Louis Goes to the Opera, 1837–1941 (St. Louis, 1946)

Managers in Distress (St. Louis, 1949)

Dear Josephine: The Theatrical Career of Josephine Hull (Norman, 1963)

LIBRARY OF CONGRESS CATALOG CARD NUMBER: 63–9958

Copyright 1963 by the University of Oklahoma Press, Publishing Division of the University. Composed and Printed at Norman, Oklahoma, U.S.A., by the University of Oklahoma Press. First edition.

22436

To My Grandchildren

Preface

One of the pleasures of publishing a book like this is that derived from saying thank you to the good people who have made it possible. Yet the situation of this present author is not without its embarrassments. The friends of Josephine Hull were like the sands of the sea, and the eagerness with which they responded to pleas for help is evidence of their affection and esteem. If I attempted to include in this acknowledgment all those who deserve honorable mention, the publisher would have to add pages to his volume. On the one hand, it seems invidious to pick out a few, and, on the other, some have given so much of their time, and indeed of themselves, that not to give them credit is unthinkable.

This too brief list must be headed by the name of Miss May Davenport Seymour of the Museum of the City of New York, for it was she who put me in touch with Mrs. Hull's nephew, Mr. Charles L. Turner, without whose co-operation the book could never have come into being. As a matter of fact, *co-operation* is a wholly inadequate word to describe what he did. He put at my disposal box on box of material—letters, pictures, reviews, programs, and the invaluable diaries his aunt had kept for over fifty years. And putting them at my disposal meant sending them a thousand miles and leaving them in my possession for months, indeed for years. Then there are Mr. and Mrs. J. Archer O'Reilly, Jr., who, on his mother's death, gave me all the letters she had received over a period of more than half a century from her classmate and devoted friend, Josephine Sherwood Hull.

What can I say of the other members of the Radcliffe Class of '99, headed by Miss Helen Tetlow and Mrs. J. Anderson Lord? Even to suggest their kindness and zeal I have no words. To Mr. Howard Teichmann I am indebted for the details of Mrs. Hull's final engagement with its pathetic but triumphant denouement. Mr. George Freedley, curator of the New York Public Library's theater collection, has responded cheerfully and effectively to every request for information. Finally, there is my wife, who, as always, has been at my side with counsel and encouragement.

As for the others, most of their names appear in the text, and I can do no more than ask them generously to accept these references in token of my very deep appreciation.

WILLIAM G. B. CARSON

St. Louis, Missouri
January 3, 1963

Contents

CONTENTS

Illustrations

DEAR JOSEPHINE

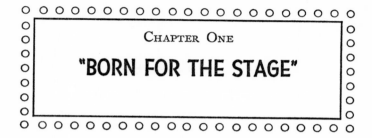

I can assure you, me dear, the crown of my success came when Miss Page (the old lady who says, "They-tell-me") put her arms about me and pressed my head to her shoulder, whispering, "My dear little girl, you were born for the stage."

Imagine my sensation, dear! Oh *you* know how I felt. I'll never make fun of Miss Page again.

PROBABLY MOST HIGH-SCHOOL GIRLS in 1895, whether they admitted it or not, would have accepted as flattery a suggestion that they were natural-born actresses, but to Mary Josephine Sherwood of Newtonville, Massachusetts, the compliment was trebly sweet. It must be confided immediately to that most understanding of souls, Caroline Eddy, a classmate who had not been so fortunate as to be on hand to share the glory.

Josephine was spending the month of August with her mother and a maiden aunt at the Cliff House, a large, rambling resort hotel perched on an eminence ninety feet above the sea near Ogunquit, Maine. Not a widely traveled young lady, she thought this the most beautiful place she had ever seen. "As you stand inside some of the rooms, and look out of the windows," she wrote Caroline, "it seems as if you were on board an ocean steamer and we hear the roar of the surf all the time."

The Cliffs, as she usually called it, was not a fashionable resort, but in spite of a regrettable scarcity of "young uns," she found the guests friendly and jolly. Now that they had revealed an unsuspected penchant for theatricals, both they and

3

the hotel were invested with charms with which she had not
credited them before. She wanted to come back summer after
summer to give them "a taste of her quality."

An Afternoon Rehearsal had been sprung on the boarders
with practically no warning, one of their number having decided that it would be fun to take them by surprise, and rehearsals had been thrillingly clandestine. Here was a captive audience ready to welcome almost any diversion. In return for
the treat afforded them, the members were expected to react
in a definite way. What that way was, they knew as well as
anyone else, and they behaved accordingly. The ballroom
resounded with plaudits, and a young gentleman presented
each curtseying actress with a gorgeous bouquet. Of course Miss
Page, whether she knew anything about acting or not, was
right. If ever anyone was born for the stage, it was Josephine
Sherwood.

Why? That is a question nobody can answer. Probably nobody ever could. It must have been some sort of spontaneous
combustion. She came of a conservative, ultrarespectable middle-class family, which she said was "long on art but short on
money," and there is no likelihood that any one of her kith or
kin had even in dreams felt the urge that stirred her emotions
every day. Her mother's Cousin Lillie, Mrs. John Laughlin
of Buffalo, gave lectures on Shakespeare, but, though sympathetic with Josephine's aspirations, she had never thought
of entering the theatrical profession herself. As for the rest of
the clan, well, the proper place for people like them was on the
right side of the footlights, and that was in the audience.

Josephine had been born in Newtonville, one of the rather
bewildering cluster of Newtons long since swallowed up physically, by the nearby metropolis of Boston. Her father, long
dead, had been a businessman. Her memories of him were at
best very hazy and she seldom referred to him in any way,
except when she occasionally put flowers on his grave in the
family plot on Decoration Day. In the diary she kept for over
fifty years her mother's wedding anniversaries are almost al-

4

ways duly noted. Just once she added, "Of course, my father's too." So much for William Henry Sherwood.

This is not surprising inasmuch as her mother completely dominated her life. Friends remember the former Mary Tewksbury as a short, rather plump little woman with dark hair and large brown eyes like her daughter's, and a warm and friendly temperament. In 1895 she had been for five years the efficient and hard-working secretary of the Newton School Committee, popular with officials and students alike. The black dress she usually wore out of deference to her widowhood belied her cheery disposition.

On the death of her husband in 1886, Mrs. Sherwood had taken her small daughter back to her old home in Newtonville and settled down with her parents and four unmarried sisters. The household on Harvard Street was distinctly of the distaff kind. True, Grandfather Tewksbury was there, but he seems to have been submerged by the seven females who constituted his family circle. His sons had married and moved away, leaving him to fend for himself. In his granddaughter's line-a-day he seldom is mentioned except on his death. Even then the ladies pursued pretty much their normal round of activities, pausing only for the funeral. This does not mean that they were callous or indifferent; they were just sensible.

Josephine's grandmother, the former Jerusha Brainerd, she describes as a "radiant spirit"; yet she has little to say about her either, except that the old lady loved music and that she used to sing for her of an evening, sometimes hymns, sometimes Wagner. With the exception of "Minnie" (as Josephine's mother Mary was called), who was the eldest, none of the "Tewksbury girls" ever married, but Fanny, the next in line, did go abroad to study art and on her return took a room out from under the paternal roof. The others stayed at home until after their mother's death. Anne kept house, a euphemistic way of saying she did the cooking, and her niece sang annual paeans to her roast turkeys on Thanksgiving and Christmas. Gertrude and Ellen taught school. The former was shy and a bit prudish, and spent most of her time in church work. (They were all devout Episcopalians.) "Nellie" (as Ellen was called), on the other hand, was gregarious and loved to bustle about in community undertakings.

Notwithstanding its Puritan background, this was a cheerful, happy household. There were the inevitable minor frictions among the spinster sisters, but everybody loved everybody else in an unabashed sentimental way. For all occasions there were family rituals. Guests were forever coming and going, Josephine's schoolmates, Aunt Nellie's fellow teachers, friends and relatives beyond counting. The numbers of aunts and uncles, Sherwoods as well as Tewksburys and Brainerds, who appear in Josephine's line-a-day are bewildering, and wherever she went, she was welcomed by doting cousins. Not even with the help of a family tree can all of them be placed. Even two unidentified "grandmothers" turn up from time to time.

In the midst of all these relatives lived Mrs. Sherwood and her daughter, wholly wrapped up in a mutual devotion and understanding rare even between affectionate mothers and daughters. Since none of her other children survived infancy, Minnie centered her every thought on her "girlie." Everything she did had but one objective, Josephine's good. When they were apart and tête-à-têtes were impossible, letters crossed each other daily in the mail even between Newtonville and Cambridge. And presents! Not only Christmas and birthdays, but Washington's Birthday, St. Patrick's Day (although they were not Irish), Easter, the Fourth of July, Hallowe'en, and Thanksgiving were remembered. Through the years, many a midnight spread which Josephine provided her fellow actors was owed to her mother. When she died, Ruth Delano, one of Josephine's friends, wrote her, "Thank God that the sorrow is yours instead of hers."

When was Josephine born? That is her secret—jealously guarded all her life and to the best of her ability afterwards. She was observing one of the sacred family traditions. Says an old friend, "I was never able to find out the age of any of the

Tewksburys." The sisters subscribed to the doctrine that on her twenty-first birthday it is the prerogative of every woman to stop turning over the pages of her personal calendar. That is precisely what Josephine did. The secret was kept even from her diary. What is more, she tore out of the first volume a page which evidently had been so indiscreet as to tell tales out of school. Thereafter, although the festivities attendant on January 3 were invariably recorded, no hint is ever to be found to suggest which birthday it is. To clinch the matter, she stipulated in her will that no date of birth was to be carved on the stone above her grave.

Years later, when her fame inspired curious speculations, for reasons of her own she arbitrarily picked 1886—the year of her father's death—for publicity purposes, a thoroughly preposterous choice. For it is certain that, clever and hard-working as she was, she did not graduate from high school at the age of nine, and from college at thirteen. Not until a very few years before her death did she relax. Then one day in an interview with a newspaperman, she admitted that she had been graduated from Radcliffe "Let's say 'about 1900.' " Suddenly, probably to her own intense surprise, she added, almost with a wink, "It really was 1899." That was an impulse she never surrendered to again. No doubt she forgot all about it.

Whenever she was born, she began her education in the Newtonville schools and continued it there until she was ready for college. One of her grammar school classmates, Mrs. J. Anderson Lord, then Elinor Carter, recalls her as "little, very pretty—with large brown eyes—gay and attractive. She was the brightest member of the class."

As the room in the highest grade was arranged, one desk and chair was in front of all the other desks, and the occupant of the chair faced the class, just as the teacher did. The boy or girl who had the highest grade in everything for any term, had the honor of sitting in that chair at that desk facing the class, for the following term. Josephine sat there facing us for three terms out of the four during that last year, of elementary school.

She was not conceited at all, was very unselfish, and jolly and beloved.

High school presented no serious problems, and she romped through the four years, getting excellent grades and having a whirl socially. Mrs. Lord can remember no dramatics. "But even at that time Josephine played easily and from ear on the piano. When our little clubs had meetings, she could be counted on to bring gaiety and fun and beauty to any gathering." She always had innumerable girl friends, Elinor Carter, Caroline Eddy, and Daisy Fillebrown, whose father, a Civil War veteran, she affectionately called "Uncle Phil." No girl with an ounce of discrimination could have asked for more congenial companions. There were always boys buzzing around too, for she was not the kind of girl any boy in his right mind would ignore. She loved football and baseball games, and when Harvard lost to Yale, she was sunk in despair—for a few minutes.

Extensive travel being out of the question, she spent her vacations almost within a stone's throw of home and found nothing to complain about. Sometimes she went up to Manchester, New Hampshire, to visit her cousin Emily Tewksbury, a girl of her own age whose death a year or two later caused the first real grief she ever knew. Then Uncle Phil and Daisy sometimes took her up to a rather primitive farm near Milford, where the two girls enjoyed playing the wheezy old melodion in the parlor, driving a somewhat contrary-minded elderly horse named Kitty, writing short stories, and, above all, acting blood-chilling melodramas in the hayloft.

> Every day we present a tragedy in the barn, throwing ourselves over precipices and leaping into space. Then we give circuses, swinging from the beams and jumping into the hay from the highest, twenty feet above. We tried somersaults in the air but were not successful, strange to say.

Daisy, it so happened, was blessed with an uncle, who in turn was blessed with two very nice sons of the proper age, a summer cottage on Great Diamond Island in Casco Bay, near Portland, and a yacht. To her delight, two summers she was invited to accompany Daisy on visits to her relatives, and did not find that she had to suffer any boredom whatsoever.

Just when it was settled that Josephine was to go on the stage, no one can tell today. Once she said in an interview that the decision was dictated by circumstances which arose a year or two after her graduation from college. It had, however, been in the cards long before it was finally settled on. It had been her dearest wish from early girlhood, but a wish she had regretfully assumed could never be realized. In a letter to Caroline Eddy, written from the Cliffs a few days before the performance that prompted old Miss Page's thrilling comment, she said:

> There is a woman doctor here, Miss Hanchett, of Syracuse, and I have had quite a talk with her. She is very interesting and she makes me more anxious than ever to be a doctor as long as I cannot be—you know what.

Caroline knew *what* very well. But the whole idea was preposterous. Her family would no more have approved of medicine than of the stage. In the 1890's gently reared young ladies, with very few exceptions, did not enter the medical profession. There were too many "indelicacies" involved. Nor had Josephine the slightest affinity for it. In fact, at this stage of her life, she could not bring herself to utter the word *leg*. So the operating room was completely unacceptable.

Whatever she was to make of herself eventually was a decision that could wait. There was, however, another that could not be postponed. With her graduation from Newton High approaching, a more immediate question had to be settled at once. Where was she to go from there?

At that time it was far from a foregone conclusion that once a young lady had emerged, diploma in hand, from a public high school or a private academy she would pursue the path of learning to loftier altitudes. Girls who went on to college were relatively few. But Josephine's case, in the opinion of her family, was a special one. Her record was so excellent that for her not to continue the cultivation of her mind was unthinkable. Sacrifices would have to be made, but there was none her mother was not prepared to face. In fact, since she had but a single aim in life, it would never occur to her that a sacrifice was involved.

To college Josephine must go and the only question was, to which one. Yet that was probably not a question at all. There were several near at hand, but it is likely that only one was considered. The girl had spent her whole life in the environment of Harvard. Her mother and her aunts had many friends in the faculty community. Where else should she go but to the "Annex"? And propinquity was not the only reason—certainly not in the eyes of Miss Sherwood.

A feature story in the *Boston Sunday Herald* a number of years later is headed by the caption: "A GIRL'S COLLEGE WHERE ANY STUDENT MAY BE AN ACTRESS." "It is said," the article begins, "that a young sub-freshman once confided to her bosom friend that the reason she wanted to go to Radcliffe was because there was a real theater there, with a stage and curtain, and anyone might act." This young subfreshman sounds suspiciously like Josephine.

"Some 25 plays are given each year at Radcliffe. Last year there were a dozen or more Idlers, four class plays, three regular open plays, including an operetta, two English and one German play, a couple of playlets coached by Prof. Baker, not to mention a vaudeville." In Josephine's day a writer could have added French, Greek, and Latin dramas. The article continues:

And what about the work and time that go into the plays? There is a story that a girl with most pardonable pride and satisfaction said that she had been to seven rehearsals that day and not a lecture cut! Another poor actress who was rehearsing four plays at once, got her lines so mixed that she talked broken English in the French play, and broken French in the English play. But for the most part, the vast amount of work is so carefully systematized and subdivided that too much seldom falls on the individual.

What sort of a place was this that permitted such goings on? Heaven, Josephine thought.

However exciting in the eyes of a stage-struck girl, these were by no means "goings on" in the eyes of the wise women who called the tunes on the Cambridge campus. They had a very serious purpose, which is set forth in an article entitled "Radcliffe Dramatics" by Elizabeth Stevens in the *Radcliffe Magazine* of March, 1901.

> Radcliffe . . . stands before the world with a presumption in favor of the study of English: the natural outgrowth of that attitude is both work and play along the line of college dramatics; and Radcliffe does not fall short in normal development. The conditions under which dramatics are produced are restricted, owing both to the small stage and the proportionately smaller auditorium; yet in spite of these two serious drawbacks, a large number of plays, many of them requiring elaborate setting, are given every year to the Radcliffe students, and, not infrequently, to a carefully selected public.

It looks as if Josephine was walking right into the lion's den, but Daniel, we may be sure, felt no such elation as hers.

How did the ménage on Harvard Street feel about the perils to which their hitherto sheltered darling was about to be exposed? They would never think of questioning the wisdom of the regal President Agassiz, the widow of one of Harvard's most famous professors and revered as Alma Mater herself; or of Dean Agnes Irwin, a descendant of Benjamin Franklin and the personification of Victorian propriety. If Josephine had any maggots in her brain, these sagacious ladies would exorcise them. After all, no Radcliffe girl had ever compromised herself by becoming a professional actress. They had nothing to worry about—yet.

Had they but known it, these same doting relatives, whose inherited prejudices imposed between her and her dearest ambition the hurdle she thought she could never take, were in the last analysis the ones who had sowed the fateful seeds. They loved the theater themselves, attended it frequently, and often had taken their small niece and seated her on their laps to be enthralled by the glamorous things that were happening across the footlights. They would have much to answer for.

CHAPTER TWO

RADCLIFFE, '99

So to Radcliffe Josephine went.

When she first stepped across the threshold of historic Fay House, although the school was nearly fifteen years old, its name was new. Had she been two or three years older, she would have been enrolled in the Society for the College Instruction of Women, or, as it was rather disrespectfully known, the Harvard Annex. But thanks to the vigor and persuasiveness of that remarkable woman, Elizabeth Cary Agassiz, it had been duly chartered and became a college in name as well as in fact, with some of the most famous professors from the nearby Yard on its faculty.

Although some of the activities carried on under the benign surveillance of its revered president may have raised the eyebrows of the orthodox, there were definite limits to her unconventionality. She exacted of her charges, all of whom she called "Dear," unfailingly "ladylike behavior in all respects," and was proud to announce that "We have had as yet no flighty students." The young ladies pursued their daily routines decorously swathed in garments which completely en-

13

veloped the human form not-always-divine now on display on almost every campus in the country. "Flightiness" would have included riding one's bicycle uncovered by one's proper hat.

It was in this environment with its fusion of good breeding and scholarly purpose that Josephine spent the next four years of her life. She became one of the Girls of '99. To this class to her dying day she was fondly linked. After her graduation, whenever she was free to do so, she returned to participate in its reunions, and her diary and letters bear witness to her delight in being again with "the girls."

What was Josephine like in September, 1895? Theater goers who knew her only in the days of her fame—of Aunt Abby Brewster, Veta Louise Simmons, and Laura Partridge—might find it hard to recognize the rotund, fluttery little lady in the slim, graceful, eager freshman of sixty-odd years ago. "I remember so well," says Mrs. George Flebbe, Beulah Dix in those days, "her beautiful dark eyes, her exquisite hands, her short, well modeled forearms, and her well-turned wrists." She was very small, with slender ankles and tiny feet, quick in her movements, her face radiant with the joy of living. She was, in short, a very delectable little person.

Although Cambridge was less than five miles from Newtonville, Mrs. Sherwood decided that it would be best for Josephine to live nearer to the school. She realized that the time had come to put some distance between the girl and the family on Harvard Street, where her every move would inevitably be discussed pro and con and she would be subjected to cross-questioning which could easily become exasperating. Since there was as yet no dormitory, a comfortable room was found with the family of Dr. Norton Folsom, whose younger daughter, Clara, soon proved to be a kindred spirit. She simply adored the theater.

It is too bad that Josephine did not begin her line-a-day until the middle of her sophomore year or that, if she did, the volumes have disappeared. She was very punctilious about it in 1897, but 1898 is a blank, as is also, unfortunately, all of 1899 except the first two months and a few days in April. Luckily her "dearest Caroline" had not followed her to Radcliffe, but had gone to faraway Smith instead, and had of course to be kept informed of what was going on. In the hurry and flurry of her new life she did not find time to write often, but when she wrote, she wrote, and the letters go on for page after page, and probably caused the recipient agonies of regret that she had not chosen her alma mater more wisely.

Despite the glittering attractions of extracurricular affairs, Josephine was far too conscientious to neglect the more formal side of her college life. She knew very well that her education was not being gained without sacrifices on her mother's part, and she would never under any circumstances fail her. Moreover, she was herself too good a Yankee not to be determined to get her money's worth. Diligent application to her studies entailed no hardship. Nature had endowed her with an unusually quick mind and a capacity for hard work as well as a well-nigh indestructible constitution. What is more, it had blessed her with phenomenal delight in everything that came her way. This did not exclude classes or teachers, as Caroline was informed shortly after the semester began.

> College is progressing finely, and I am enjoying it *so* much. I take Greek, Latin, Chemistry, French and English and I am going to take German if they will let me take six courses. [They did.] The professors are all fine, especially Prof. Greenough, who is an old dear, and the English professor Mr. Hurlburt, who looks like an actor, walks like an actor, and talks like an actor, and they say he is leading man in the Cambridge dramatic club. He is simply fine and a splendid instructor, too.

James Bradstreet Greenough continued to be a joy. When he read *Pharmio* aloud, he grew so exuberant that he sang and "made his feet go" to show the rhythm.

Life under the roof of the warmhearted Folsoms was joyous too. "We have such jolly times in the evening when we sing college songs and behave dreadfully." Dreadful in another way were the midyear examinations. In fact, they were horrid. "I am thankful they are over. They used to pass round beef tea halfway through the time, to resuscitate us." *O tempora! O mores!*

All these things were very important, of course, but Josephine knew very well that they were not what her correspondent was really yearning to hear about. Therefore she turned to more worthwhile matters, and poured forth page after page of rhapsody. Poor Caroline probably turned a livid green with envy.

First of all there was *King Arthur*. "Irving! Irving! Terry! Terry! and oh *would* that I could say Terriss!!!! I have been in a perfect trance of bliss since yesterday noon and couldn't resist the temptation of writing you all about it today." Her outpourings fill both sides of four sheets of letter paper before she turns her attention to *The Corsican Brothers*. If any stage historian thinks he needs to know more about Irving's productions, he has but to pore over this not exactly cold-blooded account.

As time went on other idols rose before Josephine's ecstatic gaze. By March there was another. "Oh Sothern! Sothern! He is divine in every way." Even the star of William Terriss was dimmed in its glory. She saw her new favorite twice in *The Prisoner of Zenda*, the first time from the second balcony where her eyes overflowed continuously, the second from down front, where, perhaps because of the proximity of a dignified male escort, she managed somehow to keep back her tears. Said escort had his own charms and he was soon to introduce her to glories she dreamt not of, but first she had to tell Caroline more about Sothern.

As good luck would have it, a friend of Aunt Fanny's had a sister who had formerly been in his company. "She says he is just as lovely off the stage as he is on, *and* he is unmarried!! I made her talk about the stage and Sothern as much as I could. She asked me to go over and see her sometime and she would tell me all about her stage life; it is too good an opportunity to miss, don't you think so?" What was Aunt Fanny thinking about to permit this?

"I have been acting a good deal," Miss Sherwood reported

in her next communiqué, "and that, as you know, is bliss." With plays going on to the right and left of her, she wasted no time in involving herself up to the eyes in them. Nor did it take those in command long to discover that in the little girl from Newtonville they had acquired something worth having. "I had charge of an entertainment given by our class to the sophomores and it was quite a success although simply terrible to get up. It took the form of *charades en costume* with scenes from Gilbert and Sullivan." Josephine, arrayed in one of Dora Drew's Chinese dresses, sang "Three Little Maids from School" and executed a fan dance.

After all was said and done, however, such affairs were of minor consequence. The really important productions were those put on by three clubs: Idler, a social club that met once every two weeks and staged numerous plays during the year; Emanuel, a non-sectarian religious group with theatrical tendencies; and the Glee Club, which in the late nineties was responsible for a number of original operettas.

With its emphasis on the study of English and all the resulting preoccupation with dramatics, it was inevitable that Radcliffe should attract young women whose interests lay primarily in the arts, especially literature, writing, music, and theater. There is no space to name here all those who in time won distinction in these fields, but mention should be made of Gertrude Stein, Helen Keller, Josephine Preston Peabody, Beulah Marie Dix, Mabel Daniels, and Rebecca Hooper. It was with the last three that Josephine was to be most closely associated, and the first of these was "Miss Dix," as she respectfully called her with the formality which extended even to girls' colleges in the nineties. This young playwright, who was making a first test of the talents which were soon to give her a national reputation and, incidentally, to introduce Douglas Fairbanks to Broadway, vividly recalls her first encounter with the future comedienne. Four days before the scheduled *première* of *The Wooing of Mistress Widdrington*, which she had written for Idler, the sophomore who had been cast in the title role "came down with a bad cold and couldn't croak a word. I was doing a triple performance as writer, producer, and leading man, and I was triply despairing."

Some one kindly said: There's a Freshman named Josephine Sherwood who has never acted in the Idler, but she's acted elsewhere in amateur things.

I'd never heard of the girl, but with a flicker of hope in my heart I paddled through the snow to the house where she boarded—and that was my first meeting with Josephine, and the beginning of a lifelong friendship.

Without boasting, simply as a calm statement of fact, she said she felt she could get up the part in four—no, it was really only three days. And she did. She always did what she said she could do. You could rely on her as you could rely on a rock. On Friday she walked on the little stage in a charming little seventeenth century frock—I never asked her where or how she got it—with an armful of jonquils and she gave a performance that made the rest of us look like (what we were) amateurs. The play was repeated by request—thanks to Josephine.

Josephine's account was dispatched to "dearest Caroline."

The play was really awfully good and very well written, and the girls liked it so much that we are going to give it again for the ladies' public Saturday afternoon. I had a very sweet part and the costume was so pretty—in the time of Charles I— Miss Dix who wrote the play took the part of my lover, and I tell you we had fun.

The Wooing of Mistress Widdrington initiated her into Idler, of which she remained a busy member until her graduation. She acted, she directed, she made up, she ushered, and she taught the other girls how to dance. "She was a generous person," continues Mrs. Flebbe. "In those early plays I never saw her try to fatten her own performance at the expense of a fellow actor. She was modest—she never tried to take over the direction of the play, tho' very likely she'd have done it better

18

than I did! And she never let herself be disturbed by the various mischances of an amateur performance. As I look back, I realize that in those college days she was amazingly mature—poised and calm, and very sure of what she wanted to do and how she meant to do it."

Josephine was, then, off to a good start—so good, indeed, that news of her successes soon spread beyond the walls of Fay House. In her first letter to Caroline after the beginning of her Radcliffe days, she mentions the fact that her English professor, Mr. Hurlburt, is the leading man of the Cambridge Dramatic Club or, to dignify it with its full name, the Cambridge Social Dramatic Club, of which the moving spirit was a young man destined to far greater fame than the rather stagy instructor of English A. This was no less a person than George Pierce Baker, at whose feet were soon to be sitting, in English 47 at Harvard, men with such names as Eugene O'Neill, Sidney Howard, Thomas Wolfe, Philip Barry, and John Mason Brown, to cite but a few. It was probably Hurlburt who spotted her and enlisted her services. Whoever it was, she had not been in Cambridge many months before she was acting with the foremost dramatic club in the vicinity in Pinero's *The School Mistress*. That, she thought when it was over, was it, but there was someone else who thought otherwise. Again we must dip into the lengthy screed she indited for the enlightenment of Caroline on March 3.

After my first appearance over here in the School Mistress with the Dramatic Club I had not supposed that I should act with them again this year, but the third performance they gave they asked me to play in a little curtain-raiser called "The Nettle" which had only two parts, the other being taken by Mr. Rolfe, whom you probably remember my speaking of. Of course I was perfectly delighted and the part was by far the best one I had ever had to take, being the only girl in the play— It was a hard part as she was never two minutes in the same mood, but I loved it and worked on it with all my might; and Mr. Rolfe was perfectly fine to act with—he is almost like a professional and quite inspired me. And what do you think? I found that he had refused to play unless I would take the part with him! It sounds terribly conceited, but I tell you everything, so do take it in the way I mean it, won't you, dear? . . . We had all but two of the rehearsals here, the other two being necessarily at the hall, and Mr. Rolfe never came emptyhanded; such flowers and candy I never expect to have again. All this would seem rather queer from most engaged men, but Mr. Rolfe is so different from other men, somehow, you never think of things like that with him. Well, the play was a grand success both at the dress rehearsal and performance and it was the "proudest moment of my life."

After the performance proper there were three curtain calls. "Of course there came the usual reaction after it, and I was in the depths of despair not to be acting, but it is a sort of pleasant despair after all."

It goes without saying that young Rolfe, though engaged, now occupied a pinnacle of favor far above those to which any of her other "gentlemen callers" had yet climbed. Chaperoned by Clara Folsom, he had been the dignified escort who had shamed away her tears over Edward Hugh Sothern, and now almost nonchalantly he played his ace of trumps. If she was not rendered speechless, it was only because nature had not made her that way.

Mr. Rolfe—she never presumed to use his Christian name, which was Charles—was one of the three sons of the celebrated scholar, William J. Rolfe, whose discreetly expurgated school editions of Shakespeare introduced a goodly portion of the American public to the dramatic masterpieces of the most illustrious of all poets. As his father's son he moved in circles up to which ordinary mortals like Josephine could only gaze from far below. It is not difficult, therefore, to imagine that young lady's state of mind when one day he asked quite casually if she and Clara had ever met Julia Marlowe and her husband, Robert Taber. Coming from anyone else, the question would have been silly, but apparently it did not seem so to him. When of course the girls said no, he just as casually inquired "if we would like to go in on Saturday afternoon and go behind the scenes and meet them!!!! Do you wonder the mere possibility quite took away my breath?"

He was as good as his word, and before the next matinee presented himself and the two palpitating freshmen at the stage door of the Hollis Street Theater. Miss Marlowe was dressing, and asked if they would mind waiting a little. The backstage regions of a real theater, which were in time to become to Josephine a second home, were in 1896 a strange new world of mystery and enticement, and she could only stare and gape, and tug at Clara's sleeve to direct her attention to this wonder and that. The members of the cast, descending from their dressing rooms, passed the two girls and smiled at them sympathetically.

Finally there appeared a god-like figure, and I fairly held my breath; Clara didn't recognize him, but I did at once—Robert Taber. He was dressed as Orlando and looked divinely handsome. Oh Caroline, imagine my sensations when Mr. Rolfe introduced him and he really shook hands with us and spoke so cordially and pleasantly. He said we must forgive his wife and him if they didn't have time to pay us much attention as they would both naturally be very busy. Then he excused himself a moment and went on to the stage, where we saw him ordering some of the men around; then he beckoned to us and led us across the stage to the very front wing on the left hand side, where he made several firemen get out of the way, and placed two chairs in the very front for Clara and me while Mr. Rolfe stood just behind us. We were right *on* the stage, although we could not be seen from the audience. Mr. Taber stood there talking with us and said anxiously he feared we would find it very stupid there and he hoped we wouldn't be bored! As if there could be anything more blissful!

In due time Julia Marlowe emerged from her dressing room, and, waiting on the opposite side for her first cue, waved at Rolfe and smiled at the girls. Later on, when she had no more costume changes to make for a while, Taber brought her over to the watchers in the wings.

Dear Julia Marlowe, she is just as sweet and fascinating and lovely near to as she is from the audience, and she was perfectly lovely to us, just as cordial and pleasant as she could be, and she made us feel that she was really glad to have us there. When she was on the stage she would smile at us if she happened to be near us and once when she was right by our wing she pulled her flower to pieces and threw it at us.

Throughout the afternoon Taber hovered solicitously close to his guests and saw to it that they missed nothing. "It didn't take away from the romance of it at all to see it as we did, and I said so to Mr. Taber."

Did she in later years remember this when, as she so often did, she opened her arms to eager young things who came backstage and stood, thrilled and awed, at her dressing room door? It is not likely that she forgot.

So Josephine's career at Radcliffe was off to a flying start. The tremendous energy and vitality which were to keep her afoot throughout her life were already at their full strength. She must also have been blessed with powers of concentration and a rare ability to budget her time; otherwise she could not have done all she did and pass her various courses creditably enough to win her a *magna cum laude* when she graduated.

Her line-a-day for 1897 shows that after the excitement of her freshman year she kept up the same pace; if anything, she accelerated it. She dashed about from one place to another, never seeming to pause to catch her breath; perhaps it would be better to say that she never lost it. By this time word of her accomplishments had spread over the whole community, and she was bombarded with pleas from, it would appear, nearly every organization that was in the business of putting on amateur plays. With the Cambridge Dramatic Club she had already identified herself, and those who steered its course had no intention of letting her go. Again and again she was invited to appear in its productions, and if she ever said no, there is no evidence of the fact. Then, closer to home were the Newtonville Players who thought she should be loyal to the place of her birth and help them on to glory. All these solicitations she took to be gracious compliments. As she had told Caroline, to act was bliss, but, though she did not advertise the fact, there was a very serious purpose underlying her ready acceptances.

Naturally the Radcliffe activities took precedence over the others; nevertheless, she could, and frequently did, effect a sort of fusion all her own. One is reminded of the girl mentioned in the *Herald* article who got her various speeches all mixed up, but that girl was not Josephine Sherwood. For instance, in May, while busy enough for any normal human being with the Glee Club and an imminent Emanuel performance of *Cranford*, she somehow managed to sandwich in a short play for the Dramatic Club.

> In the evening was the Dramatic Club, & it was perfectly *fine*. Had a glorious time & the play went finely as did the other two too. I had lovely flowers—roses from Mamma & carnations from Mr. Denny. Fine time afterwards—so sorry it is over.

In her excitement she forgot to note in the diary what the play was. As things turned out, however, the really important feature of the evening was not the forgotten playlet but Mr. Denny with his arms full of carnations. Of him, more later—much more.

Probably closest to her heart of all the various groups was the Radcliffe Glee Club. It provided an outlet for both her musical and her histrionic talents, and throughout her four college years she labored and rejoiced with it. As a junior and a senior she had the satisfaction of being its leader. Already she had begun to dabble in composition, and the first fruits of her endeavors were two operettas, *The Orientals* and then *The Princess Perfection*, both produced under her own direction.

Most Radcliffe plays and operettas had their scenes laid in remote time or space because it was of course unheard of for any modest young lady to appear in trousers even before audiences of female relatives and friends. Costume plays usually provided happy solutions. When modern pieces were presented, the answer was—bloomers. There were no bloomers in Josephine's operettas, for she kept them far away from such graceless garments.

In the midst of all this activity she found time on New Year's Day, 1899, to send her season's greetings to Caroline. The letter is only a fraction as long as those written when she was a freshman, and the passing of time had had an effect on her epistolary style.

> The operetta progresses, as I told you in that hasty moment after the Players, and it is to be given for two nights in Easter week, in Brattle Hall. We shall have a larger chorus and orchestra. The old operetta has been engaged by some Wellesley Hills people, who will adapt it, and pay me a royalty. I feel so grand!

The "old operetta" was *The Orientals*. Among the numbers in its score was one entitled "The Cat and the Sparrow," which for some time had an independent career of its own. In these supersophisticated days this ditty would not be likely to find a ready audience, but at the turn of the century it evidently caught on. Several years later while she was acting at the Gem Theater in Portland, the *Sunday Telegram* (August 12, 1906) reported in a feature story that "Only last week Miss Sherwood received payment of royalties for 500 copies from one of the musical clubs in the West, showing that its popularity still exists."

As for *Princess Perfection,* it too found favor and a publisher, the C. W. Thompson Company of Boston, which brought out eight of its songs in a special paperback edition. For over twenty years Josephine continued to put her melodic gift to good use and with it to supplement her income. Eventually, with the changing of tastes, her compositions ceased to find a market and she, a publisher.

From the foregoing it might seem that at Radcliffe she did nothing but run about the landscape, acting in and putting on plays. On the contrary, she was very serious about her studies, and applied herself diligently to them although just when she found time to do her homework is an open question. Nearly half a century later, in an interview with William Lindsay Gresham, who was preparing a "profile" of her for *Theatre Arts* (June, 1945), she put her appreciation of her college work into words.

> I had opportunities that so many other young people in the theater miss. I got so much out of college; we had George Lyman Kittredge for Chaucer and Shakespeare. And George Pierce Baker for drama history and stagecraft. And Charles Townsend Copeland — the famous "Copey" — for English "lit." Copey would have made a wonderful actor—he put so much into anything he was talking about; he had the dramatic gift. Men like these gave me a groundwork for the theater that I couldn't have gained in any other way. Everything they said made you want to go and find out more by yourself. I fell in love with the theater. But theory can take you just so far. I knew that the only way to learn to act is to do it.

She was certainly stretching the truth a bit when she said it was the inspiration of these great teachers that made her fall in love with the theater. She was head over heels in love with it long before she ever heard one of them drop his pearls of wisdom. However, they did nothing to cool her ardor. Figuratively speaking, they took her by the hand and led her on, especially Baker and Copeland. It was not until she was a senior that she and "G. P." faced each other across a desk, but the beloved Copey she encountered in her second year, when she enrolled in English 22. That was an auspicious day for her; years later when she was fighting to gain a sure foothold on the stage, he helped her more than once. "Mr. Copeland back," she wrote in the diary, "& I had an A in English, so surprised." The professor, whatever his views on the subject of higher education for women—he flatly refused to teach them argumentation—was shrewd enough to know a good thing when he saw it—even in skirts. "Josephine's themes in English 22," recalls Mrs. Alfred H. Terry (Marian Campbell), "were often read aloud to the class—a great honor. They often had little dramatic touches—a clown reading a newspaper with spectacles, in the wings—and then bounding on the stage." This was not run-of-the-mill stuff in a sophomore theme. What is more, Copey was a theater addict, another bond between them. With Baker, although she studied under him in her last year, her contacts—and they were very close—were chiefly outside the classroom and, for the most part, after her graduation.

Of the twenty-five courses she took at Radcliffe, as listed in the college records, eleven were in English, but at the same time she was wise enough to apply herself to the languages as well. Greek she left behind her, but she kept up her Latin (for one year), French, and German. She also took a year of Italian, at the end of which she was presented by Professor Charles Grandgent with a handsome copy of Dante as a reward for her application and proficiency. Her grades are classified material hidden deep in the college archives, but we know she came off with a *magna* and eventually with an honorary Phi Beta Kappa.

During these rather hectic years, by some hocus-pocus, she found time to haunt the Boston theaters, and there was exposed to some of the finest acting of the day, for few of the great stars, native or foreign, passed by the Athens of America. With intense interest and her keen perception she absorbed every detail of acting and production, and stored the memory away for future reference. She was not yet in a position to indulge very often in her later practice of seeing plays she admired over and over again so that, having recovered from the emotional impact of the first time, she could analyze and appraise dispassionately. Nor did she always have to view the luminaries across the footlights. Once, at a party, she actually met Ethel Barrymore.

26

And music! She loved symphonies, and seldom missed the weekly public rehearsal of the great Boston orchestra. All her life opera remained one of her most intense passions. She was the perfect Wagnerite, transported to the Seventh Heaven of Seventh Heavens by the *Ring* or *Parsifal*. After any one of them, like the young lovers in *Our Town*, she didn't quite hear what people said to her or see the streets along which she made her way home. Her tastes were catholic, and she reveled indiscriminately in the creations of French and Italian masters as well. Calvé left her palpitating. Singing came almost as naturally to her as speech, and many a night after a busy day she sang herself sleepy as Carmen, Isolde, or Brunnhilde.

In June came the end of her college days, and with the other Girls of '99 she became an alumna. "So sorry it is over!" Looking back nostalgically twenty-five years later, she remembered especially "Idlers, operettas, Greek tragedy, examinations and class meetings. The old gas footlights, the way the curtain fell, the little stairway for entrances, Beulah Dix, Clara Folsom, the smell of spring through the windows . . . we in our caps and gowns over white muslin."

Now she must get out into the world and seek the answers to many questions.

Chapter Three

"THE THEATER IS MY LIFE"

JUST WHAT JOSEPHINE DID during the six months that followed her graduation is for the most part not clear, since she left little evidence behind her. Such information as can be picked up today must be gleaned from casual references in her diary after she resumed it on New Year's Day, 1900. There was, however, one thing she very definitely did not do. She did not take a job which would occupy her entire time. She wanted ample freedom to prepare herself for whatever profession she eventually decided to enter. That decision was obviously still by no means made. What she wanted to do is clear enough, but she had not yet discovered that it might be feasible. Probably her mother demurred. But that, even so, she had dismissed it from her mind is incredible.

Furthermore, she wanted to be absolutely sure that she was really qualified. If she was going to take a radical step, she did not intend to fall on her face. She was much too astute to take overseriously the raptures of her friends and the plaudits of the uncritical audiences of Cambridge and Newtonville. These thrilled her, as praise always did, but she had too good a head on her shoulders to let them determine her future. There were, however, others whose judgments were neither sentimental nor emotional. Men like Charles Townsend Copeland and George Pierce Baker were not prone to bestow hollow flattery on every young lady who, after a taste of undiscriminating applause, concluded that she was destined to follow Maude Adams and Julia Marlowe to the heights. Nor was Mrs. Agassiz likely to bestow an encouraging pat on the head unless she was well satisfied that she had reason. Even so, Josephine still hesitated.

This much is clear. The choice lay between the stage and music. She herself preferred the former, her family, very positively, the latter. Accordingly she at once set about cultivating still further whatever talents she had in the two fields. One of her first steps was to enroll in the New England Conservatory of Music. She remained through two academic years. "Her subjects in the first year," according to Mr. Elwood Gaskill, the Registrar, "were Harmony with Wallace Goodrich, Theory and Musical Journalism with Louis C. Elson." During her second year she continued her study of harmony, and added instrumentation, also under Goodrich. At the same time she took private lessons in voice.

The tuition was costly, and she realized she must do something to bring in at least a little income. As soon as the schools reopened in September, she secured a position as teacher of elocution and singing at the excellent one for girls conducted by Arthur Gilman, the original sponsor of Radcliffe. Since her classes met only once a week, they interfered very little with her own studies. After the first year she taught twice a week, and in addition directed an occasional play acted by the children. Moreover, in 1901–1902 she delivered weekly pre-symphony lectures. For these services she was paid, according to notations in the back of her diary, the prodigious salary of two hundred dollars for each of the first two years. What she received for the third, she fails to say.

She had, besides, several private pupils, girls whom she trained in elocution, and also directed or managed an assortment of programs for various groups ranging from Miss Hersey's School in Boston to the Newton Masonic Hall Association. She also sometime played the organ in St. John's Episcopal Church as well as singing in the choir, but there is nothing to show that she was remunerated.

In March, 1901, she coached the first of a number of productions at Wellesley College, in this case Pinero's *The Amazons*, a comedy with which she was to have many associations, not all of them agreeable, in the years to come. Her fees for these stints were not large even for those days, sometimes $23.00, sometimes $25.00, but they added up.

All in all, her stipends ran the gamut from $5.00 for training the Grace Church girls in Japanese dances to $45.00 for directing three performances of *Jo March*, an original play by Elizabeth Lincoln Gould, based of course on Louisa May Alcott's novel. (She had the pleasure of meeting one of Miss Alcott's nephews.) Far more valuable than the very modest income she derived from this employment was the training she got herself. In the course of three years she accumulated a very respectable amount of experience that was to stand her in excellent stead for many years.

The continual demands made upon her are evidence of the recognition she had already achieved in her own community or, to be more exact, communities. Here was no prophet without honor in her own country. Never in her long life did Josephine play that role. Often she was called back to Radcliffe to help one or another of the clubs of which she had been a member. Local theatrical groups were forever drafting her, occasionally for pay, never much, occasionally for charity. She acted, she directed, she sang, she managed, she drilled dancers and choruses, she played the organ, and she gave all manner of monologues and readings. She seems to have been almost incapable of saying no, and never to have wearied overmuch. Indeed, she was having a wonderful time, and nothing stopped her, not even the deaths of people she loved. Far from unfeeling, she was throughout her life prodigal in the bestowal of her affections. She was also a realist, and she learned young that life does not stop for grief. If she was going to be a musician or an actress, she must surrender the luxury of giving in to sorrow, however poignant.

Twice in these first years death struck close to home. In April, 1901, Grandfather Tewksbury succumbed to the infirmities of age. She helped nurse the old gentleman in his last hours, and arranged the funeral. But she missed no rehearsals, and went almost straight from the graveside to a performance.

Far more tragic was the sudden death from typhoid fever of her chum, Clara Folsom, the girl who had shared with her the unforgettable experience with the Tabers. She helped the stricken family as best she could, arranged the flowers, and played the organ at the funeral. In the meantime, she went with her mother to hear the Metropolitan Opera in an exciting performance of *Otello*, temporarily forgetting her grief under the spell of Eames, Alvarez, and Scotti.

During these years Professor Baker and the Cambridge Social Dramatic Club were very much in the picture. Working with and under this remarkable man gave her experience she was always to find of the greatest service. He was a master whose genius eluded definition. "It was always easier to admire Professor Baker," says John Mason Brown, "than to explain the spell he cast or the contribution he made. He happened to have that talent for communication and that genius for igniting others essential to all great teachers." Josephine assuredly needed no igniting, but she would never have denied that he nurtured her own personal blaze.

Probably his outstanding success with the Dramatic Club was a production of *The Romancers*, a translation of Rostand's *Les Romanesques*, in which the leading roles of Percinet and Sylvette were taken by him and Josephine. This was given a public dress rehearsal on April 27, 1900, with an open performance the next evening, thus filling in a brief gap between Beulah Dix's *To Serve for Meat and Fee* and *A Copper Complication*, of which more later. The ecstasies of the heroine were no greater than those of the girl who played her.

31

April 28..... Ev'g performance of Rostand's "Romancers"—
flowers from Prof. Baker, Prof. & Mrs. Greenough, also Mr.
& Mrs. Greenough, Mr. Elliot, May Howland, Mrs. Sever &
Mamma. Exquisite. Went beautifully. Gorgeous time, dancing, etc.

There was more. Among Baker's former students was a
young man who, for the time being had turned his attention
away from matters theatrical to matters architectural, but who
was before long to return to his first love, and make for himself
a memorable place in that world. He was among those who
saw the play, and his tribute is significant.

> NORTH EASTON
> MASSACHUSETTS
> 3d May 1900

My DEAR GEORGE BAKER:

I have not yet forgotten, and I want to tell you, how much I
enjoyed the "Romancers." Honestly and thoroughly enjoyed,
from the beginning to the end, without intermission & without
any qualification. It was delightful.

The play itself seemed to me charming, and, moreover, one
which was exactly adapted for non-professional use—and I
don't believe that any professional company, in this country at
least, could have kept, as you kept, the high spirit of delicate,
playful mock-seriousness which was its life. Professional realism
would have murdered it. To call you and Miss Sherwood
"professionally" good in that play would be an insult—you
were better!

Thank you, sir, for a most delightful evening.

> Sincerely yours,
> WINTHROP AMES

So obviously was *The Romancers* a potential money-maker
that it was revived again and again, one charity after another
coming hat in hand. Josephine and Baker were always the
youthful lovers, and the young "Mr. Elliot" who had followed

Mr. Denny bearing flowers was also involved. Of him too, more later.

But already Josephine was deep in preparations for something else. Two seniors were pooling their talents in the composition and presentation of another operetta, *A Copper Complication,* for which Rebecca Hooper was providing the book, and Mabel Daniels the score. Although she was now an alumna, they included in their dramatis personae a role for their friend, and a song for her to sing.

The *Complication,* which was given four performances early in May, turned out to be another rousing hit. For the duration Josephine stayed with Jane Sever, a classmate with whom she had been becoming more and more intimate, and returned each night with armfuls of tributary blossoms. She garnered no less than seven bouquets. The practice was contagious. To the end of her days she herself scattered nosegays with a profusion which must have made the fortune of many a florist.

Summer meant no cessation, for Josephine could no more stop acting than she could stop breathing. The Severs had in nearby Kingston a wonderful old summer home that became the annual resort of many of the Girls of '99. A large house dating back to the eighteenth century, when Jane's seafaring ancestors had occupied it the year round, it had capacious rooms crammed with antiques, inside communal "plumbing" of the same kind that elicits giggles from tourists inspecting Calvin Coolidge's home at Plymouth, Vermont, and a vast attic one might think that the Severs' Puritan forebears, with an eye to the future, had designed expressly for play acting. Now it was taken over by the Radcliffe invaders, and many a good show must the startled ghosts have enjoyed. As usual Josephine was the heroine, and Ruth Delano the modestly bloomered hero. Not always were the actresses content with supernatural audiences, for on occasion they also displayed their talents for the delectation of natives and summer residents.

Autumn brought a resumption of the familiar pattern of Josephine's existence. But the second October after her graduation was marked by a step that, although no one realized it at the time, settled once and for all the question of her future.

During the third quarter of the nineteenth century, one of the most respected actresses in the United States was Catherine Mary Reignolds, known professionally as "Kate." An Englishwoman by birth, she had been brought to this country as a child, and, while still a very young girl, had so impressed Edwin Forrest that he had engaged her to support him in a performance of Sheridan Knowles' greatly admired tragedy, *Virginius*. Before very long she became leading lady at the famous Boston Museum. During the five years she remained there she made many friends in the city and married Erving Winslow, a rising young businessman. Her sojourn at the Museum was followed by two decades of touring the country as a star. Then, unobtrusively withdrawing from the stage, she settled down in Boston and established herself as a leader in the intellectual circles of the city. Her retirement, however, was not complete, for, with the example of Fanny Kemble before her, she embarked upon a series of public readings, with the difference that, whereas Mrs. Kemble had limited herself to Shakespeare, Mrs. Winslow turned her attention to the dramas of modern writers, especially those of the controversial Henrik Ibsen. The recognition gained through these adventurous programs, once they had been accepted, greatly heightened her prestige.

But occasional readings were not enough to occupy the time of so energetic a woman, and, in response to the urgings of her friends, she undertook to pass on some of her knowledge to a few carefully chosen aspirants to theatrical fame. Here was an opportunity that Josephine could not overlook, however little she could afford it financially. So on October 1, 1900, she presented herself at the Winslow doorway, and began a course of lessons whose value she can scarcely at this time have foreseen. A woman of culture and breeding, the former actress was well qualified to perceive the girl's potentialities, and to understand and sympathize with her personal problems. The two speedily became close friends, and for years the older woman served as unofficial mentor to the younger one. Her help was at times material. In later years handsome dresses from her own wardrobe found their way into Josephine's meager one.

Usually there were two lessons a week, except during the summer. Of these the brief notes in the diary tell little beyond the fact that Mrs. Winslow usually concentrated on one role at a time—Juliet, Beatrice, Ophelia, Kate Hardcastle, or Rose Trelawney among others—and also that her pupil was enthralled. With her background, it is unlikely that her style and technique were up to date. On the other hand, the woman who had dared to pioneer with Ibsen and Maeterlinck cannot have had her eyes too steadily fixed on the methods of a day that, however glamorous, was fast fading into night. Certainly she gave her student a thorough grounding in diction and in comedy. Anything Josephine may have found obsolescent she was able, thanks to her own good judgment and common sense, to adapt to her own aptitudes and to the criteria of her day.

In her odd moments Mrs. Winslow wrote books, not very good ones, for she suffered from a bad case of the current malady of sentimentality, and also evidently thought it necessary to demonstrate that the theater was, in its own way, practically an annex of the church. Perhaps it was from her that Josephine acquired the ability to shut her eyes to ugliness and pretend it did not exist. Nevertheless, Mrs. Winslow's books, whatever their weaknesses, are by no means devoid of merit. "In all great successes," she says in her *Yesterdays with Actors*, "we can trace three qualities: the power of concentration, riveting every force upon the one unwavering aim—perseverance in the pursuit of our undertaking,—and the courage to enable us to bear up under all trials, disappointments and temptations that assail us in this life of probation." All who knew Josephine as an older woman recognized these qualities in her.

Something else she never lost sight of was Mrs. Winslow's analysis of the acting of William Warren, the patriarchal comedian: "There were no sketchy bits, to be varied night after night, as inspiration might suggest or humor dictate. . . . But it was always the same; the creation was complete, uniform and fulfilled to its absolute possibilities." These precepts were

35

worth more in the molding of Josephine's art than all the hours devoted to drilling in technique.

Between her sessions with Mrs. Winslow her activities continued their dizzying pace. At least, they would have been dizzying to anyone else. She scurried about from one engagement to another, sometimes on foot or on her bicycle, sometimes by train or streetcar, sometimes even by sleigh. Whatever her conveyance, she always got there. She continued to be in every play she could squeeze into her schedule, under the surveillance of Mrs. Winslow, who meticulously reviewed her work after the curtain was down. She also saw every important actor and actress who came to Boston. How surprised she would have been could she have peered into a crystal ball and seen how close she would be to some of them in the years to come!

All this time she was slowly edging her way closer to her goal. Part of her strategy was to see to it that those who counted knew that she existed, and, with the help of certain fellow conspirators, she managed to make at least some of them aware of her presence.

> Had a special delivery letter from Mr. Copeland with a letter to Mrs. Fiske. I went in & met her & went to her rehearsal. It was *very* interesting & I gloried in it. She manages all the staging & acting. Mrs. Fiske is wonderful, and so nice. Bless Mr. C.

The next April she had an adventure that must have been as thrilling as it was unexpected. Such had been the success of *A Copper Complication* that the authorities of Adelphi College in far-off Brooklyn hit upon the idea of using it for a benefit or, rather, a series of benefits, with pretty much the original cast. So for the first time in her life she saw New York, though not much of it, for she was kept busy in Brooklyn, where she was the guest of President and Mrs. Levermore.

But at Radcliffe one operetta does not make a spring, and the team of Daniels and Hooper had not been sitting back

JOSEPHINE SHERWOOD IN COSTUME
for an amateur theatrical production at Radcliffe College

Notman Photographic Co.

JOSEPHINE SHERWOOD IN CAP AND GOWN
for her graduation from Radcliffe College

resting on its laurels. No longer undergraduates, they had written another piece, to be presented this time by alumnae, and soon everybody was immersed in rehearsals of *The Court of Hearts*, which went off "splendidly" on the eve of Decoration Day. Josephine trained the dancers, and also appeared as the Princess of Clubs, whom the audience may have been surprised to discover wandering about the forests on the planet Mars. *The Court* proved to be a hit and the following February, followed its predecessor to "dear Brooklyn."

After the usual summer visits to Kingston and the Cliffs, Josephine was treated to another grand fling, this one shared by Jane Sever. A few days after the death of President McKinley, the chums were off to Buffalo to visit Mrs. Sherwood's cousin, Mrs. John Laughlin, and her family. Cousin Lillie and her two sons welcomed their guests as if they had indeed been princesses from Mars, and devised everything they could to see that they enjoyed a genuine spree. The program included expeditions to the Pan-American Exposition and a first glimpse of Niagara Falls. But there were other pleasures than sightseeing, which are perhaps clearer today in the recollections of one of Cousin Lillie's sons, Mr. S. R. Fuller, Jr.

> Her diary tells the story well, except that she left out, which likely was quite natural, the admiration of the young gentry who surrounded her. My brother and I were mighty glad to dance attendance on her as were all our male friends of about the same age. She was as pretty as they come, vivacious and smarter than a snapping whip.
>
> To us, an admiring group of young fellows, she was just a wonder, though we stood in much honest awe of her. But how she did play us, every one of us. She probably was to all of us a thoroughly unattainable attractive human being.

But there was more in Buffalo than a world's fair and smitten youths. There was Cousin Lillie herself, a kindred spirit. No one, not even Mrs. Winslow, was more understanding of

Josephine's ambitions and of the obstacles that stood in her way; it is extremely unlikely that she did anything to discourage her. In short, Josephine had another ally.

After she returned home, she acted more and more like a young lady who knew exactly where she was going—and why. One iron promptly came most of the way out of the fire. She gave up her classes at the Conservatory and worked harder and harder with Mrs. Winslow. There can be little question that the confidence of this experienced woman with her obvious affection for Josephine swept away any doubts that may have been lingering in Mrs. Sherwood's mind.

So at last the great decision was reached and ratified. If the rest of the family saw it coming, there was nothing they could do about it. Aunt Gertrude might sit up all night weeping as she thought of the awful people her cherished niece would meet—"She will probably marry an actor!"—but her tears did her no good. The cherished niece hated to cause her pain; after all, however, it was her life, and she was old enough to decide for herself what she was going to do with it. Let it be said, in justice to Aunt Gertrude and the others, that once the matter was irrevocably settled they accepted the situation. Never so long as they lived did their great devotion waver, and time and again they were ready with help that was sorely needed. Eventually, like most converts, they became such enthusiasts that they probably forgot that they had ever felt the slightest disapproval.

One evidence of the way the wind was blowing is the persistence with which Josephine set about enlisting the support of persons whose good will would be of practical value. Copeland and Baker were already in her camp. She now turned to the mighty Kittredge. Even more helpful would be people of standing in the theater. She set about meeting all of these she could. Her efforts to reach Sir Henry Irving were futile; she was stopped dead in her tracks by Bram Stoker, who was enacting Cerberus at the gate and it did her no good to protest that she adored Sir Henry and had not missed one of his plays in years. In other quarters she had better luck. It is hardly likely that men like John Drew and E. H. Sothern would have troubled themselves about her if they had not been assured beforehand by someone whose opinion they respected that here was no ordinary aspirant.

Drew received her in his hotel and apparently was favorably impressed, for a fortnight later he sent her a letter commending her to the attention of Joseph Humphreys, Charles Frohman's general stage director. Sothern went even further. He offered her "a small position" she was unfortunately not free to accept. Quite aside from any advance publicity she may have had, these two gentlemen were certainly not blind to her obvious assets, and they knew as well as the next one that, other qualifications being present, such charms were not liabilities to a young actress.

Shortly after these interviews another piece of good fortune came her way. *A Copper Complication* was summoned back to Brooklyn, and she was asked again to go along as Nanette. Furthermore, the Ridgewood Household Club offered, not merely to pay her expenses, but to give her $25.00 besides. This was a new turn, for on her two previous trips she had considered herself lucky not to have to pay her own way.

She attended rehearsals as conscientiously as before, but she lingered no longer than necessary in "dear Brooklyn." The first morning after her arrival she crossed the river to New York, and promptly at noon presented herself at the sanctum of Daniel Frohman, with whom she had "a most pleasant talk." From D. F.'s office she hurried over to that of Bijou Fernandez, who operated an important booking office. Although these sessions led to no tangible results, as least for the moment, she had made herself known to two of the powers in the theatrical world.

At this juncture there entered into Josephine's life a man who was to be a staunch friend throughout the years in which she struggled to establish a footing in her chosen profession. How the attention of Harrison B. Hodges was first directed to her there is no one living today to explain. He was by birth a Bostonian and while still in his twenties had taught chemistry

39

and German at Harvard. Naturally he was acquainted with many people to whom she was known, possibly with some members of her family. But he had abandoned academic life for business long before she had even entered high school, and in 1902, at the age of fifty, had been for five years purchasing agent for the Long Island Railroad. One source of his interest in her was his love of the theater, which found outlets in memberships in The Players and the Amateur Comedy Club. Even before she met him after the performance of the *Complication* on May 9, she had received a letter from him, and thereafter, as she gratefully expressed it, he was "heavenly kind." It was he who put her on the train for home the following evening.

Back in Newtonville, Josephine immediately set about winding up her affairs. She was still up to her eyes in her usual activities—acting, directing, studying, and singing—but most of these were now "last times." She bade goodbye to the Gilman School and her fellow teachers, and most reluctantly to Mrs. Winslow. She also took part in the usual commencement festivities at Radcliffe, and reveled in the class reunions.

Then on the last day of July she and her mother settled down in their familiar room at the Cliffs, and in short order she was gaily going through the usual summer resort routines. But looming ahead was an uncertain future, and the two of them were facing their first real separation.

CHAPTER FOUR

THE LEAP FROM THE CLIFF

August 12. Got up at quarter of five, saw the sun rise, & had a little weep with Mother. Left the Cliffs with Alice C. & Miss A. Lacey, & went to Boston, then to New York. Comfortable trip, reaching here 4.30. Came to the Meads', 19 East 46th St., and unpacked. Very pleasant indeed. Ev'g Mr. Hodges called, fine talk.

THE LONG AWAITED MOMENT HAD COME. The leap had at last been taken, and she was off to New York to climb, she hoped, right up onto the stage. Despite her hopes and her determination it was no wonder that she shed some tears, for this trip marked a complete break with the life she had always known, and especially with her mother, without whose fostering protection she had never been before. No doubt it was made easier by the presence of an old friend like Alice Clark, whose vocation was the dance, but she went no farther than Boston.

Josephine's invasion of the theatrical center did not, as things turned out, lead to much except some contacts, of which a few eventually proved helpful. She made the rounds of the offices of managers and agents, and, for the most part, was treated with courtesy. At least, in all cases but one she got past the office boy. She "called on Daniel Frohman and had a funny interview with him," and "had a delightful interview with Mr. A. M. Palmer."

Called on Mr. Trader of the Murray Hill theater, then on

Mr. Fiske at the Manhattan, & he was lovely to me.
Called on Mr. Tyler of Liebler & Co., & tried to see Mr.
Brady but did not.
Called on Mr. Brady, no luck. Wrote & after lunch had an
interview with Mrs. Fiske & Mr. Smith.
Called on agents, Mr. Brady in vain and Mr. Palmer.

She was learning like so many other novices before and after
her that there was no open sesame. For the greater part of her
life, even after she was well known, she found herself trudging from office to office, and time after time coming away with
no more than perhaps a "lovely talk" to remember. In later
years she often grew discouraged and depressed, but in 1902
she was still undaunted.

Yet all was not dreary seeking. Mr. Hodges was standing
comfortingly by to chat with her, take her out to dinner, and
escort her to the theater. George Sever, Jane's brother, was
there too, and he "took me to dinner at the Hotel Manhattan,
& then to Madison Sq. Garden—'Japan by Night' & 'The Mi-
kado.' Great fun." She found congenial girls too among her
fellow boarders, and they saw the sights together. For one
thing, they went to see Robert Edeson in *Soldiers of Fortune*,
a piece which, like *The Prince of Pilsen* and *Sherlock Holmes*,
she apparently could never see too often. She went too, for the
first time, to the Church of the Transfiguration, the Little
Church Around the Corner, with which she was destined to
be closely identified later on in life and in death.

All in all, in spite of the disappointments, she was having a
very good time. But she could not afford to extend her stay
indefinitely just because she was amusing herself. On September 12, after a little over three weeks, she went back to
Newtonville and the waiting family circle. Perhaps it is not
unkind to suggest that some of them were not so disappointed
as she, and hoped that she was discouraged. They should have
known her better. It never crossed her mind that she had suffered anything more than a temporary setback. It would take
more than this to undermine her self-confidence.

In 1902 one of the popular local institutions was the Castle Square Theater, which four years after the demise of the Boston Museum in 1893, had opened its doors to replace as nearly as any theater could that revered predecessor. According to *Six Years of Drama*, a sort of brochure which the management published in 1903 to celebrate its own achievements:

> . . . During the three hundred and twelve weeks since the beginning of the career of the Castle Square Theater Dramatic Stock Company, May 3, 1897, there have been produced two hundred and twelve different plays, and of these, forty-six have been repeated one or more times. . . .

The range of this repertory knew practically no bounds, including anything from gloomy tragedy to frisky farce. That the company in 1902 was made up of able rather than brilliant players is evidenced by the fact that few went on to national prominence. But they were, theatrically speaking, solid citizens and accomplished their minor missions with results quite satisfactory to the local public. At this time the two leading members were Lillian Lawrence, a great favorite in a wide variety of roles, and John Craig, a young man of the matinee-idol breed who had come straight from a season with Mrs. Fiske and who a few years later became himself the proprietor.

Presiding over the actors were J. H. Emery, manager and treasurer, whose domain was the front of the house, and James R. Pitman, the stage director, who had been in the business for forty-five years and had for more than twenty-five "superintended the productions at the Boston Museum at a time when the 'Old Museum' was making stage history." It is axiomatic that the stock companies, which had been the mainstay of the American theater from its beginnings in the eighteenth century, but which were now suffering a fatal decline, were the best of all possible schools for young actors and actresses who wished to learn the fundamentals of their profession. Perhaps, therefore, Josephine would have been well advised to turn to

43

the Castle Square before trying to crash the stage doors of Broadway. At any rate she wasted no time brooding over what to others must have seemed like an ill-starred expedition, but even before unpacking her suitcase, hurried down to the theater and presented herself before Mr. Pitman.

That she was completely unknown to him is improbable. With his sensitive finger on the pulse of all affairs theatrical in the region, he can hardly have failed to hear of this unusual young woman, who was by this time very widely and favorably known in the whole community. If, like most professionals, he was dubious about the competence of any amateur, he nevertheless obviously decided that this particular one was worth a second look. He must have seen for himself that this was not just another stage-struck girl. Exactly what passed between them in this meeting on September 13, Josephine does not say, but after going to a performance of *Lady Huntworth's Experiment*, she was back in his sanctum four days later, and the next morning was on hand for a rehearsal.

Possibly she had flattered herself that, with all her training and experience, she would not be required to start at the bottom of the ladder. But the gulf between professionals and amateurs was far wider in 1902 than it is today, and, so far as Pitman was concerned, the assumption could be that she knew nothing. This misapprehension she immediately set about removing.

September 19. Went in to "Camille" rehearsal, & took notes of the business & positions.

Her approach did not escape the eye of the stage manager, as is obvious from what ensued during the following weeks.

September 21. Went to church & sang in choir. Wrote a great many letters. Shampooed my hair. Ev'g went in to rehearsal of Camille at the theater.

September 22. Wrote letters, packed dress-suit case. P. M. Went in to Castle Square Theater & went on as extra in

44

"Camille," both afternoon and evening. In between performances, went to the library & wrote, & had my supper lunch
in the station.

Thus prosaically she noted the great event of her life to
date. That she actually took any great pride or even satisfaction in its is open to question. After all the leading roles she
had played to the accompaniment of "great enthusiasm" and
armfuls of flowers a modest walk-on as one of the demimon-
daine guests of the Lady of the Camellias must have seemed
short of sensational. It did not call for inspection even by her
mother. Perhaps she was a little bit ashamed.

Nevertheless, she had no reason to feel let down. She was
being paid. She was no longer an amateur. She was a professional. Better still, she was now in a place to prove her mettle
under the critical eyes of Mr. Pitman, and, whatever humiliation she may have suffered, she had too much good sense not
to make the most of her opportunities.

In the first place she showed him that she meant business.
She intended to earn every cent of the five dollars a week
bestowed on her by the management. This involved twelve
appearances, for the members of the Castle Square Company
were not exactly idlers. They acted twice daily six days out of
the seven, with rehearsals every morning and Sunday evening.
But Josephine did not stop there. It was part of her program
to learn everything she could, and consequently rehearsals of
plays in which she was not used frequently found her sitting out
front watching, notebook in hand. Furthermore, her off-weeks
gave her welcome opportunities to study the work of others.
She saw Duse in *La Citta Morte*—"wonderful, great." There
were also Margaret Anglin, Mrs. Fiske, Ethel Barrymore,
Julia Marlowe, Henrietta Crosman, Virginia Harned, Hack-
ett, Skinner, Gillette—in the inevitable *Sherlock Holmes*—
and Henry Miller. By now she was studying the methods of
each of these with understanding, almost expert, eyes, and
storing up familiarity with a great diversity of techniques.

Meantime she continued in her role as extra—in *The Tam-*

ing of the Shrew, A Lady of Quality, Phroso, and *Lord and Lady Algy.* Diversity again.

In spite of all her good intentions, she soon was confronted with a conflict which she must have found exceedingly embarrassing. She was caught painfully between a manager she wanted tremendously to please and a family at home she was most reluctant to offend. This time victory went to the family. But it must have hurt. The cause of her quandary was *The Three Musketeers.*

When Josephine Jacoby, a young mezzo-soprano then in her heyday at the Metropolitan Opera House, was seen as Siebel in *Faust* an approving critic noted that she had two good reasons for her appearance in the role of a boy. Josephine Sherwood could, although of course she would not make the same boast. On the other hand, there were the conventions of New England gentlewomen and of her ladylike days under Mrs. Agassiz and Miss Irwin.

> October 30. I refused to play a page on account of the costume.

One may assume that this modest refusal did not sit too well with Mr. Pitman, who could scarcely be expected to be sympathetic. It could easily have destroyed everything she had built up. Yet he may have respected her courage. At any rate she was out of the cast only one week. Then came a fortnight during which she was, so far as the Castle Square Company was concerned, a lady of leisure. That, however, she could never be as long as there was a play of any description anywhere within her reach. She was on the go every minute she was not enjoying the sleep of exhaustion. Among other things there were the rehearsals of *The Christian.*

Already her musical training was proving an asset, and it continued to be so. Perhaps that was one of the reasons Pitman was willing to forget her virginal modesty. Her talents could be very useful in the Hall Caine drama. "I play the organ &

piano & lead choruses behind scenes." He paid her no more, but for the first time he put her name on the program, opposite the name of a very minor character named "Mag."

The Christian ran two weeks, thus leaving her more time to devote to her amateur activities and her busy social life. Her mother and the aunts were dutiful in their attendance at the theater, as they always were when she was in the cast, meticulously spacing their visits so that there would always be one of them on hand to chaperon her safely back to Newtonville from the slightly unsavory neighborhood of the theater.

But they must have suffered a shock just before Christmas. As a gay holiday offering intended to bring good cheer to the Bostonians, proper and otherwise, the management decided to give *Hamlet*. And here was the *Three Musketeers* problem all over again. This time the outcome was different. Whether Pitman had lectured her or she had decided on her own to have done with such foolishness, she was beheld at the Court of Elsinore in the habiliments of a page. The diary vouchsafes no comment. In the line-a-day itself she notes merely that she had tried on her costume. Only in the very back of the little red book, where she entered a record of her earnings, was the truth revealed: "Dec. 22–27. Page in 'Hamlet'—$5." Nor does she mention the effect on prim Aunt Gertrude when she took up her position as guard, on the twenty-third. The important thing was that she was ridding herself of another vestige of the amateur.

The production of William Haworth's *The Ensign* marked another step in her progress. Not only was she called upon to sing a Spanish song, but she was instructed to understudy Jane Irving as Mrs. Wilkes. Jane stayed well and Josephine stayed in the wings. Nevertheless, even though the role was small, it was clear that the manager had confidence in her.

Still better things were in store for her. Her name was not on the program of *The Ensign*, nor was it on that of Clyde Fitch's *Nathan Hale*. Yet she was noticed, and by someone whose opinion was of no little value. Henry Austin Clapp of the *Boston Home Journal,* probably at that time the outstanding local critic.

Let me add just a word regarding one of the *'extra ladies'* who appear in that well-nigh speechless last act, wherein the spectators gather in an apple orchard to see Hale hanged at daybreak. The young lady, in a somewhat dull and uninteresting costume, makes a part of the picture on the side opposite the fatal apple tree. At the moment of a little stir that betokens the coming of Hale she steps forward with parted lips and eyes full of horror. Unconsciously her hands seek her throat, she unties her hat and lets it drop to the ground. You feel aware that her heart is going like a trip hammer, and that she is nearly breathless. When Hale arrives you are not surprised to see her sink to the ground in a most artistic because quiet faint —as unlike as possible to those obstreperous faints peculiar to leading ladies who have the center of the stage to tumble on, and a lime light to show them up after they are down. Presumably the actions of the damsel are directed by the stage manager, but one so well able to convey a great deal without a word ought certainly not to remain overlong on the "extra" list.

Quite a bit of attention for a nameless "supe." In her diary Josephine noted briefly that she was pleased.

Nothing very sensational resulted at once from this flattering notice. Again she was called upon to play the organ and the piano backstage, this time for *The Parish Priest,* and in *The Greatest Thing in the World* she had her first speaking part—three whole lines. Her season was interrupted by two more trips to New York, on one of which she tried out unsuccessfully before Colonel Savage for Sidonie in her favorite *Prince of Pilsen,* and by one to Aurora, where she coached the Wells College girls in *As You Like It.* She also had a hand in an alfresco performance of *The Foresters* at Wellesley.

It was apparently Mr. Pitman's custom to use subordinates

to direct some productions. Josephine mentions one or two instances of this policy, but no credit was given on the program, where the statement simply read: "Produced under the immediate direction of J. R. Pitman." One such arrangement was of the greatest importance to her.

The Castle Square Company was not pusillanimous enough to bow before either the heat or the vacations normal to summer, but kept right on without a break or a hesitation. On June 22 it offered those of its patrons who had remained in town a chance to enjoy Hoyt's *A Contented Woman* with the following admonition: "Kindly note that in several Western states women are entitled to vote and are eligible to State and local offices." According to the diary the director was George Ober, who was listed on the program merely as "Uncle Todie." To Josephine went the role of Calliope Ayres, a "girl friend" of the heroine, with attendant songs and dances.

Once more Mr. Clapp was in the house and on the job as well, and made a point of calling the attention of his followers to an interlude in the middle of the third act.

> ... there was a comic song by Mr. Ober, and there was dancing by Miss Durant and Miss Sherwood. All these exercises proved highly acceptable to the audience. In the way of discrimination it is to be said that Miss Sherwood's dancing was exceptional in grace and modest freedom, and in nice regard for the rhythms of the accompanying music.

After the first performance she noted that her "song & dance made a hit, three encores in P. M., 4 in ev'g. Grand fun. Aunt Nellie came home with me." On the twenty-fifth her grandmother took a look, at the matinee, her mother in the evening. "My Will o' the Wisp song went finely." When *A Contented Woman* was put to rest on Saturday she could have cried. "They gave me $15. Home late, took a carriage."

One more play and her stay at the Square was over. When the last act curtain fell on *Fanchon* (in which she had played Mariette), it fell also on the apprenticeship of Josephine Sherwood. There were to be no more anonymous extras in her life. From now on she was to be a professional actress, and her name was henceforth on every program. The book was closed on another phase of her education. In a few weeks another would be opened.

"Had offer for soubrettes from Huntley-Moore Co., refused it." She felt a thrill of importance as she wrote that entry in her diary the day after *Fanchon* closed. For the first time in her life she was in a position to be "choosy." She always remained so, sometimes when she could not really afford the luxury. Never at any time did she hold herself cheap, and usually she was canny about what to pick up and what to leave alone, usually but not always.

This time, however, she was taking no risk, for she had the promise of a job that intrigued her.

July 31. Went to Boston. Telegraphed Mr. Ober accepting position in his company. Said good-bye to Castle Sq. people, they were lovely.

George Ober, the jolly fat comedian under whom she had worked in *A Contented Woman*, was going in for management under the aegis of the firm of Broadhurst and Currie, and was planning a tour with three of George Broadhurst's farces through the cities and towns of the South, where he hoped a rainbow would guide him to a pot of gold. Josephine considered herself lucky that he had chosen her to be one of his company and signed her name to her contract enthusiastically. After a week with her mother at the Cliffs and another in New York devoted to rehearsals, she was off on August 27 for Annapolis and points south.

This was to be no adventure in great art, for the repertoire was composed of three uninspired, albeit amusing, plays by a prolific dramatist who was much more concerned with the box office than with aesthetics, *What Happened to Jones, The Wrong Mr. Wright,* and *Why Smith Left Home.* She was engaged to be the ingénue and to disport herself in various specialties. In *Smith* she was to be "a bride of a day," in the other two, just housemaids. But she had nothing to complain about, especially as she would have wonderful chances to learn how to take the pulses of audiences to which she was a complete stranger.

> August 31. Wrote to Mother. Nice letter from her. Rehearsed rough places in "Jones." P. M. Sewed on costumes & rested. Another fine letter from Mother, in P. M. Ev'g our first performance of Mr. Ober's company, "What Happened to Jones," Colonial Theater, Annapolis. Fine telegrams from Mother and Stanton Elliot. Play went well. My part went smoothly.

This last was a modest understatement if the critic of the *Capital* is to be believed.

> Miss Josephine Sherwood was a typical Swedish servant girl. She had evidently made a close study of the character which she impersonated true to life, holding the mirror up to nature most cleverly. There was not much in the character, but all there was, and the very best of it, Miss Sherwood reproduced last night.

From Annapolis the troupe pushed on down through Virginia, the Carolinas, and Georgia, to Florida. Business was variable, sometimes good, sometimes wretched, usually indifferent. Mr. Ober was not filling his pockets, but his ingénue was having a gorgeous time, seeing unfamiliar sights, and singing, dancing, and acting with glee. Everywhere they went she proved to be the favorite of the company, her "specialties" being unfailing hits. When she did them in Charlottesville, the University of Virginia boys were every bit as susceptible as their Harvard brethren had been. "She was unusually good in her part," declared one of the local critics, "and as pretty as one could well wish." But there were serious moments too. In Columbia, South Carolina, she was shown over the State Capitol by "Mr. Gantt, State Secy," but was depressed by the condition of the town. In Jacksonville she went to the City Hall, and unearthed the record of her father's death there in 1886.

If she was having a good time, Mr. Ober definitely was not, and when they reached Greenville, Mississippi, on December 3, he announced that he was through. A few more performances, and Josephine was once more in New York. "So sorry it is over."

The big city was not dull. Harry Hodges was back, Stanton Elliot took her out to dinner, and a "Mr. Martin" beaued her about. Best of all, however, was the discovery that she had begun to attract the attention of those who would determine what opportunities were to be open to her. If she emerged from an agent's office still unemployed, it was her own doing. Once again she was exercising her right to be "choosy." "Had offer for 'The Heart of Chicago!' No!!"—"Had chance to go with 'Young Mrs. Winthrop,' cheap company." "Called on Col. Brown, who offered me position with 'Two Little Waifs.' " As Yul Brynner said in *The King and I*, "*Et cetera, et cetera, et cetera!*"

Once, however, she said yes when she shouldn't have. Engaged by a Mr. Plohn for a road company of *The Telephone Girl*, when she reached the designated place, she was nonchantly informed that it had all been a mistake and politely told to run along home. Indignantly she returned to the sidewalks of New York, but she did not have to pace them very long. The optimistic Mr. Ober decided that maybe New England would be more enthusiastic about Broadhurst farces than Dixie had been, and that he would have another go at the road. Unfortunately, however, New England wasn't. Nevertheless, the tour, which lasted from February 13 to March 29, was not from Josephine's point of view a complete loss. It took her through a region largely populated by Tewksbury kin and Radcliffe alumnae, who rallied about her with supper par-

SHELLEY HULL

THE SHELLEY HULLS
soon after their marriage

ties and the usual bouquets. She also garnered some gratifying notices, including one that asserted that she was both the best and the most attractive of the women involved. But her charms were not enough to pay the piper, and once again Ober had to cry, "Hold, enough!"

At this time Stanton Elliott was playing the juvenile business with the Bowser-Craven Stock Company in Springfield, Massachusetts; he apparently interceded for her with the management, for on May 2 she opened with them in *Hazel Kirke*. This engagement had one advantage. It took her within easy reach of home. Her mother was not well, and Josephine was being kept on pins and needles by frequent bulletins reporting one ailment after another. From Springfield she could easily run over to Newtonville to check on the situation for herself. Yet the outcome was not a happy one, and it wrote finis to a pleasant friendship. For one thing, the reviews were obviously not to her taste, for she preserved only one, in which she is dismissed as merely "satisfactory." It does not even tell which role she played, and she saved no programs. It would seem that for some undisclosed reason she wanted to forget the whole affair. After one week she quit. Was Stanton Elliot in some way involved? It looks as if he was.

> May 6. Dear letter from Mother, with money, etc. P. M. Stan [crossed out]—Mr. Elliott called, & we had some music, then went for a little walk.

What happened on that little walk? The next day *Mr.* Elliot took her to supper after the play and *Stanton* Elliot put her on the Boston train. Exit Stanton Elliot. Thereafter his name was forever banished from the diary. Not long after this engagement he abandoned the stage as a profession, and there is no evidence that their paths ever crossed again. She sped home to Mother.

She had been at home just a week when a new opportunity unexpectedly presented itself. She was engaged for the summer theater operated by James Moore at Portland, Maine, and four days later was installed in the Sherwood Hotel near Casco Bay.

> May 22. I went to the Portland Theater, & had a fine talk with Mr. Byron Douglas & Mr. Moore. Am to play Loey Tsing in "The First Born," and Maria in "Confusion," and am gleeful.

The First Born is a one-act play of Chinese life by Francis Powers, written, not in the usual pidgin English, but in good literate English throughout, and, at least as presented by the Douglas company, proved to be a powerful and moving drama, and this despite the fact that it was a far cry from the fare the Portlanders and their summer visitors had grown accustomed to expecting in James Moore's theater. The critics, taken just a little by surprise, were more than pleased. In all accounts the entire company comes off very creditably, but none more so than the debutante. The comment in the *Argus* of May 31 is typical. "But the strongest score was made by Josephine Sherwood as Loey Tsing, a Bond Girl whose miserable lot in life first taught her to pity Chang Wang and whose pity finally blossomed into love. As the vivacious, careless, impish creature in the first scene and the serious poetic sympathizer of Chang Wang later Miss Sherwood was equally satisfactory."

The *Evening Express* welcomed the young actress with an extended biographical sketch—not all the details stand up under close scrutiny—and a profile picture, featuring a long dark curl that reaches below her shoulder. The heading reads "MISS SHERWOOD A PROMISING COMPOSER." The article goes on to say that "several very tuneful and charming selections have been written by her," and adds that she is endowed with a fine soprano voice.

> Miss Sherwood is small, but it is an old and true saying that many good things are found in small packages and Miss Sherwood is a good example of this rule.

Her auspicious debut was not diminished by her subsequent appearances. She was cast in a great variety of parts, playing American, English, French, and other kinds of roles with skill and effectiveness. In *Blue Jeans*, for instance, "Josephine Sherwood assumed two roles, Beleene Kicker and Nell Teutwiler, but no one would have guessed it had not the house programme announced the fact, so widely differing were her drawings." Her vis-à-vis in most of her comedy parts was a cheerful youth named Bertram Yost, who often joined her in the songs and dances that transported their audiences.

This two-months' engagement, although at $35.00 a week it did not elevate her to a millionaire's status, provided her with less tangible riches in the form of experience. All accounts agree that she became a great favorite, and nothing could have thrilled her more; she had an overmastering desire for popularity or, perhaps it would be juster to say, affection. Therefore it was with great satisfaction that she saw photographs of herself distributed to the ladies in the reserved seat section at the matinees of *The Iron Master*. All this time she was managing to sandwich in, between her working hours, almost daily or nightly social engagements. Of course her mother came down to see how the land lay, and so too did no less a person than Copey of Harvard.

When it was all over, she contemplated her situation with justified contentment. There could no longer be any fears about her fitness for the career she had chosen. She even received an offer of stardom at $75.00 a week. For some reason or other nothing came of it, but the mere fact that it had been made meant a great deal.

Mrs. Sherwood was waiting for her at the Cliffs, and thither she hurried on August 1, but not for long. On the ninth came a wire to the effect that there might be an opening for her at the Grand Opera House in New Orleans, and she left for New York posthaste. Terms were quickly arranged and after a quick trip home to gather her effects together, she was off to her new job, put on the train by Aunt Nellie and Uncle Phil.

She was entering a new world, for the Ober tour had not reached Louisiana, and no young woman of her romantic disposition could have failed to respond to the Creole charm of the Crescent City. After one night at the celebrated St. Charles Hotel, she moved to a modest boarding house on Rampart Street, and settled down for the season.

One of her first visits was to Trinity Church where she paid her respects to the Reverend Beverly Warner. The next Sunday she was in a pew that she probably hoped to occupy weekly as long as she was in town. But she soon discovered that in New Orleans one did not rest from one's labors on the Sabbath. At least the actors did not. Every Sunday morning there was a scenery rehearsal, and every afternoon and evening there were performances, "the first Sunday performances I have ever had to give." Inasmuch as she was cast in every play presented during the months she was with the company—seven evenings and four matinees—there was no churchgoing for her until Lent brought a service at an irregular hour. The best she could do was paste an impressive picture of the church in her scrapbook.

This seven-and-a-half-months' season was not one of the most spectacular in Josephine's career, but it had its uses. The company was in its own way important and played most of the time to near-capacity business. As a beginner she could not hope for parts as good as those that had come her way under Ober and Moore. But she worked under the direction of a stage manager of ability and experience, Sedley Brown, and had ample opportunities to study the ways both of actors and of audiences.

The company was adequate, in some instances more than adequate. Certainly it was more creditable than the repertoire, which was made up of the trashiest farces, comedies, and melodramas Manager Charles Fourton could find at the bottom of the barrel, the best of which was probably *Charley's Aunt*. The new "ingénue and soubrette" had for the most part to be content with secondary roles, but she turned all of them to good advantage, and before many weeks had passed was one of the most popular members of the group.

On January 8 Fourton saw fit to offer his public something with real red meat on its bones. "The sensational drama, 'Nevada,'" says the critic of the *Item*, "is one of a kind that always pleases a certain type of people. It has plenty of action, good scenery, and a free and easy swing," and so on. As its name suggests, it was a lusty "meller" of the breed that faded from view when the movies took over. For some unspecified reason, the leading lady, Miss Minna Phillips, was out of the cast, and the western miner's noble child fell to the lot of the little girl from Massachusetts. All the reviews agree that she justified the confidence of the management in at last intrusting her with a lead. They disagree only on the question of whether she employed the conventional phony western dialect current on the stage at that time.

There is no space here to repeat the many kind words that came Josephine's way in New Orleans. Her parts were as a rule pretty much of a piece; so were the reviews. But there is one which in the light of past events perhaps deserves mention. The reader is asked to remember *The Three Musketeers* of her Castle Square days. In Henry Pettit's melodrama, *The Black Flag*, she was cast as "Ned, a Waif," and Ned had extremities which could not well be hidden from public scrutiny. Well, she had survived the Page in *Hamlet*—true, a not very conspicuous figure—and now she was prepared to go the whole way, especially as the poor waif was, as she said, a "splendid" part. So on she went, and, what is more, made a hit. "Barberino," the often caustic critic of a publication called *Harlequin*, pronounced her achievement exceptional. "It is so hard for a girl to do a boy's part and so easy to overdo it, that a clever graceful characterization is really a relief. A real appreciation of Miss Sherwood's art is to be found in the fact that one forgets her sex throughout the entire play." This was not the only boy's role assigned to her during the season, and, far from being distressed, she became very partial to the type. The aunts may have grieved, but, if so, they grieved at a distance, and she worried not.

Josephine had a thoroughly good time in New Orleans. Her Baedeker in hand, she explored the city, and sampled the exotic dishes in the famous restaurants. Her companions were usually Miss Minna Phillips, Bert Lytell, and Frank Sylvester, sometimes with the addition of Blanche Seymour (Dot) of the rival Baldwin-Melville Company. Nor was potential romance lacking. One of the young men fell madly in love with her and formally proposed, but in vain. One Percy Viosca, a business-man with a taste for the theater, also found her alluring, and she owed him many a good meal at Antoine's. She also acquired fans. Scarcely had she played her first part when her dressing room began to be besieged by girls, the teen-agers of the day, who paid their homage with adoring visits, candy, and flowers. Josephine glowed and made them her slaves.

It was not only the young girls, to whom crushes were among the necessities of life, who succumbed. She had hardier admirers than they in her camp. Shortly after the opening of the season New Orleans suffered a grievous humiliation. The beloved Pelicans failed to carry off the pennant of the Southern Baseball League, and all loyal citizens were in mourning. No blame was meted out to the doughty warriors—they deserved only sympathy. The villain was an evilly disposed umpire who had snatched the laurels from their brows. Something must be done to show that, despite their shame, their city loved them still. So a group of prominent citizens got together and bought an enormous cup to be publicly presented them with due cere-mony. The most fitting place for the gala occasion seemed to the committee to be the Opera House. The Pelicans were asked to choose one of their number to receive the cup on their behalf and make a suitable response. Much too modest to speak for themselves, they replied that they must have a deputy. And what better one could be found than the cute little ingénue?

So on a Monday evening their loyal supporters jammed the theater, and the shining trophy was duly bestowed on them by the respected Judge Clegg. Then, according to the *States* of the following day, "Miss Sherwood stepped blithely to the center of the stage. . . . Flushed with subdued excitement the charming little woman looked prettier than ever. In an excellently worded address full of simplicity she accepted the gift. 'Three strikes were called unjustly and you were out. The pennant may not be in our hands but you can leave here to-night with the assurance that we love the Pelicans of 1904 just as well as if they had brought the flag home.'" Cheers! Had the wicked umpire been brazen enough to show his face, he would have missed all this, for, according to the paper, he would have crawled under his seat.

The New Orleans Grand Opera Company was not another Castle Square. When the thermometer rose to uncomfortable heights, it closed its doors. In 1905 the end came on April 15.

Saturday. P. M. & ev'g farewell performances of "Ticket-of-Leave Man" & our company in New Orleans. Lovely flowers and a gold seal ring from the stage hands. Lots of calls, goodbyes, hate to say them.

Sunday. Went to Begué's for breakfast, French style with Louise, Mrs. Homans & Lytell, Mr. and Mrs. Brown. P. M. packed, lots of calls. Left New Orleans at 8.15 P. M. by the L. & N.—Heaps of girls saw me off. Sorry to leave at the last.

CHAPTER FIVE

STARS IN THEIR COURSES

JOSEPHINE WAS GENUINELY SORRY to part with her good friends; at the same time she was glad to get back to her natural habitat and to the family she had not seen for eight months. She went first to New York, for little more than a stopover, and as soon as possible went back to Newtonville, where she dedicated her freedom, theoretically, to a rest. But she was constantly on the go, paying and receiving calls, going to the theater, and, after the extraction of a wisdom tooth, having wedges driven in between her other teeth. She broke this vacation to play one week at the Square in Belasco's *The Girl I Left Behind Me,* and must have got what in the vernacular of today would be called a kick out of appearing in an honest-to-goodness part on that particular stage.

She could not afford extended leisure, and on June 11 she returned to Portland, the scene of last summer's engagement, though not to the same theater. This time she was enrolled as a member of the Gem Theater Company on Peaks Island. This island out in Casco Bay was to occupy a very special place in Josephine's affections. She always grew nostalgic when she recalled the summers she had spent there, and when war and change desecrated it, there was unwonted bitterness in her heart. "Nothing sets me up like sea air," she said when, as an old lady near the close of her long career, she came back to Portland to regain her strength. Although in 1905 there was nothing about her that needed strengthening, the chill salt-laden air was welcome after the long months in Louisiana, and then as later she delighted to sit and watch the rollers crashing in on her own particular "stern and rock-bound coast." Whatever pleasure she came in time to take in the beaches of California, whatever superlatives she might pile up in her Baedeker-like letters, nothing anywhere else was like this. "My home is in the East, and I am glad of it." So, if for a while the weather was raw and foggy and business a little slow in getting started, she was serene.

A twenty-minute sail from the mainland, Peaks Island, one of the larger islands in Casco Bay and politically a part of the city of Portland, is a favorite pleasure ground for citizens and visitors alike. The Gem itself, in spite of the raptures of its advertisements, had no architectural beauty to inspire her tender memories. Obviously a direct ancestor of the Quonset hut, its lines were no more graceful.

The season, if not the climate, was New Orleans all over again, at least so far as her roles were concerned. The plays themselves were better. There was no *Queen of Chinatown* or *Buffalo Bill* to provoke her detestation. Instead, the season opened with Henry Arthur Jones' *Mrs. Dane's Defense*—it failed to draw—and included such respectable pieces as *Dorothy Vernon of Haddon Hall* and *The Henrietta*, no masterpieces, yet decent summer fare. As in the South, the director was Sedley Brown, and he handed her, generally speaking, the same kinds of parts he had given her before. Once, however, he did vary the pattern, probably remembering how successfully she had coped with the emotional characters he had intrusted to her at the Grand Opera House.

The exception was Mary, Queen of Scots, in Paul Kester's romantic drama, *Dorothy Vernon of Haddon Hall*. Helen

Hayes, some thirty years later, was not the first diminutive Mary Stuart. Brown found that he had made no mistake. "So far this summer," wrote the critic of the *Evening Express*, "the popular actress has had a class of roles that gave room only to the lighter side of her abilities. In this play she is cast for a somber character, and she plays it as well as she has given us the ingénue heretofore. The pleasure of the audience in her work was shown last night by repeated applause, which amounted to an ovation as the actress left the stage in her final exit."

She scored again, for a different reason, when she played the comic role of Petunia Perkins in *The Brixton Burglary*, which she was asked to do on very short notice. The account in the *Express* is too long to be quoted *in toto*, but a few sentences must be repeated because they touch on a trait noted throughout her career by all who worked with her.

. . . The part is a long one and was not given to Miss Sherwood until after the performance Tuesday evening. A rehearsal was called for Wednesday morning and the pretty actress gave Mr. Brown, the stage director and her associates in the company a most enjoyable surprise by coming to the rehearsal with the part completely committed to memory and at the matinee performance it could not have been played more effectively had Miss Sherwood been performing in the piece for several months.

That evening she was rewarded "with several beautiful bouquets" and a shower of compliments. Among those in the house to applaud with particular pride were Aunt Anne, Aunt Gertrude, and Great-aunt Corrine. Aunt Gertrude's conversion was coming along nicely.

A unique event of the season was a gala performance in honor of the officers of the First Battleship Division of the North Atlantic Squadron. There were flags and flowers in abundance, and the programs displayed the Stars and Stripes in brilliant colors. No one felt more jubilant than Josephine as she waltzed and two-stepped blithely with the willing officers at the hop that came afterward. The play, Ludwig Fulda's *The Lost Paradise*, seemed almost a minor incident even though Cinders was one of her favorite roles.

The end of the month was also the end of a very gay summer with au revoirs to old friends like the Browns and Sylvesters, and to new ones like Jane Kennark—the leading lady —the Charlie Lothians, and Blanche Lawrence. They could all be nostalgic about the Gem together.

> August 25. Left the Island at 8.30 with many friends to see me off. *Sorry* to go. Mr. & Mrs. Lothian, Mr. & Mrs. Sylvester, Miss Lawrence & her mother, & I sailed on the "North Star" for New York. A rough passage, & many sick, but I found it glorious & enjoyed it all. Slept well. *Great!*

Once again Josephine was on the sidewalks of New York. She made the normal rounds from managerial office to managerial office, but she left each one of her own accord, not because she was heartlessly turned away. Of the offers made, none appealed to her, and with a little money in the bank for a change, she decided to bide her time. She did not have to wait long.

> October 4. Had an offer from Grace George's company. Went to Clyde Fitch's house, met him & read to him. P. M. went to Herald Sq. Theater, & he read "Wolfeville" to Nat Goodwin's company. He has given me the ingénue part on trial. Oh rapture.
> October 5. Rehearsed "Wolfeville" all the morning and afternoon at the Criterion Theater, under Mr. Fitch's direction. He is charming. My part has pleased him and I am to have it. Hurrah. Ev'g Cousin Frank & Herbert Norris took me to "The Ham Tree."
> October 6. Rehearsed "Wolfeville" all day. I am so happy

over this management. Signed contracts with Mr. Seymour & Frohman this morning. It seems too good to be true. I play "Sue Wilkins."

At the time there seemed to be valid cause for her to say, "Hurrah!" Here she was, engaged by the great "C. F." himself to play opposite one of the most popular stars on the current stage in a new work by one of the two or three leading American playwrights of the day. Well might she be rapturous. Unfortunately, the brightest auguries do not invariably rest on firm foundations. Josephine never looked back on *Wolfville* with any pride. After it had gone down the drain, she seldom mentioned it. There was little reason why she should, for it is a bad play, and its public life was deservedly brief and undistinguished.

The observations of the critic of the *Washington Post,* when in early November the play was put on display in the capital, have some relevance to the television repertoires of today. After listing such recent hits as *The Virginian, The Girl of the Golden West,* and *The Squaw Man,* he pondered:

> . . . How many more plays of Western life and Western character are galloping over the trail of one-night stands is not susceptible of exact mathematical demonstration, but the number cannot be inconsiderable since the tendency is to take advantage of a good thing.

He concluded unkindly that the direction of said tendency was usually downward. Despite its distinguished authorship, *Wolfville* could hardly have gone further in that direction.

At the turn of the century one of the popular purveyors of light fiction was Alfred Henry Lewis, who set out to follow the trails blazed by Bret Harte and Owen Wister in depicting life in the rough and ready communities of the Great West. But, instead of California or Wyoming, he chose as the setting for his romances an imaginary town in Arizona called "Wolfville." Of their kind, these little sketches are not wholly devoid of merit, displaying as they do originality, humor, and some observation of human nature as it—supposedly at least—manifested itself in that region, though the dialogue is painfully affected, with a lingo the reputed speakers would scarcely recognize if they heard it. When, however, the august trio composed of Clyde Fitch, Willis Steell, and Charles Frohman got through with it, few of its commendable qualities had survived. "This material has been handled in such a manner," says the *Philadelphia Record*, "as to retain but very little of the picturesque charm of Mr. Lewis' work, but to give full prominence to its bombast and its exaggeration. Omitting the incidental character touches, the play is merely a cheap melodrama, very hackneyed and very poorly constructed." This is the gist of many of the reviews preserved in the scrapbook.

Josephine must have thought that, instead of Arizona, she was back in *Nevada*. The play tells the story of Cherokee Hall, a noble and straight-shootin' gambler who comes within an ace of getting himself lynched for participation in a holdup he has not even seen, because he refuses to reveal that one of the actual culprits was none other than the lately deceased father of sweet little Sue Wilkins (Josephine), whom he loves with a pure passion. He assumes that it would make her happier to have the man she loves hanged than to have the truth about her wretched parent uncovered. Of course Sue saves him in the nick of time, and all would end happily at once if there were not still another act to go. This treats of the jealousy of Hall's partner, Faro Nell, who loves him so dearly that she would rather see him in a Boot Hill grave than in the arms of another woman, and logically joins in a plot to shoot him dead. Just before the final curtain she undergoes a change of heart and heroically saves his life by interposing herself between him and the lethal bullet. Then the kindly authors, refusing to let her die, have her linger on to enjoy the pangs of unrequited love.

If it were not for the lessons to be drawn from TV westerns, it would be incredible today that anybody could take such balderdash seriously even when it came from the pen of the white hope of the American drama. In fact, too few people took it seriously enough to make it a paying proposition. In all this, no blame attached to the actors. C.F. had hopefully assembled an excellent company. It was the opinion of the *Boston Morning Herald* that "the company was altogether too good for the play." Individual honors, all agreed, were carried off by Katherine Grey as Faro Nell, who "gave altogether a splendid portrayal of a girl whose wild passions led her to plan the murder of the man she loved." There were compliments too for Jessie Busley as the little washerwoman who returns to Wolfville a perfect lady after six months of schooling in Missouri and runs her "heathen Chinee" rival clear out of town. Goodwin himself was thought to be out of his element in melodrama, and, as for Josephine, well, she was there. One writer found her too tearful; another conceded that she did all that could be done with Sue. The consensus was that she was just "sweet and wholesome." Those were not the kind of reviews that she enjoyed pasting into the scrapbook, but she was honest about it, and there they are today.

Although Josephine was disappointed that *Wolfville* never got up enough steam to reach Broadway, it was perhaps just as well that it did not. After the initial performance in Philadelphia, Fitch himself and C.F. took over and tried to pull the play together. The trouble was that it was not the sort of thing that could be saved by pulling—even by two such experts. Yet, according to Josephine, it "went over so much better" than it had before. After a week at the National in Washington it limped into Boston, where for a fortnight it bewildered the ultraconservative clientele of the staid Colonial, and then it expired. Mrs. Sherwood and Aunt Anne dutifully attended the demise.

From this fiasco Josephine salvaged one great good, the close and enduring friendship of Katherine Grey. The bond between them lasted for many years, and, although they had not seen each other for a long time, was terminated only by "dear Katie's" death nearly half a century later. Jess Busley too remained a friend for a long time to come, but her intimacy never equaled Katie's, and she and Josephine did not by any means always see eye to eye.

After the close of the Fitch-Steell melodrama, Josephine resumed the established pattern of her New York existence, varied by a happy family Christmas at home, very different, she wrote Jane Sever, from the "unChristmas" in New Orleans the year before. Toward the end of January a brief engagement with "William J. Kelly and his Own Company of Superior Players" in Yorkville ended in unpleasantness after three weeks, and once more she was at liberty.

Whether or not this unpleasantness was entirely of a monetary nature she does not reveal—she was paid $50.00 a week—but she soon set about finding means to strengthen her depleted bank account. It is clear that she was not sufficiently embarrassed to seize upon whatever came her way, for she spurned a number of offers, some of which seem at this distance to have been not unattractive. She busied herself with her music, copying scores and doing some accompanying for Mrs. Henry De Mille, and also composing some songs of her own, which she dispatched to various publishers. Through the good offices of her cousin Edith Sherwood, she secured a job at the Horace Mann School, where she earned $15.00 directing the seniors in a German play, *Neffe als Onkel.*

During this lean period one very worthwhile opportunity presented itself, one that gave her a chance to show what she could do, however briefly, in a New York theater before a very distinguished audience.

Early in March Mrs. De Mille asked her to take part in a matinee for the benefit of the Vassar Aid Society, and she readily assented. The program consisted of three short plays: *The Mallet's Masterpiece,* by Edward Peple; *The Land of the Free,* by William C. De Mille; and *A Watteau Shepherdess,* an operetta by Harold McGrath and Fred W. Jackson. It was in the second that she was cast. Whereas the other two are fantasies, *The Land of the Free* is "a true episode of New York life." It recounts a poignant little incident on Ellis Island, and depicts the agony of a poor Sicilian, who, after saving for

67

three years to bring over his wife and two children, is told on their arrival that, because he had not sufficient income to insure their support, they must be sent back to Naples. Josephine was engaged for the role of the wife, Maria; the role of her husband was played by Robert Paton Gibbs. The piece was carefully prepared, with rehearsals under Mrs. De Mille and, for Josephine, a trip to Ellis Island, where she was shown the newly landed immigrants and the examinations to which they were subjected.

The performance took place on April 2, and is thus described in the diary:

> P. M. Matinee, Hudson Theater, for Vassar Students' Aid Society. I played Maria Ricardo in "The Land of the Free," by Wm. De Mille. Gorgeous American beauties from the Horace Mann class. Play went finely—great house, many notables there. *So happy*. Mother, Cousin Lillie, & Aunt Cassie went, & Dot. Mark Twain, Warfield, Skinner, Mary Shaw, Blanche Bates, Faversham there.

Since she evidently acquitted herself creditably, it did her no harm to be seen by such connoisseurs. According to the *Dramatic News*, "Josephine Sherwood made a pretty and effective Maria. . . . The matinee was under the auspices of Mrs. H. C. De Mille. There was a large and fashionable audience, and everybody seemed to be delighted. It was a great afternoon for the players as well as the authors."

If the *Tribune's* account is correct, no one present had a better time than the greatest celebrity of the lot. "The Governor-General of Canada and various other exalted personages waited in vain at the Museum of Natural History yesterday for Mark Twain. He did not come, for he was having the time of his life among the Vassar Alumnae at the Hudson Theater." He evidenced his appreciation of the occasion by a lavish bestowal of autographs, and of kisses on the cheeks of the delighted ushers. Too bad that Josephine was only an actress! The following afternoon and evening *The Land of the Free* was repeated at Proctor's. She had reached Broadway at last—by way of a college benefit and a vaudeville act, but she had reached it.

Nowhere does Josephine say that among the notables who saw her as Maria Ricardo was Wilton Lackaye, the celebrated Svengali of *Trilby*, but he may very well have done so and, if so, that may well account for the next chapter of her career.

Like other romantic actors of the day, Maurice Barrymore for instance, Lackaye had been for some time itching to play Jean Valjean, potentially as fat a part as any one of their number could conceive of. (Memories of James O'Neill and *The Count of Monte Cristo* danced tantalizingly in his head.) A writer in the New York Mail asserts that "this play and performance represents the consummation of the dream of the actor's life." The trouble was that in *Les Misérables* Victor Hugo had produced a novel of such mammoth proportions that it defied the "two hours' traffic of the stage." He himself is reputed to have declared that it contained material for four plays, and Lackaye admitted that a dramatization which included everything would run twenty-five hours. He asserted that he had sought to induce a number of well-known playwrights to prepare a version, but they had all shuddered and turned away. He had, therefore, been forced to rush in himself where accredited angels had feared to tread.

Sitting himself down, he read through the enormous tome three separate times. Then, after laying it aside for a time, he wrote out a synopsis of those incidents that he found had made the deepest impression on his mind. Afterward, with the novel at his elbow, he fashioned his play. He insisted that his attitude was wholly reverential, and that he endeavored to depart as little as possible from Hugo's original, a preposterous undertaking. He had no choice but to compose a condensation, wholly episodic in structure, in which all the qualities which make the novel great were completely lost. What he achieved was mere melodrama, some critics were to say, of the *Two Orphans* school. Except in the person of Valjean himself, there was no time for anything but the most superficial characterization. The supporting members of the huge cast were to be confronted with mere silhouettes that they would have to fill in according to their varying abilities. Human nature being what it is, it is not surprising that the scenes selected were those dominated by the hero.

It would be unfair to Lackaye to imply that his aim was self-exploitation. The choice was inevitable if the play was to have any unity at all. Nor were selfish motives, conscious at least, in keeping with his character. He was in 1906 in the prime of life and at the height of a conspicuously successful career. A versatile actor and a conscientious artist, he could look back on many very considerable achievements, especially as the repulsive hypnotist, Svengali, in Du Maurier's *Trilby,* which had been running for two years.

Yet he was not satisfied. He was a man of irreproachable reputation, with an exceptionally serious and altruistic outlook on life. Originally intended for the priesthood, he had adopted the stage as a profession because he saw in it an instrument that could and should be used for the betterment of society. Although an artist by instinct he was no subscriber to the dictum that art—or taste—is the only morality. In the story of Jean Valjean he perceived a powerful lesson conducive to the public good, and in William A. Brady he found a producer with the courage to go along with him.

As was said above, there is no evidence that Lackaye was among those who saw Josephine in *The Land of the Free.* Yet somehow he learned that an obscure young actress was able to handle a highly emotional role, and two weeks after the Vassar matinee she was summoned to read for him. The next day, April 19, she wrote:

> Went to rehearsal of "Les Misérables," with Wilton Lackaye's co., at Academy of Music, and rehearsed till five. . . . Mr. Lackaye thinks I can have the parts of Fantine and Cosette. A great opportunity.

On the twenty-first: "P. M. at Brady's office, & was definitely engaged for Mr. Lackaye's company." Immediately she wired her mother the great news, and, by way of celebration, was taken by Hodges to a performance by the Amateur Comedy Club, an ultraexclusive organization of which he was a pillar.

The next three weeks were almost entirely given over to rehearsals, while the star continued his run in *Trilby* and a stage version of *The Pit*. Occasionally Josephine was called to his home for individual coaching, almost imperative in view of her relatively slight experience. Lackaye must have perceived in her work possibilities that, if not necessarily undetected by her earlier directors, had seldom been exploited. As some critics were to note, she actually had three parts, not just two, to interpret: Fantine, first as a youthful grisette and later as a betrayed and degraded woman; and Cosette, Fantine's innocent daughter, the identical type that Josephine had been playing under many different names. The last must have come easily, but for the other two, in particular the older Fantine, she needed all the expert direction she could get. Meanwhile her admiration and affection for her mentor grew steadily.

On May 8 a portentous event took place. "Mr. Lackaye shaved his mustache." This was a real sacrifice to art, for there probably had not been so imposing an adornment seen on Broadway since the walrus-like appendages of Lester Wallack had made the hearts of impressionable young ladies go pitapat in the middle years of the last century. But they would have been fatal to the various guises of Jean Valjean.

Brady and Lackaye decided that it would be wise to give the play a brief tryout before dispatching it on an extended tour in the fall, prior to the Broadway opening that they hoped would lead to a long run there. Whether or not they believed that the name of the star would be sufficient to insure these happy results without benefit of an expensive cast, they certainly watched their budget when it came to assembling the twenty-eight supporting actors and actresses they required, to say nothing of the "Gendarmes, Convicts, Citizens, Flower Girls, Peasants, etc." listed among the dramatis personae.

There was also the question of a name. Lackaye loved to say in the witty curtain speeches he was almost invariably called upon to make that he had not been able to find a manager who could even pronounce *Les Misérables,* a bon mot later attributed by Ethel Barrymore to her father. Because it was probable that the public would also be perplexed, the play was rechristened *The Law and the Man,* and, thus entitled, was first presented to the waiting world at Poli's Theater in Waterbury, Connecticut, on May 14. Josephine reports "a small house," but "a big success." That first audience must have been endowed with rare powers of endurance, for Lackaye had concocted a dramaturgic marathon in a prologue made up of two scenes, followed by five acts containing eleven more of practically unrelieved gloom. It is true that no one of these episodes was long, but the necessary scenery changes consumed an unconscionable number of precious minutes. At the sixth performance, the first of two in New Haven, Act IV., "The Barricades," was dropped *in toto,* and the wilted audience was allowed to disperse shortly before midnight. The next evening, May 19, brought this experimental tour to a close after seven tentative performances. "Hate to have it over," wrote Josephine. "Lovely talk with Mr. Lackaye."

She was now free to pay a brief visit home and to go to Aurora to coach the Wells girls in a production of *A Midsummer Night's Dream,* a refreshing interlude before she returned for a second summer at the Gem. In a letter to an unidentified Portland friend, she stated that she was making something of a sacrifice. She had received offers of several summer engagements at a much higher salary, but Mr. Goding had engaged her the previous fall. "I have told all the managers I was previously engaged. It was no use to talk." She was a lady of her word. She added that she loved the Gem audiences so much that she wished she could shake hands with everybody.

The delights of Peaks Island made up for the dollars she lost by being honorable, but she did have one painful regret. She had to miss Jane Sever's wedding to Dr. Archer O'Reilly of St. Louis in the garden of the old house at Kingston. "How I long to be there!"

Besides playing several very easy roles, she was able to do

something with her music. For one thing, she orchestrated the accompaniment for an "Automobile Song" she sang in *Kindred Souls*. "Josephine Sherwood," reported the *Argus* "scored a big hit in the first act with a very clever specialty in which she sang a catchy song in an automobile costume and afterwards presented an example of serpentine and wooden shoe dancing that was most gracefully done."

But the season on the island was a short one, for Brady sent word that he wanted her for the tour of *The Law and the Man*, and she had to be off on August 12. She was one of the few survivors of the tryout cast, one of four out of the original twenty-eight, the others being Louise Everts (Epontine), Claudia Carson (one of the grisettes in the prologue), and F. Pollard (Champmathieu). Evidently Brady had concluded that the cast must be strengthened by the addition of some "names" for publicity purposes if nothing else. So he engaged the eminent English actress, Jeffreys Lewis, for the small but important role of the repulsive Mme. Thenardier, Melbourne MacDowell, who besides being a well-known actor was the widower of the great Fanny Davenport, for Valjean's nemesis, the police spy, Javert; and a good-looking juvenile, William Lamp, for Cosette's lover, Marius.

The tour opened under Brady's scrutiny at the Lyceum Theater in Harrisburg on September 3. As in Waterbury, the house was only "fair," but the reception was "enthusiastic." At least a moral victory was scored. Then the company headed for St. Louis, pausing en route in Altoona. There, "tired and dirty," they settled down for a real grind in an effort to get the unwieldy drama into some sort of acceptable form.

It was the unkind judgment of the local correspondent of the *New York Dramatic Mirror* that their struggles were futile. At the end of the week he reported that despite daily rehearsals Lackaye was still "far from having put the work into the shape required to make it a success commensurate with the effort and outlay." What was worse, he added: "No work so ambitious and in many large respects so praiseworthy was ever given here with so indifferent a cast as *The Law and the*

73

Man. Melbourne MacDowell as Javert and Josephine Sherwood as Fanchon (and later Cosette) were the only ones that saved the piece from threadbare mediocrity."

An even harsher verdict lay in store for the play when it reached Chicago at the end of the month, for lying in wait for it was Burns Mantle, then the pundit of the *Inter-Ocean*, his famous *Best Plays* still in the future. (It is a perfectly safe bet that *The Law and the Man* would not have been honored in any of those volumes.)

> If Actor Wilton Lackaye and Manager William Brady are as smart in their handling of "The Law and the Man" as they were last evening in coaxing curtain calls for its climaxes, they will strike the trail for the small town territory the day they finish their engagement in the Grand Opera-house and stay there all season.

They needed, he said, "to turn the corner of a water tank and come upon it suddenly in the opera-house at Baribou." Then, maybe they would "see the holes in it and patch them up." Yet, just or unjust, he did not frighten off his fellow citizens, for they crowded the house, perhaps to see how wrong he was.

Josephine was getting a workout. Not only was she learning how to build up widely different characters through constant repetitions, but she was also having to brace herself against contingencies that were anything but routine. Once, for instance, when she and Lackaye embarked on a very lachrymose scene, they discovered that a careless stagehand had left an unsightly feather duster on a bench between them, and there was nothing to do but act around it. They must make it invisible to the supposed-to-be tearful audience. The feat required considerable poise on the part of both, but they got away with it. That was one time when her amateur experience stood her in good stead. Lackaye was furious with the stagehand, pleased with Josephine.

On the whole, the actors fared much better with the gentlemen of the press than they had at the hands of the representative of the *Dramatic Mirror*. Usually, as in St. Louis, Josephine was singled out for particular commendation. The *St. Paul Pioneer-Express*, asserted that she was entitled to special mention for her study of the unfortunate Fantine. "She acted the difficult part with fiery and picturesque dash, and the effect was painfully realistic." The *Cincinnati Commercial* dwelt on her Cosette with its "strong contrast to her earlier assumed disguise." These compliments, thrilling as they were at the time, were to lead later to no little chagrin.

The troupe finally reached New York on December 20, serene in the confidence that they were there to stay for a long time. At first the prospects seemed favorable. "The Lambs were out in force," reported John Corbin in the *Telegraph*, "to welcome their new Shepherd after his long absence." As for Josephine, she was ecstatic.

> Flowers from Miss Lewis, wires from Mother, Howard Gore, & Mr. Swasey, notes & cards from Becky Hooper, the Georges, etc. Hd'ks, rabbit's paw, B. Lawrence. N. Y. opening *great*."

Probably not even Lackaye expected the metropolitan critics to leap from their aisle seats and toss their hats in the air—they did not—but neither did anyone foresee that almost immediately the author-star, the *raison d'être* for the whole business, would be laid low by the grippe. He was stricken on Christmas, and two days later was confined to his bed. On a few evenings he managed to drag himself to the theater and struggle through his part, but frequently he had to give in and leave Valjean to Frederick Esmelton, normally the good Bishop of Diton. Without Wilton Lackaye, *The Law and the Man* was to all practically non-existent.

The others carried on as best they could, without much encouragement. "While the actors declaimed their lines," said the *World*, "the orchestra sawed out blood-curdling music. It was a busy night for all concerned, but the busiest man of all was the one who handled the green lights." As in the provinces, Josephine attracted perhaps the greatest favor. Corbin said outright that she was "easily the best of the lot." It is not surprising that the hopes for a long run fizzled out and that, so far as Broadway was concerned. *The Law and the Man* sadly cried quits on February 2. The unhappy star's colleagues did their best to raise his drooping spirits.

> February 1. P. M. professional matinee. *Great.* Such a jammed house & wonderful enthusiasm. Ev'g performance as usual, fine house. Dinner with Mr. Hodges at the Martinique, fine time.

After this consoling send-off Lackaye led his satellites, if not exactly to the tank towns prescribed by Mantle, via several small cities, into the frozen north. But in Montreal they found that the chill in the air was by no means all outside His Majesty's Theater. The adjectives used by Josephine to describe the audiences are *small*, *wretched*, and *tiny*. One scheduled matinee was canceled "on account of wee house." Toronto, on the other hand, proved to be courteous. "Society" turned out *en masse*, and good cheer warmed the icy winds. From there the company headed south to their own national capital, where they were dismayed to find the icicles as long and sharp as those in Montreal. The handwriting was quite visible on the wall.

Long before this, Josephine had begun to pay for her flattering notices. Jeffreys Lewis was sending her no more bouquets. Indeed she was probably begrudging her the one she had contributed on the opening night. Very few people disliked Josephine, but among those few Miss Lewis wished to be "counted in." On February 9 the offender wrote, "Miss Lewis is treating me unbearably."

To do Miss Lewis justice, it must have been galling for an actress of her experience and reputation, a former star in her own right, who in her heyday had played Ophelia to the Hamlet of Edwin Booth himself, to see a young woman whom she understandably looked on as a mere novice wining the lion's share of the applause and of the critical acclamations. Furthermore, Josephine had the advantage of three sympathetic roles, whereas Miss Lewis was forced to content herself with one brief and very unpleasant one. John Corbin's words must have rankled. Another circumstance that is not likely to have soothed her feelings was the conspicuous favoritism shown by the star and his family—Mrs. Lackaye and "little Wilton"—to the younger woman. At all events, she turned in her notice and departed. Josephine—unlike her friend Louise Everts—was not one of the girls who waved her off bearing gifts.

By this time the ghost had begun not to walk. Despite the good business in Toronto, "We all received word of a cut in salary from Brady. I refused." Although Baltimore opened its arms to them, "Brady sent word we were to lay off for two weeks." So on April 13 the curtain fell to rise not again. When, three days later, Josephine went to the office to collect her salary, she learned that that was all.

Whatever the flaws in *The Law and the Man*, whatever heartbreak it may have entailed for Lackaye, it had in its eight-month's existence served Josephine Sherwood well. She had played successfully two leading roles—really three—opposite one of the most famous stars of the day, both on the road and, what was infinitely more important, in New York. Despite the opinion of Miss Lewis, she was no longer a tyro, but was now known to people who counted. For all this she had Wilton Lackaye to thank, and that debt she never forgot.

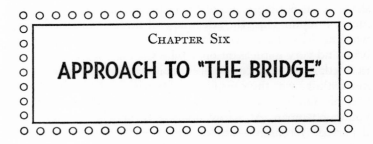

Chapter Six

APPROACH TO "THE BRIDGE"

It might be assumed that, having achieved recognition, Josephine would never again have to worry about unemployment, but any such assumption would be very wrong; in fact, it would seldom be true at any time in her career until near its end. Certainly it was not true in the spring of 1907. Unless she failed to mention them in her diary, offers simply did not come to her at this particular time. The year before, when she had not needed them, managers had looked her way, and they would do so again a year later. But not now.

If, as is probable, she did have some reserves in her bank, they were not enough to carry her for very long. Brady had paid her $60.00 a week and taken care of her railway fare, but for her living expenses she herself had been responsible, and though $60.00 went much further then than now, they did not spell riches. Her mother, anxious that Josephine not deplete her savings, sent her a generous check, or she might have faced real embarrassment.

It may not be polite to mention the fact and Josephine herself would doubtless be outraged, but, practically speaking, her friends did "come in handy." The many dinners to which she was treated by the constant Harry Hodges saved many useful pennies. While on tour, she found Radcliffe girls and other friends in city after city and as a rule was entertained royally. After Jane Sever married Archer O'Reilly and moved to St. Louis, it became a matter of course that she should stay with them. Sometimes the same hospitality was proffered by friends in other towns. Even with all these unmentionable savings her balance must have shrunk alarmingly, and it became imperative that she find other ways to earn a living.

There was her music. For some reason or other, she never included among the figures she entered in the backs of her diaries the amounts she made from it, although she often noted the receipt of royalties from Thompson in Boston. She also did little jobs of copying for Mrs. De Mille and others.

Meanwhile she wasted no time in bemoaning her unhappy lot. She had recently joined the Actors' Society, and now as a very active member she had a grand time at committee meetings and at the Actors' Fund Fair, where she had charge of a booth. As usual she went to many plays. Where the money came from is a question. Sometimes she was taken, but often she went on her own. April 23 was a red letter day.

> Went to the Ladies' Gambol of the Lambs, Actors' Theater, at one, sat in Mr. Lackaye's box with him & Mrs. L., little Wilton, and Miss Grace George. *Great.* Then Louise [Everts] & I went to Ladies' Day at the Players. Mr. Hodges fine to us, met many noted people. Ev'g saw Grace George in "Divorçons," good.

That spring she was not engaged to direct the annual Shakespeare production at Wells, nor is there any mention of overtures from the Gem. She spent a month on Peaks Island, at Trefethen's, with her mother and Aunt Anne, but did no acting. Before going to Maine she had paid a long visit to Newtonville and while there had written an article on "The Actor and the Stock Company" for the *Woman's Home Companion.*

79

It was accepted, and appeared in the October issue. In a style slightly reminiscent of Mrs. Winslow's sentimental *Yesterdays with Actors* it explains the routine operations of the stock company, whose near-extinction at the hands of the movie moguls she naturally could not foresee. Indeed she is inclined to see in the institution the hope of the theater in this country. She is on surer ground when she stresses the value of the training received by young actors under this stern discipline.

On her return to New York she tried out before Colonel Savage for a part in *The College Widow*, to no purpose. Although she was so short of funds that she was answering newspaper advertisements for a music critic and a translator, she rejected an offer of a part in something called *The Other House*. She continued to write songs and dispatch them to Thompson, but she soon found herself in such straits that she was compelled to accept two more gifts of money from her mother.

At last, on October 20, she had a windfall, thanks to George Denny and, no doubt, Harry Hodges, neither of whom can have been wholly unaware of her embarrassment. As has been said, these men were very active in the Amateur Comedy Club, the former being president, and the latter a member of the executive committee. Denny sounded her out on the possibility of her coaching the club's next production, Henry Arthur Jones's recent comedy, *Joseph Entangled*. Of course, there was not the slightest chance of her declining, and a few days later she was plugging away at the prompt copy.

At this point Irony, like one of the allegorical characters in the old morality plays, made its entrance on the stage. After all these barren months of futile trudging from office to office, now when at last she had found employment, along came an offer of a professional engagement. It was scarcely one she would have picked had she been in a position to consult her preferences, but it was too good for her to turn up her nose at it.

Of all plays, it was *Way Down East!* Today it would be incredible that this saccharine melodrama could be accepted in polite society if we did not recall the triumphs of Lillian Gish in the motion picture of 1920 and the buckets of tears that flowed down the aisles when poor long-suffering Anna was thrust out into the cruel snowstorm.[1]

Way Down East was the joint property of Brady and Joseph R. Grismer. The latter had "elaborated" Lottie Blair Parker's original in 1898, and the two had produced it with Mrs. Grismer, Phoebe Davis, as the heroine. It proved to be the hardiest of perennials, and by 1906 it was estimated that Miss Davis had suffered in more than three thousand blizzards. A year later neither she nor the play was showing any signs of weariness. But now the partners needed a new Kate, and Brady remembered his Cosette. Josephine was summoned to New Haven, where the company was performing, and put through her paces. The Grismers were satisfied, and she was hired.

But what about *Joseph Entangled?* Here luck was with her. Her services were not required till Christmas, and she was free to live up to both commitments.

The handsomely engraved program announces that the three performances of *Joseph Entangled* were the 181st, 182nd, and 183rd in the history of the club, the first having been staged in 1884. Everybody appears to have been left in good spirits, no one more so than the coach, when Denny escorted her ceremoniously down to the bank and oversaw the cashing of her check for $190.00. Moreover, by way of a bonus, he and Hodges, who had been in the cast, treated her to a dinner. To reciprocate she took Hodges to see Marie Doro and Aubrey Smith in *The Morals of Marcus.*

Way Down East was for Josephine nothing more than a time killer and a means of refilling her pockets. Kate Brewster, a rural coquette, was no challenge to her capabilities, and it was no feat to win critical approval along with the twenty-one other human members of the cast, not to mention the donkey, cows, calves, and sheep which were brought along to lend verisimilitude to the farm scenes. Six times, surprisingly enough,

[1] There was another motion picture version in 1935.

81

Mrs. Grismer condescended to relinquish the leading role and give her a chance to show what she could do in the way of patient suffering.

The tour retraced familiar routes through the Middle West. Except that Josephine saw a number of old friends, it was uninspiring, and $50.00 a week was ten less than the $60.00 Brady had paid her before. There was some consolation in being free to go to church every Sunday, but she could do that at home. After three months she decided that enough was enough, and refused to play another week. She had appeared 103 times as Kate, and six as Anna. She was tired of them both, and on March 28 bade them a relieved goodbye in Philadelphia and returned to New York.

Her situation was now greatly improved. She was again the sought-after instead of the seeker, but she bided her time. Her mother came down from Newtonville for a visit which involved the usual round of playgoing, and she found a new and stimulating companion in Walter Prichard Eaton, a brilliant young critic soon to be recognized as an authority on the stage and eventually to follow Professor Baker at Yale.

In a few weeks she was at Wells, grandly installed in the Prophet's Chamber (which took its name from the "little chamber" provided by the wealthy woman of Shunem for the Prophet Elisha) and was formally called upon by the President, Mrs. Piutie. *Twelfth Night* rehearsals were held daily, and one evening the cast gave her a dinner at the Inn. Having got everything ready for the opening, Josephine went back to New York. There seems to have been no objection to her custom of leaving before the actual performances. She put the girls on their own, and it was up to them to see things through.

For a change, she installed herself in the Hotel Latham, attended a "beautiful" service at the Little Church Around the Corner, and plunged into preparations for *The Road to Yesterday*, by Evelyn Greenleaf Sutherland and Beulah Dix, which she had seen with great pleasure some months before. The rights to this fantasy had been acquired by Jessie Bonstelle, who gave nine performances at the West End Theater in Harlem. This gifted directress had assembled her usual summer stock company, and this brief run was in the nature of a prelude to her seasons in Rochester and Buffalo. Once again Josephine was slated to be an ingénue. One would think that by this time, especially after she had proved that she was capable of better things, she would have grown weary of this typecasting, but she seems not to have done so. She probably welcomed a chance to work under Miss Bonstelle, who had begun under the Shuberts when she was only nineteen and at thirty-six already had behind her nearly twenty years of experience. She had not yet won the title of "The Maker of Stars," but she had earned wide respect for her acumen and her skill.

She opened her Rochester season on May 4 with *The Road to Yesterday*, but it was a short one, a week each of *The Road* and of Margaret Mayo's dramatization of Mrs. Humphrey Ward's *The Marriage of William Ashe*. Then she moved her cohorts on to Buffalo, where they were to stay till August 22.

Cousin Lillie received her kinswoman with open arms, and saw to it that her few idle moments were not boring ones. This solicitude was, of course, to have been expected, but not so the attentions of Richard Le Gallienne, who was spending the summer at Elbert Hubbard's Roycroft Inn in nearby East Aurora, and came frequently to the theater to see the plays and pay backstage visits to friends in the company. Twice Josephine and some of her fellow actors spent pleasant Sundays at East Aurora, attending chapel services and hearing the poet lecture. These were real treats.

Miss Bonstelle, well aware that in hot weather audiences generally prefer light fare, offered little in her repertoire to tax the mind or strain the emotions. Nevertheless, it yielded Josephine a number of parts that she enjoyed. She was, moreover, given several opportunities to display her musical talents, and made the most of them. For instance, in Mrs. Burton Harrison's *The Unwelcome Mrs. Hatch,* during a scene laid in Central Park, a group of children sang "Little Papoose," and Josephine warbled off stage another of her compositions, "Song to a Bird." Tastes have changed since those songs were

written by a sentimental young lady, and no doubt hers
changed too with the passing of time, but in 1908 they were
listened to with approbation, especially "Little Papoose,"
which she also had the gratification of hearing played by the
orchestra of a popular vaudeville house.

With the close of the season, she returned to her normal
base of operations, and, having rejected "Los Angeles stock"
and vaudeville skits, accepted a role in *The Panic,* a piece apparently of anonymous authorship. For better or for worse, it
was not fated to enjoy a long life, and after three performances
in Providence and a few more in Philadelphia, it gave up the
ghost, unwept by at least one member of the cast.

It was more fortunate than she realized at the time that
there was nothing to prevent her going home for a family
Christmas.

> Mother and I opened my stocking, great fun. Had a family
> Christmas tree, and lovely presents, heaps of 'em. Fine Xmas
> dinner & family tree.

While she was at home she and Mrs. Sherwood paid a visit
to the Colonial Theater to see Eugene Walter's *Paid in Full,*
a rather turgid melodrama which passed at the time for very
real realism. She had been exposed to it at least once before,
the previous spring, with Jessie Bonstelle and Eaton, and had
pronounced it "fine." With its emphasis on sex, it is not exactly
what one would have expected her to relish, but well-written,
tense scenes never failed to stir her, and of these *Paid in Full*
had plenty and to spare. Wagenhals and Kemper planned to
send it on tour, and on January 4 she presented herself at the
producers' office to make discreet inquiries. At the same time
she was careful not to deposit every egg in Walter's basket.

> Called on Mr. Kemper about "Paid in Full," also on Mr.
> Chapin about "Lincoln."

The next day she was still being cautious.

Rehearsed "Paid in Full," Beth Harris for Mr. Kemper, Astor Theater, A. M.—P. M. rehearsed Kate Morris in "Lincoln" for Mr. Chapin, Garden Theater.

She made such favorable impressions on both these gentlemen that the choice between Beth and Kate was hers to make. She chose Beth, and, as kismet decreed, determined then and there the course the rest of her life was to take. Had she picked Kate, there would probably never have been a Josephine Hull.

Heading the cast of *Paid in Full* was a young man from Seattle named Guy Bates Post, who had during recent seasons demonstrated that he was someone to watch. In plays like *The Virginian, Soldiers of Fortune,* and *The Heir to the Hoorah* he displayed abilities that clearly marked him as one of the rising actors of the day. So far as his latest role was concerned, however, he had to depend on the perceptions of the more observant members of his audiences rather than on the rank and file who were prone to base their opinions on charm rather than on competence, for Joe Brooks is very far removed from the hero breed. He is not even an honest-to-God villain, but just a cad. One reviewer commented that Post's "really artistic work as the husband was probably obscured to the majority of the audience on account of the thoroughly contemptible and unsympathetic part he had to play." None of the other six characters is subjected to the same ruthless realism; Joe's wife, played in this company by Julia Dean, is indeed an unbelievably noble creature straight out of the old-fashioned "mellers" in which the virtuous are almost as hard to swallow as the villainous. But such flaws did not bother a public avid in its craving for what it naïvely conceived to be the unadulterated, if repellent, truth.

It clearly appears that Josephine's esteem for *Paid in Full* did not long survive intimate acquaintance. For one thing, her own rather unattractive role may soon have begun to pall. It had little to offer an actress of her proficiency and must have grown monotonous. Although the tour, which started off in Worcester on January 23, lasted three months, she took the trouble to paste only four reviews in her scrapbook, and neglected to identify these. The fact that she usually rated little more than casual notice no doubt had something to do with this indifference. Finally a week at the Grand Opera House in New York ended the whole affair. She was presented on that occasion with a necklace by her stage mother, Miss Hattie, and with flowers by the stagehands. She always was a favorite of the stagehands.

Her mother was in New York when she got there, and the two of them had another fling of the kind they both loved before she went home on April 12.

When she had been back only a few days, she was signed up by Harrison Grey Fiske for *The Bridge*, a new play by Rupert Hughes, in which Guy Post was to be starred. It was to him that she owed this engagement, for he had recommended her to Fiske. "Josephine," says Post, "seemed suited to a very good part in the play, and Mr. Fiske liked her very much. She was the shapely young girl type. Slender little figure and a personality that radiated an inborne opulence. It was inspired by a deep reverence for all that is of the highest and most sacred." For the rest of her life she was deeply grateful to Guy Bates Post.

Rehearsals began at once, and she was in high feather. Then on May 4 suddenly her whole world changed.

> Had letters from Aunt Anne, saying that Mother had a hemorrhage of the brain yesterday & to-day continued about the same. They have a nurse. She is very ill. Phoned home at night.

Only those who know how close was the bond between the two women can grasp the severity of the shock and the anguish of mind that ensued. Every instinct told Josephine to forget all else and rush to her mother's bedside, but she stayed where she was. Beneath her deceptively soft and yielding exterior there was unbending steel. *The Bridge* was nearing readiness for its out-of-town opening, and she was needed. She knew, moreover, that her mother would have had her do nothing else. So somehow, sustained by the kindness of her associates and the solicitude of Harry Hodges, she managed to carry on. She kept in touch with Newtonville, now encouraged, now discouraged by the fluctuations in her mother's condition.

On May 9 *The Bridge* was taken to Providence. This was a godsend. From there she could reach home in a few hours, where, by this time, it was obvious that Mrs. Sherwood was dying.

> May 10. Went home early in the morning, and was with Mother all day. She knew & talked with me. Stayed till late afternoon. Back to Providence, ev'g. Opened in "The Bridge."
> May 11. Went home early morning,—with Mother all day. She is worse, did not speak, to me or anyone, except to say, "Water." There is no chance for her. Ev'g, "Bridge," Providence.

The next morning Aunt Nellie called to break the news that her mother had died in her sleep. "Had to get thro' two performances. Wrote notes." Thursday and Friday she went home by early train and made arrangements for the funeral, returning to Providence for the evening performances. On Saturday her ordeal was over. *The Bridge*, the tryout concluded, closed for the summer.

Except for a few days in Aurora, coaching the Wells girls in *As You Like It* and strolling among the columbines by the lake, she remained in Newtonville all summer. On August 7 she tore herself away and returned to New York to resume work on *The Bridge*.

CHAPTER SEVEN

SHELLEY

"1909. Shelley and I met."

IT WAS JOSEPHINE'S CUSTOM to make on appropriate pages in her line-a-day notations of important anniversaries—usually to make sure that she did not overlook them. This was not true of all, for many of them she could not conceivably have forgotten, but of the scores of entries none held for her the magic of these four short words.

As a matter of fact, although they had never met before, she had almost certainly seen Shelley Hull at least twice. Incredible as it may have seemed to her later, she had not noticed him particularly. She must have been blind. He had been in the cast, rather inconspicuously to be sure, of *Sweet Kitty Bellairs*, which she had seen twice, and perhaps he was in *The College Widow* company for which she had tried out unsuccessfully in 1907. But not till April 7, 1909, did they ever come face to face.

Guy Bates Post, the star of *The Bridge*, remembers this meeting.

I introduced Josephine to Shelley. Mr. Harrison Grey Fiske

was about to present me in a play by Rupert Hughes called "The Bridge." Mr. Fiske asked me to suggest artists for our cast. Josephine seemed suited to a very good part and Mr. Fiske liked her very much and he said, "Now where can we find the young man good enough to play opposite that girl?" We tried for a week to find someone and Mr. Fiske said no to all. Katherine Grey lived in the apartment below us and I asked Kate if she could think of anyone. She said she had seen a young man act in a one-act skit on the Orpheum circuit. It failed and she imagined he might be available. She didn't know him personally, so we contacted him through the Orpheum office and he came to see me. I felt he was right. I telephoned Mr. Fiske who said to bring him down to 12 West 40th St. Mr. Fiske took me into another office, and said, "Guy, he is it." Rehearsals started and Josephine and Shelley met.

There is no mention of Shelley in the diary until May 15, after her mother's death, then "Flowers from S. Hull." That was all. It was a very different story after rehearsals were resumed in August. She reached New York on the seventh and settled herself in the St. Hubert on West 57th Street. The next day she wrote:

Ev'g Shelley Hull called & we had a splendid talk.

That was the beginning. From then on his name is seldom missing from the pages in the little red book. There were more "splendid talks," long walks, dinners, and, after he had helped her rent a piano, evenings of music, for like her he loved to sing. Just what was going on must have been obvious to all who had eyes to see.

Josephine's emotions had not yet completely calmed down after her mother's sudden death, and her world was still dark. Now this radiant spirit, charged with life and gaiety, had come to restore her to the light. Perhaps she sometimes recalled her girlish description of Robert Taber, for Shelley Hull was another "godlike figure." He was tall and graceful in his movements, and his handsome features were marked by intelligence and sensitivity. "There was no gentler, lovelier personality in our theater," a friend was to say years later. Josephine had never lacked for men to ply her with attentions, but never before, she was convinced, had there been one like this.

Shelley was no novice in the theater. Indeed he had been in it longer than she had. On the evening of December 3, 1901, while she was in the Radcliffe Library poring over her homework for Mrs. Winslow, he was dancing and singing away merrily on the stage of the Grand Opera House in Terre Haute. He had even had the foresight to be born near Mary Anderson's childhood home on Gray Street in Louisville, where his father was for years dramatic critic of Colonel Watterson's *Courier-Journal* and had heard theater talk all his life. His older brother, Howard, had caught the contagion first and got himself a place in the chorus of a touring company of *Floradora*. When in the course of time it reached Louisville, he had no difficulty persuading the seventeen-year-old Shelley that being an actor would be much more exciting than selling railroad tickets and ushering at Macauley's Theater. John Cronin, the manager of the company, had also to be convinced. Listening to Shelley's warbling, he was not impressed by his changing voice, and advised him to return to the railroad office. But the warmhearted Irishman was touched by the boys' lugubrious faces as they made for the door, and relented. Forthwith Shelley became a chorus man. Some months later he was promoted to the famous Sextet, less because of any improvement in his vocal prowess than because of his good looks and winning ways.

After *Floradora* his progress, if not sensational, was varied. Belasco decided that he could use him, and gave him a small supporting role in *Sweet Kitty Bellairs* with Henrietta Crosman, plus a job as assistant stage manager. There were times when he also led the orchestra under the supervision of William Furst, with whom he was studying music. The season of 1906–1907 he spent in Boston as juvenile with the Castle Square Company. Josephine was then on tour with Lackaye.

After several assorted engagements, including a vaudeville stint as leading man for Virginia Harned, on Katie Grey's recommendation, he was tapped by Fiske for *The Bridge*. This gave him a chance to repay Howard by getting him a part, albeit a very small one.

The play opened at the Majestic Theater on September 4. If it did not cause the critics to hail Hughes as the long-awaited Great American Dramatist, it was received for the most part with respectful politeness, although Alan Dale of the *American* was too caustic for comfort. "*The Bridge*," he said, "shows a good deal of weakness. Some of its arches are a bit shaky. It is a bridge that won't stand much. In fact, common sense gives it a jolt." His colleagues, however, were more approving, and found much to commend. The *Herald* said it deserved success and prophesied that it would enjoy it.

Except for the injection of some rather unusual symbolism, *The Bridge* is a more or less conventional drama about capital and labor with a *Romeo and Juliet* variation. The daughter of the wealthy and haughty railroad president who is financing the construction of the mighty span falls in love with the young engineer who is abetting the workmen in their strike for a living wage. Naturally the capitalist is outraged, but in desperation he offers to meet the union demand, with the stipulation, however, that his daughter bid her young man goodbye forever. The American drama had not yet reached its pessimistic obsession with unhappy endings, and the ice about the tycoon's heart melts shortly before the curtain falls. The bridge of course symbolizes this reconciliation between the two classes. To lighten his story somewhat Hughes introduces a second pair of lovers who, although they are not free from problems of their own, add a touch of comedy. After some complications, their affairs also are straightened out, and at the end all are content. That is, all but Alan Dale.

"The noise," he complains, "almost drove me crazy. It surely must have been heard blocks away. In the street you would rush away from such an unholy racket. On the stage it was offered as beautiful realism." When the footlights revealed the bridge in all its glory with its mighty girders and towering superstructure, the audience gasped.

> Workmen toss red hot bolts, pneumatic riveters pound on the hot metal, hammers fall on the steel beams, steel cables are paid down to draw up solid beams, straddled by men in grime and overalls. (*N. Y. Press*, Sept. 5.)

Noise and all, it was like a major building job on Broadway or Fifth Avenue, and "the audience was unstinted in its applause." Other scenes rivaled this one in lavishness though not in novelty. If scenery alone could carry a production, *The Bridge* was safe.

As for the acting, if the reviewers had their reservations about the play, they had few about the excellent cast headed by Post, whose elevation to stardom was deemed fully justified. "In appearance he has a positive dignity, there is a surety of expression in his manner and voice, and an evidence of a thorough understanding of his character." There was praise too for the heroine as played by Katherine Emmet, who carried conviction as the courageous highborn maid and displayed power in her emotional scenes. Shelley and Josephine as the second young couple were called upon to do little more than be their own attractive selves.

> It is in the fourth act that Miss Sherwood shows how completely she is mistress of her art and how sympathetic is the part to which she has been assigned. She steps forth from the girl who has lived among the cinders and is transformed to the young woman of a totally unsuspected power and temperament. In this scene she develops a delicious vein of comedy which leaves with you a pleasing perfume, so to speak. (*Morning Telegraph*, Sept. 19.)

Despite the good acting and the sensational scenery, however, *The Bridge* failed to capture the fancy of the New York public, to whom girders and grimy workmen were not exactly nine-day wonders. After a month, therefore, Fiske sent it on the road, up the Hudson to Albany, Rochester, and other northern cities.

Meanwhile the two young people managed to find ways to occupy themselves agreeably.

> Sept. 30. P. M. saw Chevalier with Shelley Hull. Howard Brown came for dinner. Ev'g performance, Miss Emmet's party to Katherine Grey at the Posts'.

The evening's hostess was still formally "Miss Emmet," but soon she was to be transformed to "Callie" and enter the inner circle of Josephine's most precious friends, there to remain for over forty years.

> October 4. Albany. Took a long walk with S. Hull, out by a park, pretty streets, & the Capitol.
>
> October 7. Rochester. Ev'g very long & late performance. Shelley & I had supper with Bert Lytell.
>
> October 10 (Sunday) Shelley & I went out to a park, and had a beautiful paddle up the Genesee River. P. M. Left for Buffalo & reached here late afternoon. Hotel Touraine. Dinner at the Iroquois, & ev'g bridge with Shelley & Miss Repton.
>
> October 12. Walked out to Delaware Park with Shelley, & had a gorgeous time. Very cold & blustery, & finally snow.

Buffalo, unfortunately, produced an unpleasant interruption. Katherine Emmet had the bad luck to run afoul of a new contraption. She was run over by an automobile, one of the first actresses in the history of the American stage to suffer such humiliation. Her injuries were not serious, but she had to be out of the cast for a few evenings, and Josephine's daylight hours had to be devoted to understudy rehearsals instead of to romantic strolls and paddles. This mischance, as the next entry will show, did not affect more vital matters.

October 24. Left Toronto and had a long day's journey past Lake Ontario & Erie to Cleveland. Hotel Hollender. Played bridge in ev'g. Shelley asked me to marry him. We had a long talk.

Thus laconically was one of the great moments of Josephine's life recorded for posterity. The stoicism was for the diary only. She did not pour out her innermost feelings in the cramped space of a line-a-day, but, as Post reveals, there were other places.

On the opening night in Cleveland I was sitting in front of my mirror making up and there was a knock on my door. My valet opened it and Josephine and Shelley asked if they might come in. I said, "Of course." They backed against the door, holding hands. She said, "We have something to tell you and we feel you should be the first to know it. Shelley has asked me to marry him, and—and—" She burst into tears, and Shelley took her in his arms. I said, "It was sweet of him to ask you, and I'm sorry you feel so badly about turning him down." "Oh, no, I didn't turn him down. I said, 'Yes.' Of course I did! And I'm so happy!" I thanked them for telling me and I promised not to tell if they would go to their dressing rooms and get ready for the evening performance. It was not necessary to keep the secret. She told everybody. Just honest frankness.

Her joy was so great that she just had to share it with everyone. Even if she had said not a word, her face would certainly have given her away.

Of course Newtonville had to be told. So, two days later, "Wrote home about my engagement." The impact of this announcement upon the household on Harvard Street can easily be imagined. The awful prediction had come true; Josephine was going to marry an actor. In the diary there is no mention of a reply. Yet there must have been one, probably four, dreadful epistles to compose, especially Aunt Gertrude's. Although she was the oldest, Aunt Fanny had wider horizons than her sisters and probably had the least trouble.

The road proved to be no more enthusiastic about the conflict between romance and strikes than the supposedly more sophisticated Broadway had been, and in Cleveland the final curtain descended on *The Bridge*.

Back in New York the engaged couple found many things to do. There were formalities to be observed. Mrs. Hull was prompt in welcoming her daughter-in-law elect. Josephine hied herself out to Montclair to inform Uncle Theordore and Aunt Cassie, and the former, as her closest male relative, immediately invited Shelley to have dinner with him to give the conventional account of himself. The results of this conference were as agreeable as could have been hoped. Shelley was presented to Cousin Lillie too. But Newtonville remained, delay was out of the question, and on November 24 Josephine took her young man to Boston.

They reached there so late that they had dinner at the Essex and fortified themselves for the confrontation. Meanwhile the aunts had to brace themselves too. Whatever they felt inside, for Josephine's sake they must appear at their best. Nervous and fluttery, they waited for the sound of footsteps on the porch. It was night and the lights were all on when Josephine, aglow with happiness and pride, rang the doorbell. Then she presented all those she loved best in the world to each other. What happened? Again the diary is of no help: "In ev'g talked with family, a lovely time." The next day there was a "lovely dinner with the family" and an introduction to "dear old Uncle Phil." After that, leaving unrecorded impressions behind them, they returned to New York and the business of life.

In what frame of mind did Shelley leave his new relatives? Although nothing has been told, there is little doubt about what it was. Grandmother and her four maiden daughters, whatever they had thought of actors before, were no more impervious to this young man who radiated charm like an aura than were the teen-age girls in his audiences. He had known exactly how to handle the situation, and had proceeded accordingly. Years later, Josephine said that Aunt Gertrude *pretended* not to like to be kissed. He understood perfectly well how to behave in the presence of that virtuous modesty. "He teased her." Simply by being his natural self, he won their hearts forthwith and for all time. "After all, he is a gentleman." Let no one ever dare to say a word against Josephine's young man.

As soon as she and Shelley were back in New York, they set about looking for work, since she maintained that she had not the slightest intention of giving up her career. He found something first, in Winchell Smith's comedy, *The Fortune Hunter*. The rub was that the company was scheduled to play Chicago, and that was a long way off. On December 11, after a parting breakfast at the Knickerbocker, she saw him off. "Oh dear!" She had accepted an offer for a part in *The Call* and tried to forget her loneliness in the rehearsals.

It was no go—the blue devils took over. Without Shelley's ebullient presence, she had time for second thoughts, and conjured up unnamed fears and anxieties. Mrs. Hull hovered consolingly near, and one evening brought her youngest son, Henry, whom Josephine pronounced "a dear," to cheer her up, but she could not recapture her peace of mind. On Christmas *The Call* opened up the river in Kingston, in the midst of a snowstorm. "Wire from Shelly." In a raging blizzard, which was symbolic of her feelings, the troupe went on to Newburgh, where she sought peace of mind in church. Whatever comfort she found there, there was none for her in Red Bank, New Jersey. "Matinee in a freezing theater—awful. Ev'g ditto. A dreadful day." She could stand no more, and in Atlantic City, on her birthday, turned in her notice. "Had box from Shelley, a kimona, Music, etc. & other birthday & Xmas things sent from home & many lovely letters." Even these could not restore her equanimity.

On January 8 she returned to New York, rented a room, and went to Mrs. Hull for comfort. She was still upset. Nor were matters much better in Chicago. Shelley was greatly perturbed by her obvious unhappiness, and on the seventeenth wrote her reassuringly, but firmly. She must get hold of herself.

> I am weary for you. This day has been one long sigh. Your letter this morning telling me what I half knew already, that you were not well and unhappy put the finishing touch to a heart that was already about to burst for loneliness and longing. It has been damp and drizzly all day. Went down to rehearse at eleven, wrote you a letter and as about leaving the theater, I got that indescribably lovely little letter from you written Saturday night. It is now about five and I have been since eleven just aching and aching and aching, unable to think or act or smile. I know perfectly that it would be better to wait if we only gain something by it and I can wait as long as you are not unhappy and ill or worried.
>
> I understand, darling, all about it. Don't feel or think that you have worried me with your "trouble." That is a wrong feeling for either of us to ever have. We are too close together in soul and understanding to ever fear "troubling" each other. We mustn't feel that or think of that. But the thing to consider always is an open discussion of what is best for *us*, then we are getting at what is best for the individual.
>
> You understand don't you? All that sounds involved or foolish maybe but you are so unselfish that I think at times you need looking after. Do you understand?

This letter and perhaps others had the desired effect. Finally she was able to put by whatever perplexity had been preying on her mind, and soon was feeling well again physically. One thing now was sure. Separation was insupportable. They had given it a try, and it would not work. She would retire from the stage except when engagements would not keep them apart. As yet no definite date was set for the wedding, but it was not to be long deferred, and meanwhile there was a great deal to be done.

Mrs. Hull stood by ready to help, and on February 5 Howard put his future sister-in-law on the train to go home for a month. In Newtonville everything was in a whirl, for there had not been a wedding in the family since her mother's. The house must have resembled a dressmaker's establishment as the trousseau was planned and put together. She made a quick trip back to New York to buy a blue suit at Lord and Taylor's, and material for the wedding dress itself. Shelley buried her under an avalanche of letters and flowers, and finally set April 3 as the day. As this was less than a month off, it involved much more scurrying about. She must have worked fast, for in less than a week she was trying on the finished dress for the approval of her aunts. She was also catching up on some necessary correspondence. One person she could not neglect was Jane O'Reilly, who had to be brought up to date. She had not been able to go to Jane's wedding, and now Jane was going to miss hers.

NEWTONVILLE
March 18th

DEAREST JANE,

A flying, hastening word to you to tell you that I'm going to Chicago to be married on April 3rd at one o'clock in St. Paul's Chapel. Your very best loving and lucky thoughts, dear, please, at that time. It has been a great whirl and hustle and quite in keeping with my cyclonic way of living! The play I started out in at Xmas was a horrid affair and I left it after a couple of weeks and collapsed a bit nervously. Shelley's play made an enormous hit in Chicago and they are to continue there right thro' the summer so he's been clamoring for me to go out and get married. It seemed really the most sensible thing. This separation is awful and there's no reason for it! So Aunt Nellie is going out with me to "give me away,"—we leave on the last day of March, and she'll stay a few days after the wedding with Mrs.Hull, who is going on from New York. After our very quiet little wedding we're going to stop at May Linn's house for an informal bite and talk. That's my actress-like wedding, Jane. We'll live in a hotel the first weeks and take May's house for the summer when she comes East, but that's not settled.

Shelley has a very grand New York engagement for next winter and we hope then to find a little flat and furnish it and keep it year in and year out for our home headquarters.

Dear Jane, I hope you are well. I shall fly over to Cambridge to see your mother and Mrs. Folsom next week, but oh, it is such a rush! Got home from N. Y. Sunday and did most of my shopping there. I'm to be married in a soft green crepe afternoon gown with a yoke of point appliqué and a bit of oriental jewelled ornament, and much self embroidery. It's a peach. And a hat to go with it. Have two tailored suits a few waists (including your lovely Xmas one, all made up with hand work) and a one-piece voile gown, three hats, and lots of shoes and stockings and underwear. In the future I play when I can be with Shelley, in the same company or city,—that's all. We're going to be happy, happy happy!

Love to Archer and your darling boys and always to you, my own dear Jane. (Wish you could come to Chicago.)

JOSEPHINE

Letters flew back and forth between Newtonville and Chicago. On the twentieth she dispatched one westward, two small, unmatched pieces of notepaper, the first and larger gray with a monogrammed "J. S." in green at the head of the page.

MY DEAR Mr. SHELLEY HULL—

This is the last presentable sheet of monogrammed paper belonging to a maiden lady whose initials are as above. She wishes to give you the last remnants of maidenhood to no one but you. So here it is, *so* much of it at least. And never, nevermore will she write on paper marked JS only, she does vow hereby.

Darlingest darling, I am just home from church. Wrote endless letters this afternoon and had endless callers and phones, and some dinner invitations. Said no to all. And everyone is going to call on me. I shall go mad. Phoned my dear old Uncle Phil and changed our music to Thursday evening,—The church service was lovely and the Bishop had a fine sermon,

99

splendid and real and beautiful and practical all at once. I disgraced the community by dropping the three of diamonds out of my prayer-book into the aisle! It must have slipped in there in the chaos of my trunk. The Bishop would have loved it but he didn't see it. He's a darling.

So are you, and more of a one than any in the world. I love you, my great, big-souled love and want you. Good night, beloved. Hold your arms out to me and love me always and it will be heaven forever.

JOSEPHINE

On the twenty-fifth she "went to City hall & got the license, & arranged taxes," and addressed announcements. After a final visit to the cemetery, the last day of March found her ready.

> Left home at noon, the Dawsons, Leslie, Uncle Phil, Aunts A & G saw Aunt Nellie and me off. Flowers & presents & slippers & rice and orange blossoms.

In Chicago Shelley and his mother were waiting in the station and took them to the Elms Hotel. It must have seemed to Josephine that being married on Sunday gave the ceremony a particular benison.

> My wedding-day—sunny—Had lovely letters & wires. Shelley and I were married at St. Paul's Chapel Chicago, by Rev. Herman Page at one o'clock. Aunt Nellie gave me away. Daisy my matron of honor. Howard & Henry & Mrs. Hull, Mrs. Vaughn, the Linns, Howlands & De Witts & Lothians. Lunch at May's. Shelley & I came to the Windermere.

So Josephine "dwindled into a wife." Unlike Millamant, however, she did not do so by degrees, but all at once, as the few words of the Episcopal marriage service were read. The career to which she had aspired ever since she had been old enough to aspire to anything and to which she had dedicated the past eight years of her life was cast aside without a noticeable qualm. After all, she was getting something much better— Shelley.

The ceremony was scarcely concluded when she found herself caught up in a social whirl, for she had many friends in and near Chicago, and they kept her on the go with luncheons, calls, and sightseeing expeditions. Whenever Shelley was free, there were gaieties of every sort their well-wishers could devise. Daisy Fillebrown, now married to Geordie Murray, and May Howland, one of the Girls of '99, now the wife of the witty newspaper man and teacher, James Weber Linn, lived within easy reach. Through them the Hulls met a number of University of Chicago people, the William Nitzes and the Robert Herricks, who outdid themselves in hospitality. Josephine also came to know Louise Closser Hale, wife of an artist, and actress in her own right; immediately the two women were drawn together in a close relationship that was precious to them both. So, in spite of the hot weather, which always irritated Josephine, her honeymoon months in Chicago were all she could wish.

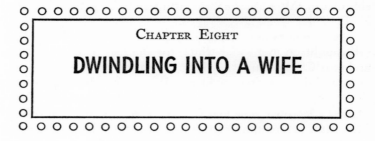

CHAPTER EIGHT

DWINDLING INTO A WIFE

FOR THE NEXT FEW YEARS the story of Josephine is the story of Shelley, of the rise of a determined and gifted young actor from relative obscurity to ultimate stardom. His wife, all her ambitions now centered on him instead of on herself, was in a sense an appendage, albeit a very important one. It was her job to further his career in every way she could, watching over his health, helping him with advice, and keeping him serene. He for his part appreciated her selfless devotion, and paid the most serious heed to her counsels. The old bromide, "My wife is my severest critic," has perhaps never been more pertinent than to them. Her advice was constructive, never depressingly destructive, taking the form of suggestions for improving his effects. She never hesitated to voice her very decided opinions and he listened to them with respect even if he did not invariably do what she said.

The life of a matinee idol's wife is not the easiest in the world. No matter how understanding she may be, how great is her confidence in her husband, she needs to be more than human to maintain at all times an attitude of tolerant detachment. And Shelley, no run-of-the-mill idol, was pretty close to unique. In the years to come his wife sometimes found the going rough, although she resolutely kept in the background and put on a good act of being deaf, dumb, and blind. Yet it was an act. Once when an inquiring reporter suggested to Shelley that Mrs. Hull might sometimes be a bit jealous, he replied with a smile, "My wife is far too sensible." Not always so sensible as he thought, she often seethed inwardly, sometimes for months on end.

"Mr. Hull can be more adorable as a lover than anyone of his years now on the American stage." If it were not for his sense of humor, "he would be too spoiled for any good use." "Isn't he a darling?" "He has the most adorable wave in his hair." "Aren't his eyes lovely?" "My dear, I'm positively thrilled. Mr. Hull is the best looking thing I've ever seen. He's cute as Christmas."

These ecstasies were by no means locked up in the palpitating bosoms of the flappers who enjoyed them, but were poured out in highly charged phrases to the object of all this adoration. It was perhaps a good thing that, at least, most of them reached him by mail.

Despite nagging ambitions for finer things, "This clever actor admits that he enjoys making love on the stage." But Shelley added, "Hugging and kissing and spouting sentimental lines on the stage is only a business, and is no more personal to me than a broker dictating a letter to his stenographer."

Even if this was true, possibly the vis-à-vis was not always so impersonal, and perhaps it would not be sensible to take for granted that she was. Philosophy now was harder than it had been in the classes at Radcliffe. But there was slight hint of all these anxieties in these first happy months, and Josephine contentedly devoted herself to learning her new part.

At the end of July Shelley withdrew temporarily from *The Fortune Hunter*, and they set out for home, not without first paying a pilgrimage to St. Paul's Chapel and taking snapshots of it for their scrapbook. What happened after that she reported to Jane O'Reilly on September 11:

. . . Since Chicago things have been in such a whirl! We left there much earlier and more hastily than we had expected,— managers whisked Shelley East at a week's notice to play a fortnight here in New York. We promptly flathunted, and have leased a darling, six rooms, at 133 West 56th St.,—and move in sometime in October, on our return from Boston for the New York run of the play. I'm selecting papers and floor-coverings and furniture and almost going mad with joy and excitement over it all. Then we went to Pleasant Valley, Conn. (the Hulls' little country home) and just rested for two weeks. It's a beautiful little mite of a village with fourteen houses and a church and a store, on one side of the street and the river on the other,—Berkshire spurs and lakes and woods, every-thing most heavenly for our belated honeymoon vacation. We were lazy and wild as could be,—then back to town for rehear-sals, and shopping morning, noon, and night. Also an influx of relatives from all quarters of the country, Hulls and Sherwoods and all their contiguous branches—till we are terribly gay and a bit tired, but having a wonderful time.

The resumed run of *The Fortune Hunter* was very brief, and then Shelley started rehearsals for *Electricity*, a new farce written by William Gillette for the lovely Marie Doro. Jose-phine found the opening in Atlantic City on September 22 an "exciting success," but said success very soon proved to have been deceptive, for the play was lucky to hold out for two months. Shelley played a rich young man who disguises him-self as an electrician in order to win the heart and hand of a nitwitted society bud who, like Lydia Languish, fancies that she wishes to marry into humble life. He, said the *World*, "struggled manfully with the desire to be poor but a gentle-man still."

By mid-December the ex-electrician was at work on another job, this time as a hotheaded French youth who is out to de-fend the honor of his family. *The Foolish Virgin*, a singularly ineffective adaptation of a none-too-good drama by Henri Ba-taille, was illuminated by the presence of a star even more famous than Miss Doro. Mrs. Patrick Campbell was inspired to show just how noble a good woman can be. As it turned out, she showed, rather, how foolish. "Unselfish devotion," commented Charles Darnton in the *Evening World*, "may be a beautiful thing, but too much of it is becoming only in dogs." Agreed that Mrs. Campbell was an actress of exceptional attainments, not even she could make New Yorkers relish the spectacle of a wife who, despite her aching heart, defended her errant husband and his foolish inamorata at their illicit rendezvous from the fury of the girl's outraged brother. The role of the avenging youth that fell to Shelley turned out to be "more ludicrous than fearful." Probably neither he nor his doting helpmeet shed any tears when, on the day after Christmas, the two weeks' notice was posted backstage.

Josephine undoubtedly knew, but regrettably she fails to reveal, just what the sharp-tongued Stella had to say about the inability of Americans to appreciate true nobility. She had a perfect chance to hear all on January 9 when she and Shelley dined with the great lady and some of her friends at the Marie Antoinette before attending a performance of *The Blue Bird*. The combination of Stella and Maeterlinck's gentle fantasy strikes one as a little incongruous. Afterward the whole party toiled up the stairs to the Hull rookery for an after-the-theater supper. It is too bad that the hostess kept her own counsel about that evening. Being the person she was, she must have had her trying moments. Being the lady she was, she would not tattle on a guest even to her diary.

With his next venture Shelley had somewhat better luck. At least the play lasted longer. Daniel Frohman, who had been "lovely" to Josephine on her first sortie into New York, now engaged her husband to support Charles Cherry in *Seven Sisters*, a farce adapted by Edith Ellis from the Hungarian of Ferencz Herczeg. The drawback was that his role, no very fat plum, was just another undistinguished representative of an amorous youth. Furthermore, no other member of the cast really had much of a chance, inasmuch as a young lady named Laurette Taylor had been engaged for the feminine lead and she proceeded to run away with the whole business. The farce, such as it was, was all hers from the start, and her colleagues, including the amiable star, could only watch what was going on with what cheer they could.

It would seem that managerial hopes dwindled during rehearsals, for when it opened at the Lyceum on February 20, Josephine reported that it met with "unexpected success," probably, though she does not say so, thanks to Miss Taylor. Even so, there were no long queues at the box office. Alan Dale, a bit peevishly, complained that it was a goulash from which the paprika required in Hungarian cooking was omitted. Consequently it did not linger long at the Lyric, but took to the road bound for Chicago. Before it started out, Josephine was engaged as understudy for at least some of the seven sisters who, protocol insisted, had to be married off in chronological order. If she ever had a chance to go on, the diary fails to note the fact.

This exodus broke in on the pattern of life that the Hulls had established while *Seven Sisters* was in rehearsal. Josephine had settled down to her housewifely duties, cooking, cleaning —whenever she had nothing else to do, she always cleaned out closets—and sewing. They had bought a rebuilt grand piano at Steinway's, and she used it to write a song entitled "The Heavens are Telling" for Thompson. Whenever they could, they went to the theater, and once enjoyed a real thrill when Shelley's brother Henry opened in Edward Sheldon's controversial play *The Nigger*, in which their friend Guy Post was starred. Henry, said his sister-in-law, was "very good." The other brother, Howard, had recently announced his engagement to Margaret Anglin, and Josephine and Shelley paid a formal call to welcome this celebrity into the family. They had to miss the wedding, which took place in St. Patrick's Cathedral, while they were in Chicago.

Although the run in that city was not very long, it had its compensations. They sentimentally returned to the Windermere, but soon moved out to the Exmoor Country Club, where a golf course was close at hand. They also saw much of the friends they had known a year before. Just before the engagement closed Cherry obligingly became ill, and Shelley had a chance to play the lead. According to his wife, he gave a "wonderful performance." Then they went home, bearing a puppy given them by Geordie.

They found New York stifling and hurried off to "the Valley," the puppy in their arms, but found little relief in Connecticut, for the thermometer soared to a record-breaking 104 degrees on the Fourth. One victim of the heat was Josephine's beloved Mrs. Winslow. Old and sick, she succumbed at her home in Concord. Being back with "the family," Josephine was able to hurry out to see the widower and son, and to accompany them to the burial in the Winslow lot at Springfield.

> Shelley & I sailed from Boston to Portland. Rough & stormy but great. Came to Headland Inn, Trefethens. Sat on rocks in ev'g. We have Mother's room.

The welcome vacation ended with a couple of days at Kingston, where Josephine, Jane, and Helen Tetlow made the rounds of neighboring classmates while Shelley went deep-sea fishing with the Sever boys.

On their return to New York he hitched his wagon to a new star, or rather, a different one, for in 1911 Minnie Maddern Fiske was not exactly new. She had not been that even when she had granted Josephine those "lovely" interviews nearly ten years before. Although Shelley probably did not realize it, the famous star was having hard sledding. For years she and her husband, Harrison Grey Fiske, had been courageously battling the Theatrical Syndicate which sought to get a stranglehold on the American theater and met with ill-deserved success. Now the Fiskes were trying to recoup losses, and having a hard time of it. Her last vehicle, Harry James Smith's *Mrs. Bumpstead-Leigh* had been close to a hit, but she had very serious doubts about the play she had undertaken to do next. An attractive young leading man might help the cause.

Langdon Mitchell had provided her with two of the greatest successes she had ever had, *Becky Sharp* and *The New York*

Idea, but about *The New Marriage* she was uneasy. Nevertheless, she went ahead, engaged an outstanding company, and in mid-September began her rehearsals.

The New Marriage, in which the author sought, according to Amy Leslie of the *Chicago News,* to "swat the suffragette," opened its tryout tour in Syracuse on October 19 and then worked its way westward through Pittsburgh to Chicago, where, it was expected, judgment would be pronounced for better or for worse. It was, very definitely for worse. As a philandering reformer Shelley showed that his acting had progressed since his appearances in *The Fortune Hunter* and *The Seven Sisters,* but when it came to the drama itself, thumbs were turned down.

Josephine, having seen the dress rehearsal, chose to remain at home in New York. Sorely as she missed Shelley, she did not languish in loneliness, for Aunt Fanny came down from Newtonville to keep her company—Aunt Anne and Aunt Gertrude had been there before her—and the two of them kept busy with a round of theatergoing and visits. Josephine also worked away like mad on her music. Shelley plied her with daily letters and on the second anniversary of their engagement sent a box of chrysanthemums and autumn leaves. Then came a very welcome "big money order" that enabled her to pay a lot of bills and treat herself to a new wardrobe under the supervision of her artistic aunt. In return she made Shelley a pair of silk pajamas.

By the middle of the month, he was back to put them on—unless they had been hidden away until Christmas—and to start work on *Mrs. Bumpstead-Leigh,* which was being revived as a sure-fire stopgap, while the next play was being shaped up. In this amusing comedy, instead of a philanderer, Shelley was a model youth, for him an unrewarding straight part. His wife was not sufficiently interested to preserve any of the reviews.

The morning after the opening, play number three went into rehearsal. Mrs. Fiske was in no mood to waste time. Then, three days before Christmas, the Hulls were packing their trunks for a tour of the provinces. "Mary and Howard came in bringing lovely things." (In the family circle Margaret Anglin was always called "Mary.") The next day they departed for Grand Rapids, leaving Mother Elinor in the flat.

All this while the star was plugging away in an effort to infuse some semblance of dramatic life into her next offering. Some months before, she had accepted a play from the pen of one of the most celebrated of contemporary novelists, Mrs. Gertrude Atherton, who wanted to try her hand at a new literary form. The authoress had anticipated no trouble, for she had airily declared that after novel writing, the composition of a play would be no trick at all. She speedily changed her mind, once she started putting *Julia France* down on paper. Having at last sent the script off, she retreated to the sunny warmth of South Carolina from whence she was summoned to ice-bound Cincinnati by the exasperated actress. Her presence was not especially helpful, for she knew nothing about the theater, didn't like it much anyway, and, although they never quarrelled, she and Minnie Fiske were not precisely congenial. Josephine, with whom she dined and spent a cosy evening at the Burnet House, found Mrs. Atherton very interesting. The *première* had originally been scheduled for the Ohio city, but the actress-manageress decided gloomily to put off the evil night, and deferred the opening till the company reached Toronto, which for some reason she hoped would not be so bitter cold.

Julia France dealt with woman's rights, a subject on which Mrs. Atherton held the strongest of opinions. With many of these the actress was by no means in agreement, but she thought the subject timely and likely to attract the good business she sorely needed. Now she wished she had never heard of the thing, and, when Fiske arrived in Toronto to cast an expert eye on the proceedings, she was not encouraged to change her mind. The grand opening was held off till the last evening in Toronto. There *Julia France* was born, and there it promptly died. Actually it was stillborn, for it never drew a healthy breath.

The debacle was witnessed by Josephine from a box where

she was the guest of the authoress. It cannot have been a pleasant evening. The forthright dramatist, however, made things a little easier by declaring at once that it was the worst play she had ever seen, and when, next day, the critics damned it, she said their opinions of it were no worse than hers.

The next evening everybody except Mrs. Atherton was in Buffalo and comfortably back in *Mrs. Bumpstead-Leigh*. Within a week Mrs. Fiske, determined to save something from the wreck, had her Manhattan Company rehearsing *Lady Patricia*, by Rudolf Besier. Like *The New Marriage*, this slight comedy in which Shelley was cast as a "cubbish young lover," had its out-of-town opening in Syracuse. Josephine was not on hand, for she had received a hurried call to Newtonville, where her grandmother was dying. She helped her aunts through the illness and the funeral, and on March 2 was back in New York in time to see Shelley on the stage of the famous Empire Theater, in his new part, and to be "very proud" of him.

Lady Patricia needed more than Josephine's wifely pride to save it, especially as Mrs. Fiske was not suited to the role of the heroine, and on March 23 she and her Manhattan Company called it quits. Minnie Fiske had had three failures in one season.

With what sensations did the Hulls look back on the year? Shelley had played four parts and played them well. He had netted some satisfactory reviews. But he had met nothing to challenge his capabilities. If there was one thing neither he nor Josephine wanted it was for him to be habitually type-cast. All he could possibly do was to differentiate one character from the ones that had gone before. With her help he had succeeded. Now he had a chance to make up for the time he had lost. Shortly before the run ended he was engaged to play leads with the Davidson Stock Company in a summer season in Milwaukee, and as Josephine had said in her *Woman's Home Companion* article, there was no better school of acting than a stock company. Playing a different part every week was grueling work, but it was the best kind of training. They were off for the West almost before the falling curtain hit the stage.

Packed trunk. Stored silver & furs & did last errands. Phoned. Cleaned house & put away lots of things. Shelley's last performance in "Lady Patricia."

Two days later they were in the Plankinton Hotel in Milwaukee, from which they moved next day to the Carlton. On the whole, they had a good summer, although it was not without its painful aspects. Shelley was not found wanting, and there was a welcome visit from Mary, Howard, and Henry, who brought them a fern as an anniversary present. Josephine was busy effacing herself, with what success is shown by an article in an unidentified newspaper, which she pasted in her scrapbook.

No, Genevieve, the fact that Shelley Hull is Margaret Anglin's brother-in-law does NOT mean that he is married. He's her brother-in-law because she married his brother. Mr. Hull is still heart whole and fancy free, but he has hopes.

Thus reassured, Genevieve could have hopes too.

Just now Josephine had a special reason for keeping to herself—she was not feeling well. She sought professional advice, and, painful treatments failing, underwent a minor operation that kept her in Lakeside Hospital for five days. Shelley was as attentive as he could be, but he had little free time; so Mother Elinor came out from New York to fill in. Josephine's relations with her medical advisers never stopped at the professional. She may have remembered Miss Hanchett at the Cliffs and her girlhood interest in the art of healing. An illness of Shelley's shortly before they left New York resulted in an intimacy with Dr. Thompson Sweeny that grew closer through the years. Now Dr. Horace Brown forthwith joined the select circle of their Milwaukee friends. On May 13 "Dr. Brown brought me home from the hospital in his car." How many physicians do that for their patients? Josephine was one of those women for whom other people, including doctors, simply fall over themselves, and her gratitude was always warm, sincere, and flattering.

For the time being at least, Dr. Brown's treatment had been successful. She was soon going about her business as actively as ever, and even paid her annual visit to Wells College in order to stage an alfresco performance of *A Midsummer Night's Dream* in which she took more than her usual pride.

On August 25 the Davidson season concluded "with speeches," but before leaving, the Hulls made a very brief and happy sortie into vaudeville at the Majestic Theater. Their vehicle was none other than Josephine's old friend, *The Nettle*, in which she had appeared with young Rolfe during her first year at Radcliffe. Milwaukee was very much pleased, especially so the critic of the *Leader*:

> In every day gab, "The Nettle," played by Shelley Hull and Josephine Sherwood, for a romantic, wholesomely senti-mental love act, is the "niftiest" and sweetest little idyll seen in vaudeville here for a long time. Because the playlet did not arrive until Thursday, only six rehearsals were given it; even so, the finer points were got at remarkably sure, the comedy touches elaborated and tripped off winningly. By Thursday or Friday the act will be one of the best, and far and high above thousands of such make-believe romance playlets. Mr. Hull, although he did not immediately strike a definite note, later gave his best to projection of the superb comedy of the piece, developing the fetching situations, by Miss Sherwood's aid, completely. Too, Miss Sherwood scored as the brother-loving sister; determined to lead a domestic existence she has absented herself from the stage glare for two years. And although a bit insecure her come-back performance was a delight, so fresh, natural and sweet; she brings an engaging personality and a bright, well-developed technique to her work that makes one forget any little short-comings.

As soon as this engagement was disposed of, they hurried home. "Shelley was engaged by Savage for a new play by Hughes," she wrote on October 10. Almost immediately he was laid low by a bad cold, but he was not one to pamper himself. He was subject to colds—Josephine called them "hard" —and she too had a great deal of trouble with her throat. But they kept on, as actors must. Again she found herself engaged as understudy, for which role she fails to say.

Before they left for the tryout in Baltimore, "Shelley signed option on land at Forest Hills." Tired of apartment dwelling, both looked forward to owning a home of their own away from the din and dust of the city. They schemed and planned and, happily, did not know that it was a dream never to come true.

What Ails You? was nothing spectacular in the way of a play, but it gave them a chance to have good times with their friends, Harry and Elise Green in Baltimore, to see something of William Courtleigh, who took over the lead before the piece reached Broadway, and it afforded Shelley the opportunity to do something a little different. He received practically unanimous critical acclaim for his restrained and tasteful performance of a drunken scene. *Vanity Fair* declared that "Shelley Hull gave the best representation of a confirmed drinker that the stage has seen this season." But he could not save *What Ails You?*, and it lasted less than a month.

Josephine had no chance to go on in the role she had been engaged to understudy, for again she was ill, this time really and seriously ill. After a consultation with Dr. Sweeny she wrote Dr. Brown, and on the twenty-seventh

> Dr. Brown came from Milwaukee, & he & Shelley talked things over with me, & had a consultation at Dr. Sweeny's. P. M. Dr. Brown dined with us at Lüchow's, and ev'g performance as usual.

They decided to wait for the closing of *What Ails You?*—a rather painfully significant title—so that he would have as much free time as possible. The trying interim they devoted to seeing their friends and getting ready for Christmas. Nothing on earth could keep Josephine from buying and wrapping up

Christmas presents, their numbers mounting into the dozens. The play closed on the seventh, and the next day Shelley took her to the Post Graduate Hospital.

> December 9. Dr. Sweeny operated on me at 8 A. M.—lasting between 2 & 3 hours. Came out of it all right. Shelley in several times.
> December 22. Got up & was dressed. Mrs. Olcutt sent her carriage & Shelley & Dr. Sweeny brought me home from the hospital. So happy.
> December 24. Did up last Xmas things & had a little tree trimmed.
> December 25. A beautiful snowy Christmas in our own home. So thankful to be alive and together.

The only shadow on their happiness was the realization that they could never have the children they both wanted. But they had much to be thankful for. They enjoyed the holidays quietly, and with Mother Elinor, Katie, and the Sweenys "watched the new year in with a toast."

During the holidays Shelley had begun an engagement as leading man with Billie Burke in Pinero's *Mind the Paint Girl*, starting an association which was to last for the greater part of three seasons. These were unsettled and unsettling years during which he appeared in four different plays (in addition to a one-act curtain raiser), and many months were spent trekking about the country from one coast line to the other, from the Canadian border to the Gulf Coast. They were not particularly happy years for Josephine. She loved to travel, especially with Shelley, but even for seasoned troupers weeks on weeks of one-night stands can grow very wearing. She had also become something of a homebody, and the periodic desertions of the flat with all her precious lares and penates did involve some pangs. Moreover prolonged absences did not bring the dream house at Forest Hills any nearer, although, before starting out, Shelley conferred with the architest so that the time need not be entirely wasted.

There were also nagging doubts as to whether, all things considered, the game was worth the candle, for the income, much as they needed it, was not all. Nothing in their lives was more important than Shelley's artistic growth and his recognition as something more than a matinee idol. His very assets constituted a danger, and they both knew it. With a single exception, the roles that fell to his lot during these seasons offered him precious little scope for the development and display of his finer talents. There was scant chance for creative friction.

The Pinero comedy had opened in September, but the leading man had withdrawn from the cast, and Shelley had been selected as his replacement. That the change enjoyed the complete approval of the star is obvious from her comments in her biography, *With a Feather on my Nose*.[1]

> Our leading man left us shortly after the opening. He was replaced by Shelley Hull, a delightful person. Shelley was a graceful actor, lithe and handsome, one of the first to play with the light and natural touch. He was whimsical, sometimes faun-like, much like a young, blond Faversham. With him was his wonderful young wife, giving no indication of her great mastery of the art of acting that she later discovered and made known to the theater as Josephine Hull.

The Mind the Paint Girl had small success in London, but Miss Burke thinks Charles Frohman believed that the British prejudice against the marriage of a peer with a very humble chorus girl would not militate against the play on this side of the Atlantic. The 136 performances at the Lyceum are evidence that he knew what he was about. Like Shelley, Miss Burke was in danger of type-casting, and was enthusiastic about her role because it allowed her to be something more than cute. She had scenes she could really get her teeth in, but no such happy chance to show the stuff that was in him came Shelley's way. As the virtuous and noble peer he had nothing to do but

[1] Page 111.

stand around, handsome and well bred, the kind of acting he and his wife were beginning to detest.

In one of the early chapters of his *Act One* Moss Hart tells of the almost frenetic passion of his first theatrical employer, Augustus Pitou, for the *Official Railway Guide*, in which he buried his head, ostrich-like, in an attempt to forget the business he hated. To anyone unfamiliar with the vagaries of play routing, the schedule evolved for the Burke tour must seem like the product of a disordered brain: Philadelphia, Baltimore, Boston, Hartford, Washington, Toronto, Chicago, St. Louis, Louisville, and Detroit. But, on the other hand, there were no one-night stands *this* time.

In every city the Hulls found welcoming friends to take them enthusiastically to their bosoms. Everywhere they went there were parties. In Boston there were the aunts and the Girls of '99; in St. Louis, not only the O'Reilly's (with whom they stayed), but Shelley's Grandmother Vaughn and the uncle whose namesake he was. In Washington his friend Bob Janney seated them on the balcony of his hotel room to watch the inaugural parade. It must have caused Josephine some sighs to watch a Democrat riding in triumph to the White House, but there are no tearstains on the pages of her diary. Even though a Democrat, Wilson was President of the United States, and her patriotism could rise above party.

This was a brief tour. The very lavishness of the production made a prolonged one prohibitive; even in 1913 it cost a lot of money—or what seemed then like a lot of money—to lug heavy wooden sets about the country. On April 20 they were back home and Shelley was rehearsing *The Amazons* in the Hotel Algonquin.

Miss Burke was keenly disappointed at having to fall back on this little Pinero farce, which had been around for nearly twenty years, but C. F. had nothing better to offer her at the moment. After her success in a real dramatic role, she felt that a return to the cuteness her public adored was a step backward. Shelley was no better off than he had been in *The Mind the Paint Girl*—again playing himself disguised as a British peer.

TWO DELIGHTFUL OLD MURDERESSES,
Josephine Hull and Jean Adair,
in the stage production of *Arsenic and Old Lace*

DISMAYED RY THE COMING OF A RIVAL MURDERER
Josephine Hull and Jean Adair appear with
Boris Karloff and Edgar Stehli
in a scene from *Arsenic and Old Lace*

The reviews show that in this role the critics were beginning to take him for granted, a consummation devoutly *not* to be wished. The piece had been so thoroughly rehearsed during the tour that it was ready to be tried out in Trenton five days after the return and was presented at the Empire three evenings later. It went well, but early in June it closed for the summer.

Meanwhile Josephine wrote songs for Thompson, saw Bernhard in one act of *Theodora* with Shelley ("wonderful"), and *Damaged Goods* with Harry Hodges ("remarkable"), staged *Much Ado* at Aurora with the Wells girls. By this time she was quite at home in the Prophet's Chamber.

When she reached home the Empire was dark, and Shelley was all set for their next adventure.

> Closed the flat, Katherine gave us breakfast & saw us off, across ferry, at Jersey City, on the Black Diamond Express. Destination, Los Angeles.

Anyone reading the entries in the diary for the next two months can easily be excused for wondering where the Hulls obtained the money to indulge themselves in a vacation among the orange groves and on the beaches of Southern California. Apparently the days as well as the evenings were given over entirely to pleasure and play. Of work, there is not the slightest hint. But if one turns from the diary to the letters Josephine found time to write "Darling Uncle Theodore and Aunt Cassie," a little light is shed on the mystery. The first is dated Los Angeles, June 28, 1913:"

> It seems such wonderful luck that Shelley and I should be enabled to take this trip alone together, not with a large company, and yet with all the advantages of having it pay for itself. They provided a stateroom for Shelley for our whole trip out, so we travelled in the most comfortable way possible, and after leaving Chicago we unpacked and got really settled in quite a homelike way in our little compartment with its dresser and

cupboards. Another great advantage it gave us—during the dusty, sandy desert stretches, by closing our windows and keeping the electric fan going, we were as clean and cool as could be, while the rest of the car got quite choking with sand and dust and very hot.

Again consulting the diary, one can see in small letters just above the entries, the word *Sapho*. Gradually the facts emerge: Shelley had been engaged by some unnamed motion picture company to star with Florence Roberts in a movie. Why Josephine never alluded to the business side of the expedition is difficult to surmise, unless it could be that she was so carried away she simply did not think to mention it. Yet that is not at all in character.

I am bursting with joy and excitement over our good fortune in being here and all that we are seeing and doing, and hardly know where to begin telling about it.

For Los Angeles it was love at first sight. Exclamation points poured from her pen.

This is a city of open air, cleanliness and beauty, besides everything fine that a big city should have in shops, buildings, traffic, etc. . . . I never saw faster speeding motors in the city streets! My, you have to jump! Even accustomed to leaping for your life in New York, I find I have to leap worse here! But except for that, it seems the sanest, loveliest city I should wish to be in,—and so beautiful!

How did Shelley find time for all the pleasure jaunts and sightseeing when he was making a picture? True, Miss Roberts was ill and unable to work for a week or so, a detail not mentioned in the diary, but the pace seems to have been furious throughout the whole five or six weeks that *Sapho* was being shot. With Miss Roberts, Blanche Bates and her husband,

George Creel, and various other friends the Hulls covered the landscape from the heights of Mount Lowe—"the most wonderful trip and views I ever saw"—to Nat Goodwin's restaurant at Santa Monica, where they "saw nothing of the disreputable Nat. (I must say when I knew him I saw only his nice and artistic side.)" They rode horseback. They went out to Catalina Island and rode in the famous glass-bottomed boats. They were driven up the San Fernando Valley, and were entranced with Hollywood, "a most charming town with big hotels, lovely homes, the usual fine schools and churches." She begged Uncle Theodore to bring Aunt Cassie out the next year so that they could both revel in the beauties of this paradise.

And yet, near the end of July, her thoughts began to turn toward home. "Shelley enjoys his work, what there is of it, and is well and we both are enjoying every moment here. In spite of all the beauty and wonder of this country, however, I'm glad the East is my home." With the end of July came the end of the shooting too, and on the first they were taken to view the results. "Very interesting," pronounced Mrs. Hull, and said no more. Not a sign of rapture.

How about Shelley? Was he any more enthusiastic than his wife? Whatever he may have told his friends, it was not till the following summer that he gave testimony that is available to us today. In an interview with the *Milwaukee Free Press* he is explicit enough to leave no doubt about the matter. The movie people had been sufficiently pleased to offer him five hundred dollars a week for his services, not a contemptible sum in 1913. "It is true, although it sounds like a 'fake' story. I was offered a year's contract at that salary. But why should I have done it? At the end of the year I should have $14,000 or $15,000 in the bank, and I should have wasted a year and lost my perspective as far as real acting is concerned. I didn't think it was worth $500 a week. Why, movie acting is not acting at all. It is just a species of pantomime." Perhaps we have here an explanation of the strange silence of the diary. Can it be that Josephine feared that he would react differently and was so opposed to the whole project that she could not bring herself to mention it? That could very well be.

Her doubts and fears laid at rest, she was able to enjoy the boat trip up the coast to San Francisco, her first sight of the Golden Gate and Mount Shasta, and the magnificent scenery along the Canadian Pacific as they covered the miles between them and the Atlantic. After a night ride down from Montreal on August 17, they were back where they had started from.

Reached N. Y. early, came home, had breakfast at Katherine's.

In September the tour of *The Amazons* was resumed, but Josephine elected not to go along. Instead she ran up to Aurora to put on an unusual fall Shakespeare performance, this time of *Much Ado About Nothing,* for which she had prepared herself by careful study and by attending productions starring John Drew and Sothern and Marlowe. At home she toiled away in the kitchen, getting ready for the fall and winter festivities. By this time she had mastered the once-foreign art of cookery, and zealously made cranberry jelly and put up spiced grapes. She might not be able to achieve Aunt Anne's eminence, but she intended to try. Early in November Shelley's tour took him to Boston, and she went up early to attend a Radcliffe alumnae tea and visit her aunts in their new homes. After Mrs. Tewksbury's death, the old house on Harvard Street was abandoned, and the sisters separated. Fanny was already on her own. Now Nellie moved in with two schoolteacher friends, and the other two settled in the Marion Apartment House. Wherever they were, they were seldom off their niece's mind, and never were to be as long as they lived. Nor was she off theirs. Keeping step with her had given them new outlooks on life, and Aunt Gertrude was able to enjoy the young Amazons in their knickerbockers without blushing.

After a week Josephine hurried back to New York to prepare for Henry's wedding to Juliet Frémont, a granddaughter of the famous General John C. and his brilliant wife, Jessie

Benton. The wedding was to take place on the 30th and, as Mother Elinor was in Europe, Josephine's services were needed.

Shelley came home early. We put laurel and ground-pine everywhere. Henry came. Cable from Elinor, telegrams. Henry & Julie were married at Church of All Angels, 2.30, and had reception here, 35 people.

By this time *The Amazons* had run its course, and Miss Burke was rehearsing a play of very different quality, *The Land of Promise*, a comedy by Somerset Maugham. She welcomed it, as did Shelley, because like *The Mind the Paint Girl* it afforded them an opportunity to get away from the kind of roles they feared they might be tied to for life. The comedy is an amalgam of *The Taming of the Shrew* and *The Great Divide*. An English girl, finding herself penniless, takes refuge on the Canadian ranch of her brother, subduing as well as she can her resentment of his marriage to a waitress. "Here we find the Dresden china Billie ironing blouses and washing dishes, clumsily and petulantly, under the nagging guidance of the wife who so resents the 'society' manner of the wretched Norah that fearful ructions result." Again the girl takes flight, this time to the cabin of an uncouth young neighbor with whom she contracts a platonic marriage. She finds that she has merely jumped from the frying pan into the fire. The young farmer has more in him of the domineering Petruchio than of the more considerate Stephen Ghent, and sets out to tame his rebellious bride. It takes no seventh son of a seventh son to predict the outcome. Maugham had been anticipated by Shakespeare and Moody.

The roles delighted the two players, but not their admirers, and despite critical acclaim, the Burke fans manifested their displeasure in the only way they knew—they stayed away from the theater. *The Land of Promise*, which had opened on Christmas, lasted less than three months, and the disgusted star soon found herself back in the old groove.

Shortly after New Year's Aunt Cassie died, and Josephine found herself with a new responsibility, Uncle Theodore, who of all her male relatives was closest to her. With another niece, Edith Sherwood, she took charge of the funeral, and then kept the lonely old man under her eye until she got him settled in a single room with his possessions about him.

March 28 marked the beginning of one of Josephine's personal purgatories. Miss Burke's new vehicle, Catherine Chisolm Cushing's *Jerry*, after being "tried out on the dogs" in New Jersey and Pennsylvania, was put on display in New York. The wife of the leading man registered no enthusiasm.

> Stormy. Shelley came home from Easton at noon & rehearsed—After an early dinner went to his opening in 'Jerry' at the Lyceum—It is a poor part. Usual brilliant opening. Supper at Katherine Grey's.

It was a poor part that had fallen to Shelley's lot. There can be no doubt about that. The only good thing about it from his point of view was that it required him to assume the role of a man of forty instead of a youngster in his twenties, but even that boon was qualified by the gentleman's determination to preserve his youth. Heretofore Shelley's characters had, for all their sameness, at least been likable, but this man is an out-and-out cad.

For twenty years he has been engaged to Jerry's handsome aunt, but has proceeded no further than to remind her annually of the passage of time by sending her an orchid for each fruitless year. Upon this "brute," as the *Telegraph* calls him, Jerry fixes her predatory gaze, and with the help of a bewitching pair of pink pajamas and a fake suicide attempt, she gets her man. "Shelley Hull," wrote Lewis Sherwin in the *Globe and Commercial Advertiser*, "accomplishes competently what he has to do, but he is about the only person on the stage who has no good lines to deliver. If there ever were any in his role they evidently got mislaid at rehearsals." Little wonder that Josephine was glum! And so far as *Jerry* was concerned, she was to remain glum a long time.

The play was all Billie Burke, "Billie Burke raised to the nth power, Billie Burke laid on thick, Billie Burke much overdone." It was hinted by one critic that, as originally written, the principal role had been that of the aunt, played beautifully by Gladys Hanson, but the whole thing had been rewritten under Frohman's orders to exploit the undeniable attractions of his star. Perhaps still smarting after the failure of *The Land of Promise,* he was resolutely determined to cash in on every charm she possessed. Ruthlessly he kept her center stage, whether she belonged there or not, and saw to it that she pulled out all the stops. Maybe she didn't like it. Maybe, on the other hand, she did. One thing is certain—without Billie Burke this very slight comedy would have had slight excuse for being. As it was, the critics thought it had none too much. C. F. thought otherwise, and so, as events proved, did the public.

Probably it could have lingered profitably on Broadway for months to come, but the young star had defied her infuriated managers by marrying Florenz Ziegfeld, and they vengefully decided to break up the honeymoon by separating the happy pair. At least that is her belief, and whether she is right or not, Messrs. Frohman and Hayman achieved the result she thinks they desired. They arbitrarily cut short the New York run and dispatched the company to Chicago.

Josephine, however, did not go with them. She had another alfresco production at Wells to direct and an overdue visit to pay to Newtonville. By the time she was ready to join her husband, *Jerry* had stopped for "the pause that refreshes," and he had moved on to Milwaukee for another summer with the Davidson forces. In a sense this was also a "refresher course," for he was freed for a time from the strait jacket of an uninspired and uninspiring role. She reached Milwaukee on June 19. "Shelley met me. Oh, so good to be with him!"

Perhaps the best thing about this summer season was that it brought them into close association with that gentle couple, the

Priestly Morrisons, who in the years to come were among Josephine's most precious and loyal friends. Priestly was to steady her hand when she was beset by perplexity and grief, and Mary was to be one of the last to stand by her bedside when life was ebbing away. He was not only a kindly, understanding man, but a shrewd and experienced director, and his guidance brought fresh insights into the young actor's consciousness. Out of the theater the four of them spent much time together, often driving out after the play to Ma Heiser's, an excellent restaurant away from the heart of town, whose genial hostess was another of Shelley's devotees.

While in Milwaukee Josephine twice emerged from the backstage shadows and appeared in two plays. The first time she was seen as Ruth Sumner in *The Rainbow,* and according to her own judgment was "dreadfully bad." She did not venture again until the eleventh and last week of the season, when she tried her hand at Nancy Valier in *The Runaway.* The critic of the *Sentinel* commented that Shelley had "little opportunity," but was impressed by his wife's performance even if he did get her name wrong.

> His wife, Dorothy Sherwood, is doing a delightful bit of light comedy acting as a fascinating actress. She is as happily cast in this part as she was unhappily cast in "The Rainbow," and the light and shade of the scenes between Miss Sherwood and Mr. Hull give the production its most artistic touch.

During their stay in Milwaukee the First World War exploded, but, although actually deeply concerned about current events, Josephine saw no reason for recording in her line-a-day something that was common knowledge. So she dismissed this calamity with a few brief words.

On August 24, having said their goodbyes to their friends and to their public, the Hulls turned their faces homeward and returned to their flat for the last time. This was a melancholy business for anyone as sentimental as Josephine, but they could not afford to keep it unoccupied for nearly a year. After a short excursion to Pleasant Valley, they set about the job of packing their furniture and other effects. On September 10, she wrote:

> Had one hour's sleep,—up early. Packers & movers here before 8. Worked all day. . . . Last things out at 7.30 P. M., & we left our first home for good. Spent night at Great Northern.

This painful break accomplished, they sailed off for Long Branch, where on the twenty-fourth the despised *Jerry* was restored to life, with a cast that included only two survivors of the earlier run. Much as she loved to travel, Josephine had few happy anticipations. At the same time, no power on earth could have kept her at home.

Miss Burke believes that her vengeful managers had re-solved to punish her still further by sending her up and down the country, across the continent and halfway back, where her bridegroom could not follow her. Whatever the motive that inspired these gentlemen, they assuredly were wholly success-ful in achieving the designs she ascribes to them. In nine months the weary company played in 121 cities, in 32 states, 2 Canadian provinces, and the District of Columbia. Miss Burke says there were no less than 72 one-night stands. Jose-phine's meticulous tally adds 9 more. Sometimes their travels resembled nothing so much as a game of hopscotch.

As *Jerry* was a relatively short play, the management de-cided to open each evening with a curtain raiser. The first one tried out, something called *Poor Jo*, proved to be a poor thing, and was later replaced by *The Philosopher in the Apple Or-chard*, but that too left much to be desired, and finally a solu-tion was found in a revision of the fourth act of *Jerry*, which seems to have turned the trick and also, happily, greatly im-proved Shelley's part.

Catching her breath during a week's run in St. Louis, Jose-phine, from her comfortable haven at the O'Reillys', wrote a report to Uncle Theodore shortly before Thanksgiving.

We had such a strenuous week, last week, that I was unable
to get letters written. Altho' the cities looked quite near one another on the map, the railroad connections are very poor, ne-
cessitating changes, long waits at junctions, and weird hours
of leaving and arriving. Three nights we traveled by sleeper,
and other days we got up by starlight and left at dawn. In several cities we arrived so late and left immediately after the play,
that we did not even go to a hotel, but used the theater dressing-
room as our temporary abode. But it was very interesting, even
if it was tiresome by the end of the week.

It had also been bitter cold in Iowa. At Davenport, they
shivered in zero weather as they watched the sun rise magnificently over the Mississippi.

It was not, however, unrelieved hardship. There were the
usual welcomes in various cities, and in St. Louis, where Henry
was playing in stock, there was a family Thanksgiving dinner
at the Jefferson Hotel. In Louisville Shelley was received like
a prodigal son and conquering hero in one, and they were
feted right and left. She was entranced by the noble bluegrass
plantations and especially by one of their hosts, General Halde-
man, "who *ought* to be a 'Colonel,' *I* think, for he is the ideal
Kentucky colonel type—white hair, mustache and goatee, pink
skin, very courtly, old-school manner—and his wife is like an
old portrait." All this was wonderful, and partly compensated
for other conditions she found it impossible to take philosoph-
ically. This was one of the times when she was not being "sensible." Her bereaved uncle, whom she did really want to cheer,
must have been somewhat startled by the outburst that came to
him on the monogrammed stationery of the Hotel Gibson in
Cincinnati:

> This unfeeling management and especially this star have no
> regard at all for their actors as human beings. The company
> rehearses nearly every day for something or other, which is very
> trying,—and now, both the women in the company (there are

only two besides Miss Burke) have received their two weeks
notice for no reason at all except that she doesn't like them,—
and then that means two new people to come on and be broken
in and *many* rehearsals. It is horrid. Miss Burke might well sing
the old song—"I care for nobody, no not I, and nobody cares
for me. . . . Shelley says the same thing. But we try to forget
her as much as possible, and we do, except when something
special makes us wrathy like suddenly turning these two good
actresses adrift in the middle of a shaky season. We do record-
breaking business everywhere, but we hear other tales of other
companies all about us.

It doubtless did her soul good to write "And Shelley says
the same thing." At the same time, it is very obvious that
plenty of people did care for Miss Burke. Having got this off
her chest, the jealous wife calmed down sufficiently to caution
the old gentleman about going to the cemetery in bad weather
and to invite him to spend Christmas with them in Atlantic City.

He accepted the invitation and they all enjoyed the holiday
together. Then the company plunged into the deep South,
where, contrary to Josephine's expectations, there was relief
enough from the pestiferous rehearsals to permit her and Shelley to do Richmond, Charleston, and other entrancing places
together.

Hard times did not prevent the pleasure-loving citizens from
packing the theater to see Billie Burke—seventeen hundred
dollars in the house, that one performance. In poverty-stricken
Columbia. She is breaking the records in all these places, and
ought to be enormously wealthy after this tour.

When we leave by sleeper, I spend the evening in Shelley's
dressing-room, as we do not take a room at a hotel. Otherwise I spend the evening in getting our bags housecleaned,
socks washed out, handkerchiefs ditto,—that we may not have
to carry soiled laundry any longer than necessary, and fresh-
ening up our clothes, which show the wear and tear of travel
unless I keep at them constantly.

Assuredly Josephine had "dwindled into a wife."

She had another problem, a most inopportune one at this particular time. She was getting fat. The Tewksburys were all short and, except Aunt Gertrude—shall we say—comfortably plump? That was all right for them, but it simply would not do for her. A year before, she had begun experimenting with a buttermilk diet, but that she stuck to it is doubtful. In Philadelphia, during January, she had embarked on a regimen of morning exercises and salt baths. Now from Macon she wrote her uncle: "I have been on a strict diet for two weeks now, and have lost several pounds, and feel *very* much lighter and spryer. I do hate to be heavy, and shall do my best to get light and stay so." With all her determination it was hard, very hard, for no one ever loved good, rich food more than Josephine Hull.

From Dixie the company went to Texas, and then north through Oklahoma, Kansas, Nebraska, and Iowa to Minnesota. Then it headed for the great Northwest, Oregon, Washington, and British Columbia, fifteen one-night stands, before they stopped for breath in Victoria. Mr. Ziegfeld was a long way off. At last the performances seem to have jelled and there was time for plenty of long walks, golf, and boat rides. At Portland Josephine was kidnaped by her Uncle Will Tewksbury and carried off for a blissful night on his ranch.

> Up at 5, fed the chickens, went over Uncle Will's ranch,—and that of the Robbins. Picked strawberries and flowers, wild cornflowers and shushullas. After dinner walked to the Paddocks'. Mr. P. drove us all around the loop of the valley,—mts., fir woods, great apple ranches, 2 snow peaks, & cascades.

Then on southward by the Shasta Route. "Got out at waystations for lunch & dinner,—cider & ice cream cones. Played hearts." What about that diet? Josephine never learned to resist ice cream. She must have been tried again in the famous restaurants of San Francisco. There they found the Exposition in full blast and visited it nearly every day. The fire chief took them around the bay in his boat. In Los Angeles they found California-born Katie waiting to act as guide. The long tour was approaching its end.

At last, on July 8, they pulled into Denver, and near the arch over Seventeenth Street the Weber Linns waited. Two days later Josephine made the happiest entry her diary had known in years: "End of 'Jerry.' "

CHAPTER NINE

WAR AND PEACE

WITH THE EARNINGS of *Jerry* safely in the bank, the Hulls felt that they were in a position to enjoy a new luxury—an automobile—and after much deliberation Shelley decided that a Dodge would fill the bill. On the way back to New York he got off the train at Detroit to pick one up and drive it proudly home. For such a satisfying reason Josephine accepted the separation and, impatient to be home, sped on her way alone. Nine days later she wrote with some satisfaction: "We had our first puncture during a moonlight evening ride." They had been duly initiated. That Dodge put in a strenuous summer, for they drove it all over the landscape, dropping in on relatives here and friends there, and taking the delighted aunts on a trip to Gloucester and Salem.

But even more than an automobile they needed a home. They undertook to canvass their old neighborhood, and finally selected another aerie, this time in the Rutland on West Fifty-seventh Street. Into it they moved with all their chattels on September 25.

By this time Shelley was in another play, *Rolling Stones,*

"A Melodramatic Comedy of City Life," by Edgar Selwyn. It had been running for some time at the Harris Theater, and they went to look it over before Shelley became involved. Probably for reasons that had nothing to do with art or aesthetics, he allowed himself to be persuaded to join the cast for a while. As we know, what Josephine did not like, Josephine did not see. She was mistress of the art of ignoring. Not a single review of *Rolling Stone* or Shelley's part in it did she paste in her scrapbook, and she mentioned it only twice more in her diary, when he joined up and when it closed. It deserved no further notice.

Fortunately *Rolling Stones* ceased from troubling in December, and Shelley went on to better things, greatly to his wife's satisfaction. His next venture suited her to a T.

> So let my voice ring out for one
> Who has no fame for great deeds done.
> He rules no realm—he's more than king;
> A woman's joy his harvesting
> He spins no song, he rears no dome;
> Out of his heart he builds a home.

"The above bit of verse was the inspiration of Edward Childs Carpenter's four-act play, 'The Cinderella Man,' which was produced at the Apollo Theater last night by Oliver Morosco," according to the *Atlantic City Press* of January 4, 1916. It had opened in Washington on Christmas Eve, and Josephine had been on hand to welcome it. Sentimentalist that she was, this gentle comedy was exactly to her taste. She stayed with it throughout the brief pre-Broadway tour, and according to the leading lady, Phoebe Foster (now Mrs. Harold LeRoy Whitney), occasionally carefully inserted a finger in the pie.

"She would be ever so quiet in the back of the theater, taking notes both during rehearsals and at the performances. Very occasionally she would throw me a word of advice, or tell Shelley to tell me. He would stick to his own way if he did not agree with the manager, but he never went against anything

Josephine said. He said she knew more about the theater than he did."

The Cinderella Man tells of a poor little rich girl who plays fairy godmother to a destitute young poet who is starving in a nearby attic. *The Washington Post* called it "an exquisite romance of youth." The acting was delightful, and Shelley was complimented for avoiding the supersentimentality and effeminacy lurking beneath the surface of his role, that would have totally destroyed the delicate charm of the play. As for Miss Foster, everyone agreed with Josephine that she was "a very charming actress." To add to the contentment of the Hulls there was also their old friend Frank Bacon of *Fortune Hunter* days in a very appealing role.

After the New York *première* on January 17, they happily celebrated with a real party, fifty people toiling up the three flights of stairs. "There was an open fireplace in the living-room, and big soft chairs and a long sofa." Miss Foster remembers too that the food was "beautiful."

Memories of *Jerry* were fading away, and all was right with the Hulls, except that Josephine was having trouble with her throat. Her tonsils were pronounced the cause, and in April she went down to Dr. Reik's sanitarium in Baltimore to get rid of them. The operation was a success, but by no means put an end to her throat troubles, which continued to plague her for the rest of her life. Then there was a familiar annoyance. "She was always a little worried about her figure," remembers Miss Foster, "which was like a neat little rubber ball. She always had a *new* diet."

It is not in the order of things that a handsome and popular young actor should be allowed to twiddle his thumbs in idle solitude. Shelley and Josephine were inevitably caught up in a round of social engagements, many of them with people who today would be called VIP's. For instance on Sunday evening, April 30, she reported:

S. & I went to the Hippodrome, McCormack's concert, &

CARY GRANT JOINS JOSEPHINE HULL AND JEAN ADAIR
in the motion picture production of *Arsenic and Old Lace*

AS PENNY SYCAMORE
Josephine Hull in *You Can't Take It With You*

to supper with the McCormacks at the Plaza—Howard &
Mary, Mr. Schneider, the Ditrichsteins & Kreislers, etc. Delightful!

That was a tableful of celebrities in the Plaza dining room,
and it is not surprising that she went home in a glow. What
would she have thought in her Radcliffe days if she had been
able to foresee this evening? Poignant memories of those days
must have been awakened a month later, for she cannot have
forgotten Clara Folsom.

Shelley & I went to Julia Marlow's farewell to the stage,—
benefit performance. She read magnificently, tremendously
moving occasion,—Sothern & a good program.

The Dodge too contributed to the excitements of the season,
for, first, Shelley got himself fined $5.00 for speeding, and
then the car was stolen and they had to go to court about it.

On July 1 *The Cinderella Man* closed for the summer, and
the Dodge was hard at work again until the play went on tour
in September. An unusually agreeable feature of this tour was
a long engagement in Boston, so long, indeed, that they took
their colored maid, Margaret, up from New York and installed
her in an apartment. This run lasted till the first of the year.

Almost at once Shelley started work on *The Willow Tree*,
a pseudo-Japanese fantasy by Harrison Rhodes and J. Harry
Benrimo—whose *The Yellow Jacket* had recently caught popular as well as critical fancy. Mounted with exquisite taste it
was as beautiful a spectacle as the New York public had been
treated to in years, and Fay Bainter as an Oriental Galatea was
as exquisite as the production. Yet the whole thing was rather
self-conscious-arty and its Japanese version of pidgin English
was unkindly mocked by more than one unsympathetic critic.
Shelley was all that anyone could have asked for as the young
American who has a romance with the lengendary maiden, but
once again he found himself somewhat outshone.

133

At this point the whole picture changed. The United States was drawn into the War. It would have been impossible for Josephine with her patriotic and humanitarian instincts, to keep out of the activities that now boiled up all over the place. For some time she had been devoting many hours to various enterprises devoted to Allied relief; now the need became more personal and immediate. Emotional impetus was given by the visits of French, British, and Italian leaders, and she thrilled to the sight of Joffre, Balfour, Viviani riding under the kaleidoscope array of flags along Fifth Avenue. She joined with zest in the work of the newly-formed Stage Women's War Relief and set about making surgical dressings and knitting socks and helmets with a determination some may have equaled, but no one exceeded.

At the same time she was busy with different projects intended to swell the family exchequer. She was teaching classes in elocution at St. Agatha's, and directing plays for the Comedy Club as well as keeping a watchful eye on Uncle Theodore and looking after Shelley's needs. For most women all this running about and up and down stairs would have been utterly exhausting, but she throve on it. What is more, she loved it.

Somehow, despite its pictorial appeal, *The Willow Tree* did not turn out to be another *Yellow Jacket,* and on the first of June, Shelley once more found himself a gentleman of potential leisure. Undoubtedly both he and Josephine would have benefited by an extended vacation, but neither would have felt justified in taking the rest they really needed. She dashed up to Wells for her annual Shakespearean visit, enjoying, aside from the welcome fee, only a change of scene. Shelley had no respite at all, for within a matter of days he was rehearsing *The Lassoo,* an inconsequential comedy by Victor Mapes. This bit of froth opened in Stamford on July 1 and Josephine thought the auguries were favorable. But her own history has shown that auguries are not always to be taken without plenty of salt, and these were not of the trustworthy variety. In two months *The Lassoo* went into limbo, leaving the Hulls and their friend

Phoebe Foster richer by little except the friendship of Victor and Anna Mapes.

Once more they were caught up in the maelstrom of wartime activities, at a steadily accelerated pace. They were obviously trying to do too many things in too many places at the same time. Of course, as they would have pointed out, they were by no means alone in this. The strain, miraculously, left her unscathed, but Shelley, although he was undeniably "a fine figure of a man" and kept himself in good condition by playing golf and squash, did not have her stamina. He suffered from one frightful cold after another, some so bad that she put him to bed and kept him there except when he was on the stage. No matter how he felt, he could not at this time reconcile himself to idleness, and in November involved himself injudiciously in another play.

The word *injudiciously* is used advisedly, because it was not worth the trouble. *Among Those Present* was a *Raffles* concoction in which Shelley appeared as a dangerously attractive gentleman-thief. The bait that lured him on was the promise of the producer, George Tyler, that he would be "featured." Josephine was delighted by this recognition of his worth, but she must have had her private doubts all the same. "The choice between sound repute and the mere adventitious flash of advertising," observed the *Philadelphia Public Ledger*, "is here suggested to Shelley Hull." It was not that his acting did not do him credit, but that it was all to very little purpose. However, *Among Those Present* did not endure long enough to do him any real harm, for it lasted only a month, and never appeared on Broadway.

His inclusion in the cast of *Why Marry?*, the next play with which he was identified, was an accident, a happy accident, as it turned out. His friend Mapes was working on a successor to *The Lassoo*, but he had not nearly finished, and Shelley felt that he could not afford to waste the interim. So he signed up for a temporary engagement with Selwyn and Company. The new play was pronounced by Darnton of the *World* "the best

American comedy that has found its way to the stage in years."
Shelley had the satisfaction of having been in the cast of the
play that subsequently won the first Pulitzer Prize.

> Marriage as an institution, marriage as a convenience, mar-
> riage as a necessity, marriage as an experience, marriage as a
> comedy, marriage as a tragedy, marriage solemnized by the
> church, marriage in the sight of God, marriage according to
> Blackstone, Sherwin, Nathan, Shaw, Williams, Sinclair, Hop-
> per, Goldwyn, Trotsky, the Kaiser, Lloyd George and Nat
> Goodwin—marriage viewed practically from all angles was
> placed entertainingly on trial at the Astor Theater last night
> in a comedy new to New York, written by Jesse Lynch Wil-
> liams, and called "Why Marry?" (Mantle, *Evening Mail.*)

The question in the title is posed by two young people, an
ultraserious scientist and a girl who does not propose to be
ruled by what she considers archaic conventions. In her opinion
marriage is a handicap to those who submit to it, and she wins
the young man over to her point of view because he is in love
with her. They decide to go their way without benefit of clergy,
and the three acts are devoted, as Burns Mantle says, to a dis-
section of the merits and demerits of the institution they intend
to ignore. The dialogue is clever, but Williams, perhaps because he could find no other way out of the dilemma he has
created, ends the plot with a trick. By present-day standards
Why Marry? falls sort of being a masterpiece; in 1917, compared with other dramatic works of American authorship, it
well deserved the encomiums heaped upon it.

It opened in Columbus on the first of November, and then
went to Chicago for a run of ten weeks, where Shelley joined
the excellent cast, assuming the role of the scientist. The girl
in the case was the gifted young actress, Estelle Winwood. The
judge-uncle who serves rather crudely as the Euripidian *deux
ex machina* of the final curtain was none other than Josephine's
old associate of *Wolfville* days, Nat Goodwin, who certainly
was equipped by experience to discuss the subject at hand. Shel-

ley met with the approval that by this time he was justified in expecting, except that one critic thought he looked too healthy for a scientist and immediately was chastised in a sarcastic letter from Walter Prichard Eaton. *Why Marry?*, which had opened in New York on Christmas, kept Shelley busy till May, the longest run he had taken part in since *Jerry*. The Mapes play did not materialize, but even so he did not sign up for the fall reopening.

The New Year saw no letup in their manifold activities. Shelley had joined the Actors' Equity Association shortly after its founding in 1913, had been elected to the Council two years later, and now, being in New York, was able to give considerable time to its affairs. He was also a member of the board of The Players, the actors' club founded by Edwin Booth and housed in his old home on Gramercy Square, and he attended frequent meetings there. He did not permit professional responsibilities to limit his participation in the larger events of the day. His draft number had not been called, but he was on the go all the time, making speeches, selling Liberty Bonds, helping the police round up draft dodgers, lending a hand to Josephine with some benefits, and appearing in others. In no way did he spare himself.

As for Josephine, the leaders of S.W.W.R. soon discovered that she had unsuspected talents, and proceeded to make use of them. First she was elevated to the board, and then elected treasurer. In the latter capacity she was largely responsible for the innumerable benefits that followed so fast one after the other that she had no sooner added up the earnings of one than she was making preparations for another. Daily she padded about the streets from office to office, to the workroom, to banks, and sometimes to hospitals.

She and Shelley had of late been seeing a good deal of Laurette Taylor and her playwright husband, Hartley Manners. That spring Laurette decided to see for herself and to show the world what she could do with Shakespeare. Accordingly she arranged to present herself, at special matinees, in a series of scenes from his plays. One of the excerpts was from *The*

Taming of the Shrew, and for her Petruchio she tapped Shelley. Her announcement of her plans had elevated many professional eyebrows, and the first performance elevated them still further. Among those on hand, near the back of the theater, were Sothern and Marlowe. Just what they thought of what they saw and heard is not on record. What Petruchio's real-life wife thought is: "Shelley very good as Petruchio—Laurette dreadful." That was the consensus. The star braved three more matinees on successive Fridays, and then bade the Bard adieu forever. She had found out what she wanted to know. So had her public.

Confronted with the imminent closing of *Why Marry?*, Shelley looked about for something else. Al Woods was tempting him with a promising role, but he shied away from it, sensing the danger that he would again find himself playing second fiddle to a glamorous prima donna. Then Woods suggested another piece, an import from London, which he declared would not involve any such risk. Again the actor was wary, but agreed, before making up his mind, to have his wife take a look at the play, which was being tried out at Stamford, under the title of *My Boy*.

Went to Stamford at night to see 'My Boy' for Shelley.

That was on May 10. Three days later, Shelley "signed with Woods for 'My Boy' for next season."

The present season still had a few weeks to run, and the family exchequer could do with a little improvement; consequently Shelley accepted an opportunity to support Ruth Chatterton in a brief tour in *Come Out of the Kitchen*, a pleasant way of picking up a little needed cash.

Although the Hulls were not extravagant in their habits, neither were they in any way parsimonious. They had exchanged their Dodge for a more impressive Cadillac, and also engaged an assistant maid to help Margaret. She needed help because their parties, while not lavish, were many, and sometimes involved fairly long guest lists. The pages of the guest-book and of the diary are filled with the names of innumerable friends, some famous, some not, with whom they somehow managed to squeeze in engagements between chores. Mother Elinor, Uncle Theodore, Henry and Julie represented the family most often, but from time to time one or more of the aunts descended on them, for a brief visit. Then there were Tom Dobson (the young singer), the Mapeses, Laurette and her husband, Lynn Fontanne, George Denny, and many others. One familiar name, however, was missing. Harry Hodges had married—a bit belatedly—two years before, and had faded out of the picture. In her war work Josephine was thrown more and more with Louise Closser Hale and Rachel Crothers, especially the former. The pages of the diary are enough to make the reader's head swim.

On July 22 rehearsals of the new play, now rechristened *Under Orders*, got under way, and on August 11 it opened, appropriately, in Washington. "Shelley at his best."

A quarter of a century later John Van Druten created something of a stir by writing a play in which, except for one brief scene, only two actors appeared. From the ensuing pother one might well conclude that such a feat had never been accomplished before. With the difference that in *Under Orders* there were only two actors to interpret four characters, the same thing was done by Berte Thomas. As a matter of fact, some years earlier Nazimova had been seen in a similar piece called *Madam Coquette*, by Robert Bracco.

Under Orders had already been seen in England under the title of *Out of Hell*, and was now being launched on what its producers hoped would prove to be a long run in this country. It is the story of twin sisters, one married and living in England, the other married to a German, and of their two sons, who happen to be the same age. The German son comes to England, and, because of his resemblance to his cousin, succeeds in passing himself off even on his aunt until he gives himself away by playing the piano, something his cousin has never learned to do. When threatened with exposure, he tells her that if she betrays him, her own son, who is being held as a hostage in Germany, will be shot. She does, nevertheless, call the police, and then, thinking herself responsible for her son's death, loses her mind. In the last act the American boy returns unscathed and restores his mother to sanity.

The roles of the two sisters were admirably played by the veteran actress, Effie Shannon, and those of the sons by Shelley. Although the critics did not unite their voices in a unanimous paean of praise, most of them found at least something to commend, and the play was soon established as a hit. Among the enthusiasts was Dorothy Parker, who wrote a lengthy review in *Vanity Fair*.

> I strive, of course, to be open-minded about the thing, but it is certainly going to be difficult to convince me that I will ever see a better war play than "Under Orders." . . . When a trick play can be so intensely absorbing that you forget all about the trick part and think only of the play itself, I would like to suggest that that is indeed something.

She was most favorably impressed by the performance too. "I can think of no actor—other than Mr. Hull—who could rush out of the door as an American, and come back through the window as a German, and not make the entire audience dash out to the box office and demand their money back."

The final act, however, bothered her.

> It is an act you know all about before it even gets started. You have positive inside information, somehow, that the returning son is going to restore the mother's reason. I could have gone out into the night a different woman if they hadn't had that last act. And yet I suppose it had to be done: it's much better propaganda to have it all end happily.
>
> And, besides, you know that if the author had let Shelley Hull get killed, not a woman in the audience would ever have smiled again.

Josephine undoubtedly shared these sentiments, but on September 20 she had no time to sit and ponder over alternative endings, better or not.

> At War Relief all day, awfully busy on benefits & Fete. Had executive meeting. Shelley opened at night in 'Under Orders' & gave a very fine performance & had to make a speech. The Mapes, G. Denny, J. Yates, T. Thorne, & Katherine here afterwards. So proud & happy.

The play settled down comfortably, and Shelley, despite one of his "hard colds" kept on winning golden opinions. On October 13, his wife's pride and happiness soared to new heights, for "Papers announce *Shelley as a star for the first time.*" Just how Miss Shannon reacted to this arrangement no one has revealed, but possibly she was content to be "featured."

When the war was over, peace had no effect on the popularity of *Under Orders,* nor, for that matter, on Josephine's preoccupation with her relief activities, nor, indeed, on their social life. The only cloud was the influenza epidemic, which by this time was reaching dreadful proportions. The tragedy of it was brought home to them by the death of their young friend, Tom Dobson, whose funeral they attended on November 13. If they saw in it any threat to themselves, they did not allow it to slow them down, and continued, despite it, to enjoy their good fortune.

> Christmas Day. Stocking from family. We had a wee tree. . . . Mother E. & Uncle T. for dinner. Lovely swarm of people in all afternoon & ev'g till nearly dawn. Shelley's fur & dressing-gown, perfume & books—and lovely box from family,—Heaps of cards, flowers. Lovely, lovely day & people.

She could not have been more blissful. Her spirits were not dampened even when Shelley celebrated Founder's Day at his beloved Players, instead of seeing the New Year in at home with her. His recognition by this revered club was one of her greatest satisfactions. With the understanding Aunt Nellie, who had come down for a brief visit, she listened happily to the horns and bells and welcomed 1919 in.

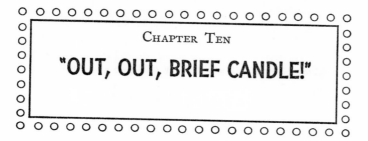

CHAPTER TEN

"OUT, OUT, BRIEF CANDLE!"

Shelley Hull, star of "Under Orders," has evolved a set of rules through the observance of which he thinks he can avoid having influenza. They are,

> Keep clean.
> Keep warm.
> Don't be afraid of it.
> —Clipping from unidentified paper.

ON JANUARY 8, Josephine wrote: "Shelley has a temperature. He played at night, but then took medicine, foot-bath & rub & got to bed."

The next day it was obvious that he had influenza. So had she. Her case was light; his was not. Mother Elinor came in to take charge, and Dr. Sweeny managed to get two nurses. Terrified, and loath to leave him even for a moment, Josephine lay by his side till evening, when the doctor moved her into the little front room. What happened from then on we shall leave it to her to tell, as she did later when she had enough strength and courage.

January 12. Both nurses continuing. Shelley's case so serious, Thompson called in Dr. Warren Coleman—reassuring. So anxious & agonized for Shelley, but better physically myself. Everyone kind & helpful.

January 13. Shelley about the same, but it is the dreadful pneumonia-influenza. Praying for him, listening to him from my little front room, longing so to help him. Oh such agony not to be with him.

January 14. Had three nurses. Shelley struggling for life all day. Dr. Coleman in again. Oxygen, drugs—they are fighting for him. At between 5 & 6 I went to him, had a sweet little talk, followed by a few words later when he asked for me. He died at 6:55.—My beloved, my life.—Dr. Reiland, Henry, Mother, Jack Yates, Louise Hale, Etta & Jack—everyone kind.

That evening the lights on Broadway were dimmed.

"Shelley looks so young, so beautiful, I want to be with him always." Years later, writing of the death of a friend, Louise Hale said, "She and Shelley are the only two of the dear dead I have ever seen who changed not at all."

In the little apartment Josephine was surrounded by people who loved her and who, unmindful of themselves, tried—futilely, as they knew—to help her. Weak as she was from the effects of her own illness and from shock, her indomitable spirit was not destroyed. Even in her anguish her New England courage and her unshakeable faith in the goodness of God triumphed.

In Newtonville the four aunts were distraught with grief and anxiety. Before they received Josephine's wire, Aunt Fanny read the news in the paper. "I am so broken up that I can hardly write," said Aunt Anne in a hurried letter, "but you know how we all loved Shelley." Aunt Gertrude was so distracted that her sisters sent her off to school, as they thought "she would be better there."

It was not only to his family and friends that Shelley's death came as a stunning blow. The world of the theater was shocked as it had seldom been before. "It seems incredible!" Otis Skinner wrote his wife. "He was one of the most glorious of the young men of our stage! and pretty nearly its 'white hope.' " He had been so young, so vital and buoyant, that he had seemed beyond the reach of death. Messages of love and sympathy poured in by the hundred.

"OUT, OUT, BRIEF CANDLE!"

In Josephine's scrapbook the reviews of *Under Orders* are followed by fifteen pages of obituaries and eulogies clipped from papers all over the country. The tone was all the same. In the *New York Evening World* Louis De Foe wrote:

> Right conduct in private life, unfailing generosity to his professional associates, and a genial sunny nature which radiated the warmth of good fellowship made him beloved by all with whom he came in contact.

Later in The Players Memorial, Jack Yates spoke for the members of his favorite club:

> To his great devotion to his wife was added the realization of her help in his work and his reliance on her judgment. In his attitude toward life the characteristics which stood out most clearly were his cleanness of mind and the courage and strength of his convictions. As a friend he was entirely unselfish.

The funeral, conducted by Dr. Reiland, was held at St. George's with all its happy memories, at noon on the sixteenth. "A great throng of loving, grieving people. Tom Safford's music beautiful. Dr. Reiland and his wife heavenly kind, took us into their home till it was time to leave." She had decided on burial in the Sherwood lot, and, together with Mother Elinor, Howard—Henry could not leave his play—and Shelley's close friends, Russell Churchill, Jack Warren, and Ernest Hunter, she took the four o'clock train to Boston. There, at the Hotel Bellevue, Aunt Anne and Aunt Nellie were waiting for her. Interment took place the next day.

> Shelley's burial, Newton cemetery at noon. Drove out by Babcock St., & dear familiar roads & scenes—Friends at cemetery. Mr. Loring read service. Home to Marion with my aunts & Daisy, who spent P. M. Spent night with them. Wonderful flood of love for Shelley from everywhere. Cannot make it all seem real. Like a dreadful nightmare.

The services were covered by the press.

> More than four hundred floral pieces from all parts of the
> country were massed in the chapel of the Newton Cemetery
> at noon today when funeral services were held for Shelley Hull,
> the actor, who died in New York. . . . A number of theatrical
> people were included in the gathering at the brief service, which
> was conducted by the Rev. Richard T. Loring, rector of St.
> John's Church, Newtonville.

Although invited by the aunts to stay with them, Mrs. Hull
returned to New York with Howard. Next morning Josephine
with Aunt Anne and Aunt Nellie went back to the cemetery
to see the flowers once more. "Brought all from N. Y., more
came here." That afternoon she took the train to New York.

Weakened and exhausted, when she reached the apartment,
the stairs had never seemed so steep, and she shrank from facing the familiar rooms with their dreadful memories. When
she opened the door, the air was heavy with the fragrance of
flowers. Everywhere she looked there were vases filled with
them, and on the tables piles of letters and telegrams, hundreds
of them. All traces of the recent illness had been cleared away
by Margaret, but nothing seemed real. Before long Mother
Elinor came, and bleakly they sat down to dinner with the
maid hovering about. In their desolation the two women,
deeply devoted as they had been for years, were drawn closer
to each other than ever before. During the dreary months that
followed they were seldom apart.

Somehow Josephine got through the first lonely night in
what was now for her the empty apartment. The next day was
Sunday, but she could not muster up the courage to go to
church, especially to St. George's. "Mother E. & I walked
down to Howard & Mary's for dinner. Home on bus."

Dazed and bewildered, she found herself in a situation she
had never allowed herself to imagine. In less than a week
everything that gave her life meaning had been swept away,
and the future seemed like one of Aunt Nellie's jigsaw puzzles,

the pieces of which she must fit together. Fortunately there were many to help her. The Hulls, Uncle Theodore, Katie, Callie Emmet, Louise Hale, and countless others hovered about. To advise her about the practical matters of business confronting her there was Shelley's friend, Jack Yates, kindly and understanding. John Carrington Yates, a young Englishman who came to this country as an actor, soon quit the theater for the world of business, and was at this time on the staff of Vincent Astor. Although no longer on the stage, he had retained his membership in The Players and had been a crony of Shelley's there. It was he who wrote the obituary Josephine always treasured.

The situation he uncovered would have dismayed her if anything had seemed to matter. Shelley had evidently never faced up to the fact that he might not live out his allotted span, and had never seen any pressing need for laying by assets against unforeseen contingencies. This, as the *World* pointed out a few weeks later, was a common failing with theatrical folk. Nat Goodwin, who died only a fortnight after Shelley, was reputed to have left but $6,000, and the great Charles Frohman himself, only $451. The article then goes on to cite Shelley as another example, saying that when his widow filed his will, "she estimated that his property was worth only $500," although at the time of his death he had been receiving a salary of $750 a week.

This account is, however, inexact. In the first place, Shelley had never bothered to write a will. Nor was the situation by any means as bad as it was pictured. An inventory of the estate published in the *Morning Telegraph* eight months later gives the net value as $7,903.40, the gross being $13,004.60. This included some small bank deposits, thirty-five shares of United Cigar Store stock, and the Cadillac, which was appraised at $1,600. There had been heavy expenses, especially in connection with the funeral and interment, and there were still a number of unpaid bills. The Surrogate Court appointed Josephine administratrix, and the Hulls signed releases. Accordingly what there was went to her. She had enough, then, to provide her with a respite while she got her bearings. Under Jack's supervision she was able by degrees to straighten out the trying problems of administration and of transferring Shelley's meager assets to herself. In the disposition of his clothes and costumes she had Henry's assistance. She retrieved his skates from "Iceland," but, when she went out to the Scarsdale Country Club to get his golfing clothes, she found that the clubhouse had burned and all his effects, except his clubs, had burned with it. At the office of the Sage Foundation "I signed papers closing up Shelley's & my contract for Forest Hills Gardens. He gave me a check, which I deposited." This marked the end of a long-cherished hope. She neglected to say who gave her the check.

All these tasks, as she said, "kept her mercifully busy," and left her little leisure for brooding. But again and again she confided her heartbreak to the diary.

> Valentines from my dear aunts & Uncle T. Puzzles from Aunt N. & salted nuts from Aunt A. I had spring flowers put at Shelley's grave. What a world's difference this Valentines day. Oh, my beloved!

Yet whatever she felt, she did what had to be done to the best of her ability. Four days after the burial she went with Mother Elinor, Katie, Louise, and Laura Bacon, whose husband she had asked to design a headstone, to see a motion picture in which Shelley appeared. He had not recanted his decision to keep out of the movies, but when a worthy cause was to be served, he had been ready as always.

The members of S.W.W.R. had made up their minds not to close shop with the end of hostilities. They had rightly concluded that for months to come they could be of service to the boys returning from overseas, and particularly wanted to maintain their theater in the Grand Central Debarkation Hospital No. 5. Carl Laemmle, president of Universal Pictures, had told them that the surest way to raise the necessary funds would be to produce a series of film plays featuring prominent actors, preferably some who had never been in pictures before. The suggestion was quickly adopted and, under the leadership of Rachel Crothers, the call for volunteers went out. The first person asked was Shelley. "He not only promised to be in the films himself," said Miss Crothers, "but took an untold interest in the project." Today it is not unusual to see the dead moving on the screen, but in 1919 it was something new. It must have been an ordeal for Shelley's wife, and his mother as well, although she described it as "a wonderful, sweet experience."

Every time Josephine returned to the apartment she was confronted by the stacks of messages that had continued to pour in for weeks after January 14. Obviously they could not all be acknowledged, but there were some she had not the heart to neglect. "Getting along slowly with the huge piles of letters & answers." One of these was Jane O'Reilly's, and she summoned up the fortitude to answer it.

> I am so glad to have my wonderful memories and so thankful for having had Shelley even for these nine years. It has been ideal, wonderful enough to last me always in this world. . . . I suppose in the great scheme of things, hard as it is to understand, Shelley was more needed There than Here. At least he never knew any real sorrow in his life and went out triumphant, and left a wonderful heritage of love and sunshine and radiant beauty. I am sure I shall be all right, indeed I think Shelley is helping me. But it seems another world and I have not yet found any real rudder to steer by.

A rudder she must find to replace the one she had lost. She did not realize that her rudder had been less her husband himself than the need to look after him. After she had put aside her own career that had given her life its purpose. Now that it was gone, she had to find some means of keeping herself alive, unimportant as that seemed at the moment, and she tried to submerge her sorrow in service to others. At this juncture the thought of returning to the stage seems not to have occurred to her. She had put it by and had no heart to go back. But whatever she was to do with her life, she could not wait long to decide.

There was always the S.W.W.R., and she returned to the office on February 20. "Everyone dear and lovely." Soon she was deeply involved in the treasurer's business again; fortunately, there were no more benefits to be managed. She was elected to fill Shelley's empty seat on the Executive Council of the Actors' Equity Association and appreciated this vote of confidence as much as she was capable of appreciating any compliment at this time. Of course she took hold at once. "She always did what she said she could do."

These two jobs were invaluable in keeping her mind occupied, but they brought in no dollars and cents. (A check from the Comedy Club in remuneration for directing *The Village* she sent back "as a memorial for Shelley.") She turned down a request to coach a children's play, but accepted one to supervise a scene from *The Yellow Jacket* to be given by the Colony Club as part of a Chinese fete, and one to direct a play for an amateur club in Plainfield. So she was finding at least part of a rudder.

Meantime she was constantly on the go. She and "Mother E." frequently went to concerts and plays. Aunt Anne and Aunt Gertrude came down for a visit, and she took them to Henry's opening in Rachel Crothers' *39 East,* a "brilliant event." Then she went home with them so that she could take flowers to the cemetery on her wedding anniversary. She had approved the design for a monument by her friend Henry Bacon, the architect of the Lincoln Memorial in Washington, but it would not be completed until June.

By this time she had been taken over completely by a new obsession: the overpowering determination somehow, if such a thing was possible, to get in touch with Shelley in the world beyond the grave. Never for one moment had she doubted the actuality of life after death. Otherwise she could never have reconciled herself to the deaths of Emily, Clara, and, of course, her mother. Now, with Shelley "over there," the need to reach him was overwhelming, and she was ready to try anything, however dubious, that might conceivably bring her the contact she craved. Her first moves were somewhat tentative and a bit suspicious, but she grew steadily more desperate and more reckless.

In the wake of the First World War and the influenza epidemic thousands of the bereaved, mostly women, sought pitifully for some assurance that the dear ones they had lost were continuing in another sphere, and for messages from their departed husbands, sons, or lovers. Josephine was but one of thousands. It was inevitable that this great hunger should evoke responses of many sorts, some no doubt sincere, but others quite the reverse, as hundreds of charlatans seized upon this opportunity to batten on the sorrows of the stricken. Houdini had not yet published his warning revelations. Canny as she normally was, Josephine, in her present state of mind, was fair prey for almost anyone who promised to open the mystical doors to Eternity.

She began by reading books on the subject, starting with Conan Doyle's *The New Revelation*. Next came *The Letters of a Living Dead Man*, which impressed her as "fakey, but interesting," and then *On the Treshold of the Unseen*. Twice she went to the Spiritualist Church, was disappointed, and did not go again. She did, on the other hand, find satisfaction in the Institute of Psychical Research, which claimed her loyalty for years. At this point she met a woman bearing the euphonious name of "Mrs. Tubby," who gave lectures on "the scientific séance," and a Mrs. Hesse, a medium. She went from one to the other, always hoping. She did entertain some doubts about Mrs. Hesse after discovering that the lady had operated under an assortment of different names. Charitably Josephine concluded that it was a case of many husbands; still, disquieting suspicion nagged her.

Then, on June 5, she found her answer. At a dinner at the home of Jesse Lynch Williams, she met a Mrs. Gavit. When the ladies retired to another room to leave the men to their cigars and their anecdotes, Mrs. Gavit introduced her for the first time to the wonders of "automatic writing." Josephine kept, carefully preserved among her papers, a transcription of this miraculous demonstration to which she later added pages and pages describing other sessions during that tragic year.

Mrs. Gavit addressed the invisible spirits, and asked them to sign their names. She held a pencil loosely between her fingers and the spirits "wrote." She explained to the women that the room was full of them and that they loved their friends who were trying to establish contact. "Then the pencil jumped & flew about."

> Mrs. G. "This is a new personality, a very strong one. Who is it?"
> Pencil wrote a large letter *S* and then stuck.
> Mrs. G. "Who knows anyone beginning with S?"
> I. "Could it be Shelley? I always feel he is near."
> Pencil danced all round, made big circles, then wrote rapidly.
> "I am here I am here you said I was near you and I am."

S. directed her to try using the pencil herself. "I will love to write for you." She did try, but her arms tingled so and she was so upset that she had to return the pencil to Mrs. Gavit, and the message continued through her medium. Thus it all began.

She quickly learned how to manage for herself, and during the rest of the year she had writing after writing. Usually she was alone, but she soon had Mother Elinor and gradually other relatives and friends join her. None of them, however, was able to "get through." Mrs. Hull, wavering on the edge of conviction, tried a number of times, and, although she never succeeded, seems to have been persuaded that the messages were genuine. She told Josephine that some of the information she received could not possibly have been known. Howard declined to have anything to do with the séances, but Henry and Julie, sympathetically, at least pretended to believe. Jack and Helen Yates, however, were so incredulous that S. instructed Josephine never to let them be present at another attempt.

Thompson Sweeny told her to keep on, but to "keep her feet on the ground." His attitude is revealed by the one question he put. He told her to ask Shelley if he was glad to have missed prohibition.

Obviously the lengthy transcriptions she preserved cannot have been written down at the time, but are the conversations as she recalled them. Her arms always tingled while she was writing and often she wept bitterly. The phraseology of Shelley's remarks and those of others with whom she later communicated are usually Josephine's own when she was at her most sentimental. She attributed to him, quite unwittingly of course, the things she yearned to hear him say. Two or three times she admits, "That did not sound like Shelley." Once she suggests that something she wrote may really have originated in her own subconscious mind. But such doubts she hastily put aside. Gradually the circle of the communicants was enlarged to include her mother, Shelley's sister Edith, Cousin Lillie, Uncle Phil, and many others who had gone on ahead. Almost invariably she put her own thoughts and wishes into their messages. She accepted them all without question and she resented interruptions—those of a John Saltonstall, for instance, who kept breaking in to enlist her help in reaching his still earthbound wife. Only a mind nearly irrational with grief could have accepted seriously all the farrago of nonsense she transcribed. Yet for years to come, when doubts presented themselves, she quickly thrust them from her and, nonsense or not, the whole thing helped to preserve her sanity. In a way she did follow her doctor's admonition to keep her feet on the ground.

Gradually with the passing of the years the craze released its grip on her. Eventually she confided to Callie that its hold had been getting too strong, and that, moreover, "Perhaps there are some things we are not supposed to know." Instead she relied more and more on her conventional religion. Yet she never, so long as she lived, lost the faith that her adored husband was close at hand. She always spoke as if he were in the next room. "She was a bit of a 'psychic,'" says her cousin, Mrs.

Allerton Brooks, "and told me that she could always bring Shelley to her—at certain times of the day." He was always there to share her joys and sustain her in her trials. On anniversaries and holidays she festooned his pictures with flowers, and the surest way to win her favor was to tell her what a great actor he had been.

All this while she was picking up the pieces of her puzzle and halfheartedly trying to fit them together into some sort of picture. In June she went to Boston, where she met Mother E., who had come up from Connecticut. They joined the aunts at the Marion in Newtonville, and next day, Shelley's birthday, together with Russell Churchill, took flowers out to the cemetery. "The memorial is in place & so beautiful." A day or so later Mrs. Hull returned to "the Valley," and thither Josephine followed her for a quiet, if melancholy, fortnight. Then Henry drove her and Julie back to New York.

One of the first things she had to do was to find a new home. The apartment was too big for her needs, and she set about hunting another. She chose Guy Post's old one, on the top floor of 137 West Fifty-sixth Street, next door to the building in which she and Shelley had first set up housekeeping, and was pleased because of memories of happy evenings spent there with Shelley, Jane, and Guy. Many years later when Frank Rowan pointed her windows out to another friend, the latter exclaimed, "She climbed all those stairs!" She did—for years—but at that time she did not have so much weight to lift as when he knew her.

She had been back in the city only a few weeks when something happened to jolt her out of her apathy and galvanize her into such action as she had not dreamed of since January. Equity called its famous strike.

Actors' Equity Association had been organized in 1913 to improve the unfair conditions under which members of the profession had suffered from time immemorial. The actors banded together to present a united front to the managers who had theretofore had their own way because they could deal with their employees individually. Whether the members mentioned the fact or not, it was in essence a labor union. During the six years of its existence it had succeeded in bringing about considerable betterment of the situation, but further ameliora- tion was still called for. In order to defend their position the managers followed suit, and banded together in the Producing Managers' Association, a hard core of resolute men who, con- fident of their ability to bend the recalcitrant players to their will, assumed a granite-like stand. Of Equity, Alfred Harding says in his *The Revolt of the Actors:*

> The Association had now approximately three thousand members. They represented between forty and fifty per cent of all the actors and actresses in the legitimate theater of the country. But in many respects they were the flower of the field, the best, most prosperous, most responsible of the players. If they would agree to stand together and to play only in such companies where all members were Equity members in good standing, the remaining actors would have to come in and stay in; for the Equity actors were the sort the managers considered the backbone of their companies, and there were not enough such actors outside of Equity to supply the casts of many first class productions.

Obviously this, though called "Equity Shop," was Closed Shop. At swallowing this the managers gagged. They flatly refused, not only to sign a contract containing any such pro- vision, but to have any dealings whatsoever with the offending union. David Belasco said he would withdraw from the theater before he would submit. So did George M. Cohan. And many others.

Josephine was aquiver with excitement, for she loved a good fight provided it was in behalf of a principle she believed in and was carried on chivalrously.

> August 7. Had Equity meeting at Astor, & called strike, great excitement. . . . 12 theaters closed by A. E. A. strike.
> August 8. All Broadway wild over the strike. Evening had instruction meeting at Rehearsal Club.

155

August 13. At Equity Rooms all day working on relief and aid committee. Greatest excitement & continuous new developments over the strike.

August 14. Went to A. E. A. headquarters, working on relief committee, & in P. M. to rally at the Astor with wonderspeakers & enthusiasm.

Josephine's enthusiasm was by no means shared by all American actors. Some were aghast. Sothern, foreseeing the doom of the theater he adored, struggled furiously to bring about some sort of reconciliation. From Long's Peak Inn in Colorado an outraged Otis Skinner telegraphed his resignation from Equity. "I find I am a striker!" he exclaimed. He believed that injustice was being worked in the name of justice on managers who had never offended. Moreover, to many, labor unions were anathema, and they felt that their art was being degraded by affiliation with the American Federation of Labor. To touch pitch is to be defiled. When Samuel Gompers attended an Equity meeting and threw the whole weight of his organization behind the strikers, that was too much.

August 23. At Equity all day, hard work, very inspiring and thrilling occurrences. Council meeting in evening. . . . Pretty tired but so enthusiastic over work.

In the matter of cold figures, she had every right to be enthusiastic over her part in the fray. The managers were banking smugly on the inability of the striking actors to hold out, but Josephine gave them something to think about. "It was, therefore, a considerable jolt to this confidence," writes Harding, "when Mrs. Shelley Hull, in charge of Equity's Relief and Aid Fund, announced at this time that her treasury now contained $40,000 and that there had been only three calls on her for assistance."

The dissident actors now rallied to form their own group in opposition to Equity, electing Cohan president, rather an anomalous choice because he was a violently partisan member of

P. M. A. The strife now took on the aspect of a minor civil war with hitherto devoted friends glaring at each other from the opposing camps. It was John Drew and the Barrymores, Francis Wilson, Frank Bacon et al. *vs.* Sothern, Skinner, Mrs. Fiske, Blanche Bates, and their sympathizers. Many of Josephine's best friends became enthusiastic members of Actors' Fidelity League. That was all right with her if that was the way they felt. Everyone should do what his conscience directed. Her heart was wholly on the other side, but there was no rancor or bitterness in her reactions. One of her opponents was Gladys Hanson, who had been a member of the original *Jerry* company, and for whom she had felt a warm affection ever since. Miss Hanson still has vivid memories of the "embattled" Josephine of those hectic days.

> In thinking of Josephine I think—I see—her radiance—and feel her understanding—and kindness—her sense of fun & humour—her high intelligence—her keen sense of right & wrong which she applied to herself as well as others.
>
> We used to laugh in remembering the Actors Strike (ancient history, indeed)—Josephine stood on one side of the Battle line—with flaming sword in hand—I stood on the other side as definite in my belief as she—and yet our separate meetings being at the same hour, I always stopped by to pick her up and drop her at Equity headquarters—then went my way across town to the Fidelity meeting. Never once did we attack either the cause or the personal attitude of the other.

That was the way Josephine liked to fight, if one can call it "fighting." And what was true of one of the adversaries was just as true of the other. Each respected the right of the other to disagree.

At last, after many engagements and counterengagements, many denunciations and counterdenunciations, peace was declared on September 6. P. M. A. surrendered, and despite its many defiant pronunciamentos, it signed the Equity contract on the dotted line, and Equity Shop was accepted. The actors had won and, until radio and television presented new menaces, they enjoyed a security they had never known before. Yet for a few "Something went out when the unions came in."

With the restoration of peace, Josephine's thoughts were once more free to return to her troubles. She must resume her search for a rudder. But, first, she had to move. With the help of Mother E. and Henry, she got things ready for the packers. They came on September 20.

> Last night in Shelley's & my darling home. Had fire in dining-room fireplace for memories.

Next day she moved temporarily to the Great Northern Hotel. It was not till October 16 that she and Margaret spent their first night under their new roof.

The rest of the year was uninspiring except for one happy event. A new Shelley Hull was born on December 10. In giving him the name they did, Julie and Henry also gave Josephine the best Christmas present she received. In other ways her life returned to its familiar pattern. She was offered at least one chance to return to the stage, but she seems not to have given it serious consideration. She and her mother-in-law continued their playgoing and she saw much of her friends. But it was all tame.

On New Year's Eve she began her custom of sending a telegram of greetings to The Players. "After Shelley's death," writes Howard Lindsay, "at our annual ceremony of Founder's Night, when we celebrate the founding of the club by Edwin Booth, we never failed to receive a telegram from Josephine Hull. This message was more warmly applauded than any of the other messages read on this annual occasion."

> Opened windows in front room to let New Year in. Oh my Shelley!

CHAPTER ELEVEN

A RUDDER TO STEER BY

DURING THE FIRST MONTHS of 1920 Josephine rather fumbled about without any over-all purpose. She did some teaching and coaching at St. Agatha's, did various odd jobs of direction, and gave desultory lessons to a few private pupils. She managed in this way to keep her mind off her grief part of the time, but not to bring in much cash. She was still marking time in a rather half-hearted way. She kept up her work on the Equity Council and with S.W.W.R., and went almost regularly to plays and concerts. Where the money came from to finance these pleasures she does not say. Once she escorted Ethel Barrymore to a luncheon of the Women's Trade Union League, where the latter gave a talk. Evenings at home were usually dedicated to the comfort-giving "writings," which gave her the support she needed to carry on.

In May, however, thanks no doubt to Henry, something concrete turned up. The Shuberts were planning to star him in a new play by Leighton Osmun, and she was engaged to direct it. "This was my first professional directing job as such." The original title of the drama, *The Crucible,* was changed before the opening to *Greater Love*. As soon as the script was put in her hands, she turned for help to Priestly Morrison, and under his experienced guidance worked out the scene plots, with Mrs. Morrison standing by and helping with dinner, since Margaret, her maid, was off on one of her several short-lived trials of more lucrative jobs. (These were always of short duration because she could not endure long separations from Josephine.) "Mr. Morrison really 'taught' Josephine the fundamentals of directing and helped her get established as a director," said his widow.

There were occasional pleasant breaks in her routine, the usual excursions to the theater or an agreeable supper party. On June 25 after a long day of work, "Howard & Mary came to dinner, bringing some lobsters, nice visit with them." The pleasant evening, however, had an unpleasant aftermath—she was sick all night. This was not the last such mishap in her life, for when offered a lobster, a crab, or an oyster, Josephine was prone to let discretion wait upon enjoyment. By morning she was again in good form, and ready to tackle *Greater Love*.

By the opening date, July 5, when Osmun's *opus* was presented in the Shubert Crescent Theater in Brooklyn, everything was under control. The fluttery, bewildered little person the public came in later years to identify with Josephine Hull was just about as far as anything could be from the real article. Once she saw clearly what she wanted to do, there was no uncertainty and there was no fumbling. Nor was there any weakness. Although never unreasonable, she could be as firm as any of her Puritan forebears. She got her way, according to the late Clarence Derwent, not by shouting or having tantrums, but by politely asserting her will; and he considered the results excellent. Under no circumstances did she ever forget that she was, first of all, a New England lady. However, there is no law that says New England ladies cannot be stubborn—in the nicest possible way, of course.

Despite the "raves" in the Brooklyn press, *Greater Love* failed to measure up to the hopes of its producers. To tell the truth, it was not really worthy of either its star or its director.

It started out with a prologue that held promise of good things to come, but the promise was not adequately fulfilled. Conferences with Osmun, Henry, and Priestly were followed by revisions, and still paying customers did not see fit to fill the seats in the Shubert Crescent. The excessive heat may have been partly to blame. Whatever the reason, *Greater Love* soon moved from Brooklyn to the warehouse without ever having seen the Great White Way. This was disappointing; nevertheless, so far as Josephine was concerned, it was by no means a total loss. She got her check from the Shuberts. Under Priestly's tutelage she had gained invaluable experience.

By November she was again, as in her first postgraduate days, juggling three balls in the air at the same time. That is, she was coaching three amateur plays. The only difference was that distances were greater in New York than in Boston, and for a while she was in a state of perpetual motion, shuttling back and forth between Brooklyn (the Junior League) and Plainfield (the Dramatic Club) with stopovers in Manhattan (Barnard College). The winter was largely given over to such coaching jobs, including an exceptionally congenial one with the Snarks, a woman's club. She was "not pleased" with the dress rehearsals, but the performances "went beautifully." She greatly enjoyed her contacts with these women, some of whom became lifelong friends.

While she was still busy with the Snarks, her affairs took a very definite turn, one that was to influence the whole course of her life. She had a call from Jessie Bonstelle, the upshot of which was that she was engaged to return to her company in Detroit the following summer, this time, however, not as ingénue, but as director. Here at last was a real rudder to steer by. It gave her self-confidence an invaluable boost, for it assured her that her abilities were recognized and needed.

There now followed a great deal of rushing about, to enable her to leave everything reasonably shipshape. She applied the finishing touches to *Mrs. Bumpstead Leigh,* and Priestly came over to help her. "He came to see me one afternoon with a brief case full of scene plots and lighting plots, which he went over with me." One of the invaluable bits of advice he gave her was always to stand her ground in the face of the carpenters' protests that certain things she wanted done were impossible. They could be done and would be if she held firm and convinced the workmen that she knew what she was talking about. She was to find out that he was right. Mother E. and Margaret helped her swathe the furniture in its ghostly summer wrappings, and she flew about town attending to numberless little odds and ends. At last on May 7, somewhat out of breath, she sank down in her berth on the train to Buffalo and braced herself against the morrow with a good night's rest.

In the morning she descended briskly from her Pullman; to her delight she found Guy Post and Effie Shannon stopping at the same Buffalo hotel. Without more ado Josephine initiated the rehearsals of Salisbury Field's *Wedding Bells*, the play scheduled to open the Detroit season. "Seems like old times to be trouping again." But she had little time for sentimental reunions or any other diversions during her five days in Buffalo, for she was kept hard at work shaping up the production under the critical supervision of Miss Bonstelle, who wanted to see how her new director got along. When she was around, that title was a courtesy one, for the actress-manager held the reins tightly in her own hands. She divided her time between her two theaters, playing the leads in whichever city she was in, and maintained viceroys to control events during her absences. In Buffalo this functionary was Adams Rice; in Detroit it was to be Josephine. It did not take Miss Bonstelle long to discover that in the latter at least she had exactly what she wanted. Nor was the viceroy slow to realize, not for the last time, that being second in command is not exactly a sinecure.

For Josephine this summer season proved to be a definite turning point, one of the most important in her life. She was back in the professional theater. Her activities with the college and other dramatic clubs had been well enough in their way. They had given her experience and self-confidence, but they had not attracted the attention of any producers and they bore the damning stigma of amateur. This Detroit engagement was something else again. It was in the commercial theater, and the gentlemen who called the turns there had the greatest respect for the judgment of Jessie Bonstelle.

On May 14 the Detroit contingent moved on to base, and two evenings later the doors of the Garrick Theater were flung open for the initial production, *Wedding Bells*, with Miss Bonstelle taking her first bow of the season.

> Three events of prime importance annually claim the attention of Detroiters. One is the opening baseball game, another the first symphony concert, and the third the opening of the Bonstelle summer stock season at the Garrick. *(Detroit Times* May 17.)

According to the *News* it was as "cosy as a family party on Thanksgiving Day. Society turned out in force to welcome back old friends and greet the newcomers. The narrow lobby was glutted with bouquets of flowers, and after the final curtain the services of every usher in the house commandeered to convey the posies to the stage." There were compliments enough for everybody and a particular one for Mrs. Shelley Hull, whose "stage direction was agreeably out of sight." The lady in question was delighted with the "splendid house and performance." Then "work late" on *Bab*.

"The Maker of Stars" had as usual surrounded herself with a group of promising young people, for several of whom bright futures lay in store. In Buffalo the heroines were usually played by Letha Walters unless they were ingénues, in which case the beneficiary was the lovely young Sylvia Field, as in *Bab* for instance. Later in the season some of the "leading business" fell to the lot of Edith Meiser. The leading man was Frank Morgan, and the juvenile, Kenneth MacKenna. All in all, it was a competent and likable aggregation for Josephine to shepherd. For her assistant and Handy Andy she had young Jo Mielziner, "honor pupil" at the Pennsylvania Academy of Fine Arts. The scene designer that summer was Lou Bromberg.

Wedding Bells felicitously opened Miss Bonstelle's twelfth

163

season in Detroit, and, except for a couple of disappointments—
in the plays rather than the productions—it was a season she
could look back on with satisfaction. "The Bonstelle Co.," recalls Sylvia Field (now Mrs. Ernest Truex), "was a place of
hard work, 10 performances a week—three matinees and Sunday night—new play each week." Apparently the young people
did not overflow with enthusiasm over "Bonnie's" rather fussy
rule, for they found her difficult to please. "But every other
week she went to Buffalo. Then Mrs. Hull directed, and we
all had a wonderful time. It was fun." Mielziner says, "She
would laugh defensively about her overplump body, which she
moved with the agility and lightness of a sparrow. But the
quickest way to her heart was to comment on her tiny and
beautifully shaped feet." Once when the three of them were
on a shopping expedition in quest of properties, Bromberg
"made the tactical error late in the day when we were fatigued
and footsore of suggesting that Josephine would be better off
with 'larger shoes.' This remark got over like a lead balloon."

The members of the company were not the only ones to recognize her merits. The newspaper men assigned to cover the
Garrick—Forrest Davis of the *Times*, Al Weeks of the *News*,
and Lem Shaw of the *Free Press*—instead of maintaining the
approved judicial distance, immediately moved right into her
camp. Without even trying, she captured the heart of almost
any man she smiled on, and, like Browning's duchess, she had
smiles for everyone. She would lower her head, and then gaze
up with her large brown eyes as if the man talking to her was
a giant who had her at his mercy. Even the carpenters and ele-
tricians succumbed. They call her "Mamma," and put up
none of the resistance predicted by Priestly. She had a way
with stagehands too. Time and again those with whom she
had worked in the past would pay their respects at her dressing
room door.

But back to the gentlemen of the press. Shaw was irritated
by what he considered the cynical indifference of the Garrick
audiences to all the hard work Josephine and her colleagues
had put in just to entertain their idle moments. He became

her champion, and took his typewriter in hand to enlighten them. The play of the week when he interviewed the director was *The Sign on the Door*, and he had her tell him—and the public—just what she had done.

After Miss Bonstelle and I had gone over the script and selected the players, I took it a week ago last Thursday and read it carefully. Friday I went over it again, jotting down the properties required, costumes, lights and general idea of the setting. Saturday I drew to scale the ground plots, or, in other words, the blueprints from which the carpenter built the scenery.

Sunday she worked over details with the carpenter, electrician, and property man. (She did not see the inside of a church in Detroit.) Monday was given over entirely to the play slated to open that evening, dress and scene rehearsal and first performance.

Tuesday we began work in earnest . . . We had a complete reading of the play, the actors reciting from their various parts, while I held the script. . . . Wednesday we rehearsed all day.

Thursday there were two performances, but when they were not on stage or memorizing their parts, the actors were at liberty to divert themselves in any way they preferred. After going home—she had a room at the Borrowood—Josephine settled down to begin the process all over again with the next week's play. "As I have no time during a performance to read a manuscript, it means that Thursday, Friday and Saturday nights I must work from the moment the curtain comes down until any old time the next morning, not infrequently close to daylight." Once more she had three balls in the air—the play currently on the stage, the one in rehearsal, and the one due to be put in rehearsal the following week.

Yet this was not all she did in Detroit. She also acted. She appeared in four of the fourteen plays produced—as Mrs. Martyn in *Clarence*, Hilda in *My Lady Friends*, Mandy Dicks in *That Night at Dolan's,* and Myrtle in *39 East.* These were all small parts, it is true, but merely learning the lines consumed time. On the other hand, she was back *on* the stage, not just behind the scenes. In an interview with Davis, she said, "I was an ingénue before I was married and then I became fat, and I decided to abandon the stage before it abandoned me."

The routine outlined by Shaw did not leave room for a great deal of frivolity, but Josephine managed to get in a few sprees, as they must have seemed to her, a College Club tea for the company and a "charming lawn dinner at Miss Dyars' " in Grosse Pointe, at which she added to the gaiety of the occasion by unexpectedly playing a solo on a cornet.

By the end of August she was quite ready to cry, "Hold! Enough!" She was not only tired, she was hot, and she detested heat.

> Last days of our stock season. Finished packing trunks, left the Borrowood, did last errands, & had last matinée, 'Turn to the Right.' Bonstelle here, curtain-calls, gifts, etc. Gave co. dinner at Dixieland & last performance at night.—Speeches, flowers from Kenneth MacKenna and Harold Moulton, pencil from Phyllis Loughren. Supper at Miss Kimball's. Left at 3 A.M.

Just how much richer was she when the last curtain fell? There is no telling. Her salary had been $65.00 a week and the season had run fourteen weeks, not counting the five days of rehearsals in Buffalo. There had been little time for extravagance; on the other hand, when it came to food, Josephine was not wont to count pennies, and that Dixieland dinner must have consumed many of her dollars. The state of her finances was one of the secrets she kept even from her line-a-day.

Except for brief sorties to Newton and New Ipswich, New Hampshire, where Aunt Nellie had bought a house, she spent the following months more or less uneventfully in New York. She continued her assiduous playgoing, seeing for instance eight performances of Clemence Dane's *Bill of Divorcement,* with Katherine Cornell and Allan Pollock. When The Players gave a supper in the latter's honor, she journeyed down to Gramercy Square, bearing champagne, how many bottles she does not say. Of course she could not afford this gesture, but Allan had been a crony of Shelley's, and this was no occasion for economy. She did not go up to Massachusetts for Christmas, but stayed quietly at home. "Margaret & I sang carols & opened presents in front of the fire."

On January 8 the death of Uncle Theodore severed another tie. In his will he left her one-fourth of the residue of his estate, amounting after taxes to a little over twenty thousand dollars.

By April she was getting ready for another run in Detroit. After preliminary conferences with "Bonnie," she began holding rehearsals of *The Boomerang* at the Playhouse, and going over scene designs with Stephen Nastfogel. On May 5 Katy saw her off with her cohorts, and the next day she was ensconced in a pleasant room at the Hotel Tuller.

There had been many changes in the personnel of the company. Frank Morgan was back, but Sylvia Field had been replaced by Ann Harding, transferred from the Buffalo company, and there were altogether more newcomers than old-timers. They were all "lovely" to work with. Once more, as she had foreseen, she had let herself in for a season of exhaustion, but "The labor we delight in physics pain." Although she had no regrets, when all was over she had drunk her fill, and not all of "Bonnie's" cajoling—in person, by letter, or by wire —could tempt her again. This was one of the times when she would not budge.

She probably had a number of reasons for her determination. In the first place, she no doubt began to feel a bit restive in her subordinate position. She must have known that at least some of the actors thought her a better director than "Bonnie"; she may even have suspected that they were right. Nor was "Bonnie" by any means always governed by sweet reason. Moreover, Detroit was not New York, and it was a long, long way from Broadway. She was not provincial enough to join in the

167

ditty in *The Ham Tree* which says that "When you leave old New York Town, you're only camping out"; nevertheless, she could not be happy for very long anywhere else. Newton with the aunts, and Pleasant Valley with its rustic delights were wonderful when she was tired, but it was only in Manhattan that she could be in touch with the theater, and, joy of joys, spend heavenly evenings talking shop with her innumerable friends.

There was, however, another reason even more potent, and it came out of hiding in another interview with Lem Shaw. He came backstage after she had given an amazing performance in the melodramatic *Broken Wing*, to add his tribute to that of another critic who had already said his say:

> But there is one triumphant, because wholly incongruous achievement, and that is Mrs. Shelley Hull as the keeper of a tough Chinese joint in Hell's Kitchen. Who would believe she could do it unless they had seen it. She must have paraphrased Lady Macbeth's petition "Come, unsex me here" after this fashion: "Come, all ye attributes that I have not, and clothe me with your strange habiliments." Nothing is the same except her lovely speaking voice.

How did she do it? But what Shaw really wanted to know was which she liked better—directing or acting.

> "If you were to ask me what I do best, with particular reference to this week's production," she shot back, and there was more than the suggestion of a twinkle in the eyes that looked out good naturedly from under a becoming little hat, "if you were going to ask me what I do best, I should say without any hesitation, directing. . . .
>
> "When I gave up acting I lost my youth [a statement that can be successfully challenged] and my figure," Mrs. Hull went on with a chuckle as she appraised the lines that are, of a truth, a trifle plump. "It is all right in direction for one to be

168

fat and healthy, but imagine me doing 'Lady Macbeth' or 'The Second Mrs. Tanqueray' or some similar role.

"Just the same, I am hoping that some day I will find a part which fits me—or that I can fit," and again there was a musical laugh. "I don't mean slapstick comedy, or burlesque, but something really serious, a modest little Mrs. Fiske, as it were. Then I am going to quit directing, for a time at least."

Here then was the chief reason why she wanted to get back to New York. In the months that followed Shelley's death, she could not face a return to the stage. Now these two summers had given her a taste of the fruit she had been denying herself, and she had found it as sweet as ever. The hybrid arrangement under the Bonstelle banner was no longer satisfactory. She must get back to Broadway where the theaters and the casting offices were.

Before the season had spent itself she played one more role, a "sweet-faced aunt" in *Wait Till We're Married*, and that presented no problems. She had plenty of models. She worked hard, too hard, and for two days was sick in bed, attended by a doctor and a nurse. Outraged because she had to miss rehearsals and a performance, she still did not break her record, since fortunately she was not in the cast that week. There were pleasant breaks too—a refreshing picnic in the woods by Turtle Lake, and two birthday parties, a backstage one for young, fair Ann Harding, and a surprise one for Phyllis Loughren, her fifteenth, at her home.

At that age, incredible as it may seem, Phyllis was Josephine's stage manager. She had been assistant for two years, and now occupied the top post herself. She was efficiency personified. "I do not know what I would do," Josephine was quoted as saying in the *Journal* July 5, "with the mass of detail a director of stock companies encounters if I did not have Phyllis to look after a great share of it. Once it is turned over to her, it is a closed book so far as I am concerned. Phyllis never fails."

There can be no question that, professionally, the two summers in Detroit were of great benefit to Josephine and advanced her far toward her return to the stage as an actress. That side of the picture was bright. But there was a darker aspect. The reason is made quite clear by Mielziner.

> When I joined the company in early spring, I was well aware that Miss Bonstelle was a woman of great drive, shrewd in business and able in administration. But I soon discovered that one of the ruling passions of her life had to do with the world of spirits. She was attracted to many different cults, some of them of Eastern origin. I do recall that she and Josephine had many interests in common, including going to séances.

His brother, Kenneth MacKenna, has his recollections too, especially of the production of *The Triumph of X,* by Carlos Wupperman.

> I do remember something of the Triumph of X. Carlos Wupperman was the deceased younger brother of Frank Morgan who was our leading man. This gave Jessie, a spiritualist herself, the chance to give the company a serious talk, urging us to open our hearts and let Carlos, who was somewhere in the wings, direct the play himself. Being an irreverent youngster this did not impress me as a sound plan, especially as when I bounded onto the stage for its opening scene, Jessie immediately reverted to her accustomed didactic and forceful style of direction and stopped me to correct the reading. I couldn't resist the temptation to credit my version to Carlos! If Josephine was herself under the local mediums my words must have hurt her. But I don't remember that she ever allowed me to know that side of her interests.

By the summer of 1922, Shelley had been in his grave two and a half years, and he should have been permitted to rest there in peace. But, like Queen Victoria, Josephine clung to her grief, seemingly in the belief that to let it quiet down would be disloyal. She was forever stirring it up with little rituals, the rereading of his love letters, and various spiritualistic experiments. All these things, which she was entirely convinced brought her consolation of a sort, actually kept her in a state of inner turmoil.

Here in Detroit "Bonnie" shovelled fuel on the fire. She introduced Josephine to two women of similar interests, and the four of them indulged their fancies in séances, table tipping, and automatic writing. It is not surprising that Josephine's sick spell followed hard upon one of these sessions. We know by her own testimony that during her writings she shook all over and often wept bitterly. Her stomach was her weak point, and, despite the best of resolutions, she subjected it to much stress and strain. When a highly emotional orgy followed a hearty meal, the result was likely to be painful. So it was a very good thing that, the season ended, she resolved to part with Miss Bonstelle, although it is unlikely that the latter's occult interests were included among the reasons.

When Josephine got back to New York, the Comedy Club and the Plainfield Dramatic Club soon sought her out and, whatever her preferences, she soon found herself once more backstage instead of behind the footlights. She was in no position to refuse even if she wanted to. Not yet able to draw on her inheritance from Uncle Theodore and without any other considerable resources, she probably was depending chiefly on what was left of the thirteen hundred dollars she had earned in Detroit. It was a nuisance to have to travel over to New Jersey for rehearsals, but she liked the club members there, and greatly enjoyed her associations with George Denny, the Steinways, and others, at the Comedy Club.

At this point a new interest was injected into her life, one which, while it paid nothing in sorely needed dollars and cents, added impetus to her progress toward her present goal in life. Ever since the successful conclusion of the strike three years before, Equity had wanted to establish an actors' theater but not until 1922 were circumstances propitious. Now at last the

Forty-eighth Street Theater was rented and the first play, the Quinteros Brothers' *Malvaloca*, was launched with Jane Cowl as the star. This example of modern Spanish dramatic literature proved to be an artistic success, but the public failed to respond, and at the end of six lean weeks it was laid aside. The next attraction, *Hospitality*, by Leon Cunningham, fared no better and shortly followed *Malvaloca* into the discard. In a few weeks the determined Equity Players were poised for another try.

This time the piece selected was *Why Not?*, a high comedy by Jesse Lynch Williams. Whether at his suggestion or not— for they were close friends—Josephine was picked for the director's role. To her intense annoyance, at this unpropitious moment, she suffered another slump, and, at Thompson Sweeny's insistence, underwent unpleasant treatments with X ray. She does not tell what these revealed, but, inasmuch as she was subject to repeated spells of nausea and pain so intense as to call for codeine, her troubles probably were again digestive in origin. She carried on valiantly, and if anyone asked how she was, the answer was "Fine."

For *Why Not?* she got herself a good cast, headed by Tom Powers, but in so doing was obliged to perform a duty as unpleasant as the X ray ordeals. "Had to give notice to one of the co.—one of the hardest things I ever had to do." A requirement of these Equity productions that must have entailed a good deal of strain for all involved was a run-through under the scrutiny of the board. The director and the players knew full well that they were being put through their paces by a group of eagle-eyed, if not unsympathetic, experts. The opening occurred on Christmas evening, the fifth anniversary of Shelley's first appearance in *Why Marry?* With its contrived situations and rather stilted dialogue, *Why Not?* does not make for impressive reading today, but standards were different in 1922, and the comedy was well received. Josephine could justifiably wear a feather in her hat.

Unfortunately, though the blame could not fairly be saddled on her, the feather soon had to be taken off and stored away for future use. It had not been intended that she should direct *Roger Bloomer*, but Augustin Duncan, who was to have done so, became ill, and the job was turned over to her. Her social and political views being what they were, it is unlikely that the play was much to her taste, and it is clear from mutterings in the diary that she did not welcome her assignment with glee. But she was never one to shun a responsibility. In *Roger Bloomer* she found herself dealing with a play as different from *Why Not?* as John Howard Lawson was different from Jesse Lynch Williams. The latter composed sophisticated, ultrapolite comedies of manners with satirical overtones. Lawson was the 1922 prototype of the "Angry Young Man" of today. He wrote plays of protest, and did not concern himself greatly with the Williams brand of urbanity. He also experimented with new techniques that taxed the director's ingenuity. None of this was exactly Josephine's meat, but she took a deep breath, and lavished upon the production every bit of skill and every ounce of strength she possessed.

The drama opened on March 2, and went better than she had hoped. The company was good. Henry, who had the title role, could always be counted on to do himself credit. In the cast, too, was one of his colleagues of stock days in St. Louis, a young actor named Louis Calhern. Nothing had been omitted. It was probably no one's fault, but the public just was not yet ready for what Burns Mantle describes as a "weirdly impressionistic drama of adolescence written in the continental style." The play, so far as the Actors' Theater was concerned, was closed on the tenth, but it then found a haven in Greenwich Village, where it ran for several weeks.

Obviously the Equity Players' board did not hold Josephine responsible for their disappointment, for in a month she was called on again. This time they decided to play safe, and projected an all-star revival of *The Rivals*, which they hoped would reduce the operating deficit to a moderate sum. (According to *Equity Magazine*, she was "assistant director," but this title does not gibe either with the diary or with Burns Mantle.) In selecting her to preside over an array of "names" like Francis Wilson, James T. Powers, Sydney Blackmer, Maclyn Arbuckle, Mary Shaw, Violet Heming, and Eva Le Gallienne the board showed gratifying confidence in her and her ability. By some strange quirk of Fate, the Fag was none other than John Craig, who had been the leading man of the Castle Square Company when she made her first appearance on a professional stage as an anonymous démimondaine in *Camille*. What must have been the feelings of the two when they met under circumstances so different from those of twenty years before? Josephine could now take her feather out of the closet and pin it back on her hat, for the Sheridan comedy was loudly applauded and played to full houses for the twenty-four performances allotted to it.

When the next fall came around and with it a new theatrical season, she edged herself a little closer to the place she wanted most of all to be. The optimistic Players were trying again, this time with *Queen Victoria*, "a chronicle play," by David Carb and Walter Prichard Eaton, and Josephine was engaged to understudy Beryl Mercer as Her Britannic Majesty. This historical drama is good literature, but it lacked the theatrical qualities of the later *Victoria Regina*—it also lacked Helen Hayes—and held out for only forty-four performances. What is more, Miss Mercer proved to be enjoying the best of health, and her potential substitute remained perforce in the wings. But there were consolations. Her friend Grant Mitchell and his nieces took her to the Annual Equity Ball at the Astor. "Home at seven in the morning."

Despite the discouraging sequence of failures, broken only by *The Rivals*, the Equity Players persisted, and in December set to work on an unpretentious, folksy little comedy by Leon Cunningham, first called *Small Town Stuff*, but by opening night, *Neighbors*. This time Josephine was at last rewarded with a nice little character part, Mrs. Hicks, which, while it gave no scope for her as yet unsuspected abilities, did give her a chance to act in the big city. It was thirteen years since she had last played on a Broadway stage. The private showing for members came as a joyous climax for her least unhappy Christmas since Shelley's death. "Exciting, love playing again."

Neighbors, though not without its merits, proved no more attractive than its predecessors, and all too soon Josephine had to bid Mrs. Hicks a regretful adieu. Nevertheless, it proved to have been another steppingstone in the right direction. While helping shape up the next luckless venture, *The New Englander,* she could report that

> Miss Helburn of the Theater Guild sent for me & talked with me about a part in their next play. Met Philip Moeller.

A part in a Guild production she may have dreamed about, but it was nothing she had expected to come her way so soon. Now, probably thanks to Mrs. Hicks, it had, as it were, dropped unsought for in her lap. For the first time in years she wrote "Very happy" in her line-a-day. The play was *Fata Morgana,* a comedy by the Hungarian Ernest Vajda, and she was cast as the hero's mother. The cast was headed by the beautiful and temperamental Emily Stevens, cousin and pet of Mrs. Fiske. George, Josephine's stage son, was Morgan Farley, and present too were Armina Marshall, Helen Westley, Edith Meiser, and others it was a pleasure to be with.

By September, after some six months, *Fata* began to show symptoms of going into a decline, but a producer by the name of Leftwich believed that it had possibilities for the road, and arranged to back a tour. Presumably on the recommendation of Guild authorities, Josephine was engaged to direct. What that meant was that she was to supervise the second company in the production as originally laid out by Moeller. Miss Stevens was to continue as Mathilda Fay, and Miss Marshall was to take over Josephine's role. Rehearsals were carried on in various theaters, but just before the new company left, it was permitted to give two performances in the place of the original one, thus ending the run. The tour opened successfully at the Adelphi Theater in Philadelphia on October 13, and two days

175

later Josephine was back in Fifty-sixth Street. The trouble was that once more she was unemployed.

Unemployed she remained until May. This was not the first time, nor was it to be the last. Yet it seems to have been one of the most distressing. Perhaps after *Fata Morgana* she had expected to get another engagement in short order. But none came her way, and no matter what front she may have shown most of her friends, privately her morale was at its lowest. Only desperation could explain her next move. Mr. James A. Farrell, an attorney whose children attended the same private school as Henry's son, had recently lost his wife, and was in search of a housekeeper or governess.

> Josephine heard of my plight and came to my office to apply for the post. She was deep in grief and felt she would never act again. We talked for an hour at least. She wept and got a great deal off her mind. She said I encouraged her to go on. She was to think over coming to me, but I was sure she would rally with a little time, as she apparently did.

Probably in the end she would not have taken the position, but the mere fact that she considered it shows to what depths of depression she had sunk. If her friends suspected nothing of the truth it was because she was constantly on the go. Both S.W.W.R. and the Equity Players made demands on her, and she saw a great deal of many people. What is more, there was no lapse in her playgoing, and no matter what her financial straits, she could not forego the matinee Ring Cycle at the Metropolitan. There was no medicine like Wagner, and she was willing to give up other luxuries to enjoy it. Just what she gave up is not disclosed in her line-a-day—it certainly was not the Institute of Psychical Research. She haunted its offices, attended lectures and séances, and entertained Dr. Prince at dinner. The question is, did this help her or not?

With spring her affairs took a turn for the better. She was engaged by Philip Goodman to play Madame Helseth in a revival of *Rosmersholm,* which opened on May 3. Madame

Hellseth, though not, as words or "sides" go, a long part, supplied greater opportunities than had come her way for some time to probe beneath the surface; and, moreover, she knew that there were usually professionals in the audience. The more of them who saw her, the better. By June the heat became oppressive, and both Ibsen's drama and Josephine wilted in a hurry. Notices went up, the play closed, and again she was on her own. With nothing to detain her, she took off for Pleasant Valley on the first day of July.

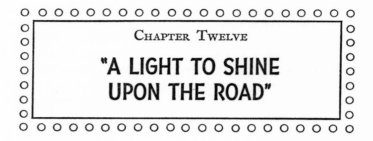

CHAPTER TWELVE

"A LIGHT TO SHINE UPON THE ROAD"

AMONG THE MEMENTOS of a long friendship, preserved by Miss Alice Clark for nearly thirty-five years, is a letter written from the Valley on August 8. Miss Clark had recently opened a tearoom at Bellport on Long Island; Josephine sent her good wishes, and at the same time told her friend about her own affairs.

This summer I am having a real vacation, the first one in some years that I've been able to take. I came here late in June, to the little Hull place Shelley loved so, with his Mother. Three weeks I spent up in New Ipswich, New Hampshire, where Aunt Nellie (Tewksbury) has a lovely old made-over house and pool and flowers and vegetable garden; in the house are many of the familiar things I grew up with,—the cuckoo-clock, spinning-wheel, piano, and many pieces of furniture, pictures, and pet books, etc. It is as sweet as it can be and she loves it so, and has thus provided a real home in which my aunts can spend their old age. At present she still teaches in Newton and just

178

goes up there summers. My other aunts were there and we had a wonderful time together.

The place is high and the air bracing. I borrowed a Ford and drove round in it; we have a little one here which I drive too. All this rest and chance to renew vitality and nerves is the happy result of my securing work for next season, so that I could take some time off with an easy mind. So much of my work,—as a director of the Actors' Theater, for instance—is voluntary that I am feeling very lucky to have a regular job ahead. It is to be a part in "Craig's Wife," a new play by the author of "The Show-off," and rehearsals start around September first.

Fortunately I always am busy, even when it is not very lucrative, and so I have kept interested and alive. I live alone in the old apartment on 56th St. next-door to where we first kept house. It seems so homelike and I am confortable, if shabby. And it pleases me to see continual signs of my gradual improvement in getting good work for it wasn't easy to get back in the game after so long an absence. I hope to build up a place for myself again in time. My aunts come over to visit me sometimes, and I take great joy in Henry's three children, the second of whom is a darling Shelley, aged five.

On September 8 she presented herself at the Playhouse for the first rehearsal of *Craig's Wife*, under the direction of the author. George Kelly already had to his credit not only *The Show Off*, which had missed the Pulitzer Prize by a fluke, but also *The Torchbearers*, a hilarious if slightly acid satire on amateur dramatics, and he was definitely one of the outstanding American playwrights of the day. Whereas in *The Show Off* he had centered his attention on a man, in his new drama, he concentrated on a woman.

Craig's Wife relates ruthlessly the story of an unscrupulously possessive woman who marries "a romantic fool," as she calls him, in order to assure her own security. The symbol of her domination is her house to which even he is admitted only on sufferance. It is beautiful, immaculate, the joy of any interior decorator. But Walter's aunt, who has been unhappily living under its roof, describes it as "a house which has died and been laid out." Harriet is obsessed with the conviction that the neighbors are all seeking, by one pretext or another, to gain admittance to her holy of holies so that they may satisfy their vulgar curiosity. She especially resents the visits of a Mrs. Frazier who occasionally drops in to consult Auntie Austin about a pattern or to bring her roses from her garden. One of her calls provokes an explosion that leads to Miss Austin's unmasking the infuriated Harriet before the eyes of her incredulous husband. The curtain falls as Mrs. Craig, having alienated everyone belonging to her, wanders about the house, staring blankly into space, and heedlessly scattering the petals from an armful of Mrs. Frazier's roses on the polished floor.

Mrs. Craig was played by Chrystal Herne, who so completely immersed her own character in the part, that audiences were inclined to believe that she and Harriet were one, whereas in real life she was exactly the reverse and in a few years quit the stage because she believed that her career was interfering with that of her journalist husband. The disillusioned Walter was in the hands of Charles Trowbridge, and Miss Austin was the handsome, imposing Anne Sutherland, who thriftily operated a tearoom as a side venture. Josephine was the Lady of the Roses. Although Kelly was not acquainted with her when he wrote the play, the role might easily have been tailored expressly to fit her. The garrulous, warmhearted, roly-poly little lady with her big brown eyes and her musical voice was an unforgettable figure as she stood at the door, her arms full of roses, completely unconscious of her hostess' antagonism. Only Josephine could make her banalities endurable, but as she poured them forth, they became pearls of great price. Mrs. Frazier was Josephine. Josephine was Mrs. Frazier.

"Enjoy this work with Mr. Kelley so much." It was hard work, but she never objected to that if it did not represent wasted effort. Kelly's direction was meticulous and his actors were always amazed at how much he knew about a character. Frank Rowan says that Chrystal Herne told him that, no matter how often she played Mrs. Craig, she was always aware that (generally) standing in the entrance was a better Mrs. Craig. If his actors were physically worn out, mentally and emotionally they were always stimulated.

Craig's Wife was one of the best things that ever happened to Josephine. Not only did it give her a chance to show what she could do with a rich part in an important play, but it introduced her to a new coterie of friends who were to constitute what she called her "gang." There were George Kelly, the author, Rosalie Stewart, the producer, and three members of her staff, Florence Johnson, Frances French, and Nat Pilling. These were cheerful, zestful young people, who were interested in the present, not the past, in this world, not the next. They worked earnestly and enthusiastically, and played with healthy gaiety. Caught up in the swirl of their activities, Josephine was gradually weaned away from her preoccupation with the world of spirits, and became again absorbed in more mundane pursuits. Less and less often did she haunt the Bureau of Psychical Research. Fewer and fewer evenings did she sit trembling with a pencil in her hand, taking down ghostly messages.

There were gay dinner parties in various restaurants, and night after night after the play, they would all troop up the stairs for cheerful little snacks. Sometimes Rosalie would spend the night, or George would chat before the fire. Smiling down on these jollifications was the handsome face of Shelley, the frame of his picture decked with flowers on holidays and lighted by candles on anniversaries. Hand in hand with these warmhearted friends, Josephine emerged at last from the shadowed valley in which she had dwelt for six years. Her exuberance radiates from every page of her diary.

> September 26. Mother E. came for me at six, we dined at the Alps, & she saw me off with the co. at 9.10.

The play opened in Buffalo and "went wonderfully." They were off to a good start. The New York opening on October

12 was one of the big evenings of the season, with the house crammed with a glittering audience that included many notables. "Heaps of friends there, & all came home for supper." How she crowded all those people into her four rooms only those invited to be there can explain. "Thrilling evening." Five evenings later "Chrystal's name went up in lights—had little party in her dressing room at night."

The season was for Josephine one of almost unqualified delight. There being no rehearsals, she was free to make cranberry jelly and other delicacies, to teach once a week at St. Agatha's, and go to a Snarks' party at which she played for one of the stunts. Best of all, perhaps, she could now gorge herself on Wagner with a free conscience. She was on hand for all the *Ring* matinees, and shepherded Rosalie, Florence, Anne, Jess Busley, and George to *Parsifal*. On March 27 came the exciting news that *Craig's Wife* had won the Pulitzer Prize. Meanwhile the play went on and on, and each week she contentedly pocketed her $125.00. Then a new prospect opened.

> August 2. Rosalie called me to her office & took me out to lunch, & told me definitely I am to open in G. K.'s new play in October.

So when *Craig's Wife* went on tour in the fall, there would be a new Mrs. Frazier.

> August 21. Last day of our wonderful play.
> August 22. Left at 10 on the boat, "Calvin Austin," for Portland. Anne Sutherland on boat too, we had lovely trip together on top deck & at meals. Moon nearly full. Fairly rough trip, wonderful. Slept eight hours.

Fortunately she did not know it, but when the curtain fell on *Craig's Wife*, it also fell on Josephine's streak of luck—for a long intermission. Ten years were to pass before she would find herself in another hit. During that heartbreaking decade she was to be in a dismal succession of failures, a number of them out and out flops that did not make the grade even as far as Broadway. A few of them, it is true, she loved; others she detested. Of course this meant weary days of rehearsing, to little or no purpose. It also meant a very light pocketbook, so light, in fact, that at least once the aunts, who had received an inheritance from a grateful cousin, came to her rescue. It was not that she was not wanted by producers. It was simply that the plays in which they cast her were failures. Personally she had the satisfaction of getting excellent reviews, but what good did they do her when the play itself was damned into oblivion? At times she became so discouraged that again she was tempted to throw up the sponge. She even contemplated retiring to New Ipswich and teaching music. Yet, despite her frustrations and disappointments, she seldom turned back to spiritualism for comfort.

The first thing she did on getting back to New York after a refreshing vacation in which she had paid sentimental pilgrimages to familiar landmarks, including the "beloved old Gem" and the Cliffs, was to journey up to the Riviera Theater to greet her friends who were playing a pre-tour run of *Craig's Wife* there. Then on September 20 work was started on *Daisy Mayme*. "Lovely co. & joyous rehearsing." They were interrupted, however, by the death of the author's mother. With Rosalie, her brother Stuart, Florence, Frances, and Frank Rowan, who had a part in the new play, Josephine went over to Philadelphia for a call of condolence. After the funeral they all returned to New York, where rehearsals were resumed.

By October 11 the play was ready to be "tried out on the dogs," the dogs being in this case the worthy citizens of Rochester. Each performance was carefully checked by George and Rosalie, and changes were made here and there as suggested by the responses of the audience. Why hadn't this line got an expected laugh? Why had a certain scene or piece of business not gone over? All this meant a great deal of experimenting and, as is inevitable under such circumstances, tensions mounted. It is a little surprising, however, that some of the disagreements were between Josephine and the greatly admired author-director. Rowan's recollections of these slightly hectic days show something of the way Josephine went at the job of building up a character and also of her rock-bound stubbornness.

The differences with George Kelly were never very serious. There was one slight situation while we were opening out of town. It seems that Josephine didn't feel comfortable with a piece of business that G. K. had given her and couldn't bring herself to perform it. This of course led to whispered conferences with the master. Then, when she did do it, she would become obviously unhappy and there would be days she would not join us at dinner or after the show for laughs and conferences at some restaurant. She was such an instinctive actress that she couldn't do a wrong thing to a character, and nothing was ever forced or labored. She knew what kind of woman she was playing, and it was uncanny the way she could project the details of a character. I think that the situation resolved itself in a compromise—half of what G. K. wanted and half of what J. wanted, and it seems to me that, as time went on, it was all of what J. wanted or, I should say, what she simply had to do to feel right.

George was tireless, and if a company didn't like him, they'd call him merciless. He would keep us on our feet for hours and get so absorbed that he'd forget about a five minute rest. So very often nerves became taut and tempers frayed, and there'd be groans. Josephine was almost as tireless as G. K. and she'd toil till something came to life; even tho it was a tiny bit of business, she'd perfect it before going on to the next scene. G. K. used to give her her head in these matters (as why shouldn't he?) and when she had achieved something, he'd stand there and laugh his head off just as the audience was to do later.

When *Daisy Mayme* opened at the Playhouse, October 25, it was soon painfully evident that Kelly had somehow failed to repeat his earlier successes. Perhaps the explanation is to be found in the appraisal of Brooks Atkinson, who described it as "a remorseless, unpleasant drama of the suburbs and middle-class life." Joseph Wood Krutch put it in another way. "Mr. Kelly refuses to stay put and was determined to accentuate those aspects of his attitude which were the least familiar and the least acceptable to his audience."

The play tells the story of a young unmarried woman, Daisy Mayme Plunkett, who thwarts the attempt of a selfishly conniving widow to gain complete control of her bachelor brother and install herself as undisputed mistress of his household. Cliff, the intended victim, and his niece, May, whose mother has recently died, have met Daisy at Atlantic City, and on the girl's insistence she returns with them for a few days' visit. She quickly takes the rapacious sister's measure and, knowing what will happen to May if she succeeds, openly and without the slightest hypocrisy undertakes to defeat her. In the end the field is hers and she knows it is to remain so, since Cliff asks her to marry him. But she derives little happiness from this outcome because she realizes that he has proposed, not because he is in love with her, but because May has begged him to and because he knows that it will be a sensible arrangement. Possibly audiences found Daisy Mayme, most convincingly played by Jessie Busley, too brash and outspoken for comfort; or perhaps they were let down by the final curtain, when Cliff, instead of giving Daisy the embrace and kiss the situation calls for, smilingly blows smoke at her from his cigar, and she looks wistfully off into the distance.

Josephine's role was that of Mrs. Olly Kipax, another sister, "one of those fussy fatties that never has a well day—to hear her tell it," whom Ruth tries to enlist in the execution of her scheme. But Olly is made of less stern stuff, and soon changes sides. There was much business with a magnificent black crepe veil which was a forerunner of another Josephine was to display in a more famous play fourteen years later. According to Atkinson she gave as "the slightly obese, sentimental and light-headed Mrs. Olly Kipax . . . a luminous performance, instinct with understanding." Rowan feels that she made the character sympathetic, as all comedy characters ought to be. Yet, despite the best efforts of this excellent company, the public could not be won over.

While business dwindled, Josephine occupied herself with her own affairs, teaching, entertaining Aunt Nellie, and hearing all the good music she could possibly afford. By the end of February the play had run its course on Broadway, and on March 12 sadly made its final surrender to public apathy.

Last two performances of Daisy Mayme at Bronx Opera House. Jess & I dined at the Hofbrau. Goodbyes—sorry to stop playing Ollie & that the play could not win longer season.

CHAPTER THIRTEEN

BLIND ALLEYS

DESPITE THIS CONTRETEMPS, Josephine was not left to twiddle her thumbs—there was plenty to keep her occupied. For one thing, Mary was projecting a lavish production of Sophocles' *Electra* at the Metropolitan Opera House, and, having an experienced stage manager in the family, she saw no reason for seeking further afield.

The disparity between the positions of the sisters-in-law was decided. Margaret Anglin was one of the great ladies of the theater and one of the grand ladies as well. She had begun life in the grand manner by being born in the speaker's chamber of the Houses of Parliament in Ottawa while her father was speaker of the House of Commons, and was accustomed to social prestige. She had been a star since the early years of the century, when Josephine, fresh out of college, used to gaze down on her in admiration from her lofty perch in the gallery. She took both the theater and herself very seriously, and long before 1926 had achieved a status of commanding eminence, especially in the field of classical drama. Her interpretations of Shakespeare's heroines, both in tragedy and in comedy, were highly esteemed, and, except by Josephine's friend, Edith Wynne Matthison, she was unchallenged in the Greek dramas. Having reached these summits, she believed, understandably enough, that she was entitled to certain rights and privileges, and expected them to be recognized. In the words of a colleague, "She was as difficult to handle as she was fine."

Obviously no such grandeur was enjoyed by Josephine. She was simply a lovable little character actress respected by her peers, but, so far as the public at large was concerned, scarcely even a name. As she had told Lem Shaw in Detroit, the great parts like Lady Macbeth and Paula Tanqueray were not for her, still less Antigone and Electra.

Out of the theater, the relations between the two women were warm, even affectionate. The Hull family was a close one, and Shelley's death had in no way weakened Josephine's ties with his relatives; if possible, she felt even nearer to them than she had when he was alive. She saw Mary and Howard frequently when they were in town, and they often brought or sent her welcome gifts of flowers and vegetables from their country place at Katonah. For her sister-in-law's artistic attainments she felt unqualified admiration, and stood ready whenever she could to help her to the limit of her ability. At the same time, Mary's calm acceptance of the gap between their positions did occasionally get under her skin. Usually she kept her own counsel and silently did what was expected of her, but every now and then, when tried too far, would confide in her diary or her sympathetic mother-in-law. When in later years her own fortunes rose and Mary's declined, her heart was touched and her loyalty was unabated. Mary, beset by many trials, would run in for comforting talks, "sweet and sisterly." And in her last months, though she was too ill to know it, no small amount of the care she enjoyed she owed to a legacy from her little sister-in-law.

When it came to Mary's *Electra* productions, Josephine might well have joined her voice with Figaro's in "Largo al factotum." The star was her own director, and Josephine a

short-of-glorified stage manager. It was she who got on the
telephone and called actors to come for interviews. She blocked
out the action and stood by during rehearsals. With Mary and
Howard, who acted as his wife's manager, she inspected the
stages where the performances were to be given—it was a novel
experience for her to stand on the vast stage of the Metropolitan instead of peering down at it from a great height—and then
superintended the placing of the scenery and the assembling
of such few properties as Sophocles requires. This time there
were two performances before "enormous, brilliant" houses,
but whether she got anything more out of the adventure than
aesthetic satisfaction she does not say.

Since one good house deserves another, Mary decided to
give another performance, and Josephine went to the Shubert
office and re-engaged the cast. The next day, after a conference
at the Barclay Hotel, Mary changed her mind and canceled
all her plans. She did not, however, abandon *Electra,* but, to
the good fortune of American drama lovers, gave them further
opportunities to see her admirable productions of the tragedy.
With only two of these was Josephine concerned, one the next
December in the Gallo Theater in New York, and another six
months later in a park in Providence. Whatever she got or did
not get out of these productions in a material way, she undoubtedly derived great gratification from having been a part
of them.

The summer of 1927 brought the first of the long line of
professional disappointments that were to come close to breaking down her morale. She was engaged by Philip Goodman for
a role in *The Wild Man of Borneo,* not the type of play the
title would lead one to expect, but a very slight piece by Marc
Connelly and Herman Mankiewicz about a pathetic little man
who tries to pass himself off on his family as an important big-
time actor, but is exposed as nothing but a medicine show freak.
Whatever optimism Josephine may have cherished at the beginning evaporated soon after the opening in Asbury Park
on September 5. Although she found her fellow actors pleas-

ant and things went not too badly at first, she was "not pleased
with direction or outlook of this play." When they reached
New York, there were "ructions with Connelly and Goodman,"
whose ructions she does not specify. If she was involved, as
she probably was not, since it would have been distinctly out
of character for her to engage in backstage squabbles, all was
soon forgotten and forgiven on both sides, because in three
years she and Connelly were negotiating happily about an
excellent part for her in a play he was writing.

When *The Wild Man* opened at the Bijou Theater, she received her usual good notices, but these were not enough to
attract, and after fifteen performances her services were once
more on the market. She did not yet find the prospects so alarm-
ing that she felt constrained to accept anything that came
along; nevertheless, she had nothing to be jubilant about. After
her next venture, she had even less.

Brady had contracted to produce a play by Don Marquis at
first called *The Smiths,* soon rechristened *The Skinners,* and
employed Josephine and Frank Keenan for leading roles. At
this point everything looked propitious, for the Marquis name
would unquestionably be an asset, even though he lacked experience in playwriting, and the director, Lumsden Hare, knew
what he was about. Josephine was soon assailed again by serious
misgivings, and rehearsals became "very trying and tiring."
Keenan was going through a very upsetting period in his life,
and was not in what might be termed a "dependable" condition. For one thing he could not learn his lines. Inasmuch
as most of his scenes were with Josephine, this weakness was
extremely hard on her. Then Brady came down to see how
things were progressing, saw very clearly, and proceeded to
go into one of his well-known rages. The cause of his ire was
of course Keenan, but since he struck out in all directions, the
resultant suffering was not limited to the guilty party. The
locale of these embroilments was Wilmington, Delaware,
which was to be honored with the out-of-town *première*. Thither Josephine, attended by Margaret, had repaired immediately
after Christmas, to be in good time for the first performance

on the twenty-ninth. When the turmoil subsided for the time being and she was at last permitted to retire to her room, her exasperation was reaching fever heights.

> Rehearsed all day, but no dress rehearsal. Opened at night, terrible opening. Brady kept us late at night for cuts.
> Rehearsed all day with Brady butchering the play, cutting it to pieces.

While the producer fumed and slashed, Hare and the actors could only stand about helplessly, and obey orders. The only man who might have been able to save the situation, the author himself, was not on hand to see what was being done to his handiwork.

> Rehearsed & gave two performances. Sort of a nightmare, this whole thing. After playing at night had little sandwich & sherry in my room, Margaret & I.

The next stop was Atlantic City, one of Josephine's favorite resorts, but the only comforts she found there were the waves pounding the beach, and the Shelburne Hotel—"nicer than ever." For the first time in her life her birthday came and went unnoticed (except by Margaret), and, to add to her distresses, she read in the papers of the deaths of Emily Stevens and Dorothy Donnelly. Her spirits dropped almost to the zero point. From Atlantic City *The Skinners* staggered over to Long Island for two exposures at Great Neck, and gasped out its life at Mamaroneck. After that Josephine took to her bed for several days and thought about Shelley.

The next six weeks were passed in uneasy idleness. Then her hopes were raised when Charles L. Wagner decided that the time was ripe for a revival of Harry Wagstaffe Gribble's *March Hares*, and asked her to be the Mrs. Janet Rodmey. Almost before she knew it, she was back on the premises where *The Skinners* had expired. Nevertheless, she dared permit herself a little optimism, for, after all, the comedy had done well in its earlier incarnation. After the opening at the Little Theater on April 2 she noted that her friends were wonderful as usual, and again the notices were "good for me personally." Yet the pattern was unchanged, and after about a week the company moved sadly on to Rochester and Buffalo, where all was soon over.

The days continued to be depressing, but she maintained her outward bravado and occupied herself with Mary's Providence *Electra*, and also with The Players' annual all-star benefit. This time the play was *The Beaux' Stratagem*, in which she was happy to have a bit part—very "bit." She loved contact with the great of her profession, and The Players had, of course, been Shelley's favorite club.

Her next two ventures did not detain her long. In fact, they scarcely succeeded in getting off the ground. Just what theatrical connoisseurs like Brock Pemberton and Antoinette Perry saw in *Hotbed*, an early play by Paul Osborne, to justify all the money and effort they squandered on it they probably knew, but they have not taken posterity into their confidence. It concerns itself with scandal on a college campus and the fulminations of a thoroughly repulsive dean, who discovers too late that chickens sometimes come home to roost. The opening on November 1, in New Rochelle this time, by way of variety, "went well considering no prop, set or dress rehearsal," a haphazard procedure that was poison to the painstaking lady from Radcliffe. Despite this unpropitious take-off, the play looked well enough at the Klaw a week later to fool her into believing that at last her luck had changed. She found out soon enough that it had not. After the unpleasant dean had been thwarted nineteen times, he and his victims joined Josephine's other hopes in the graveyard.

Before her next chance to appear behind the footlights she had to endure another exasperating wait, the more trying because negotiations had begun some time before, only to be suspended. Yet occasionally a reluctant sun managed to peer through the clouds. For one thing, Hoover was elected. She was not given to flaunting her politics in public, but in private she took them very hard, and the thought of a Democrat in the White House was never to be contemplated without pain. Now she could dismiss the awful fear that the brash Al Smith and his brown derby would move into the rooms sanctified by Lincoln and Theodore Roosevelt.

The interim was also partly filled by a completely novel experience. She had from time to time taken part in radio broadcasts, but as yet the screen had remained terra incognita. No doubt Shelley's prejudices still lingered in her mind. Now, however, the motion picture industry was taking a sensational step. For the first time it was recognizing the existence of the human voice. This innovation, which would in short order seal the fate of many an idol of the silent days, would open strange doors to the legitimate actors, who had voices and knew how to use them. Among these, of course, was Josephine, to whom the new art would before she died bring widespread fame the legitimate stage could never have given. But in 1928 little did she foresee this future.

On November 20, with the imminent demise of *Hotbed* staring her balefully in the face, she "went to see Mr. Yorke about a movie-tone engagement & arranged to do it." *Movie-tone* was an early name for what later became known as a *talkie*. The picture was to be a short one entitled *The Bishop's Candle Sticks*, an old story to her because it was a scene from *Les Misérables*. The director was none other than the fabulous George Abbott, and her fellow actors were Walter Huston and Charles Abbé. So she knew she was in excellent company. Rehearsals were held on the paramount lot in Astoria, and she was fascinated by the novel experience. Every minute brought her delight. The resulting picture, which she saw at the Criterion Theater the following May, was, according to Abbott, "Fairly successful." For her and her associates it was a milestone.

Once the gaiety had been interrupted, and Josephine's thoughts had traveled back a quarter of a century. After the dress rehearsal, "Out to Hollis, to dear Harry Hodges' funeral service, memories." Well might there be memories, for she never had a stauncher friend.

The movie-tone, unfortunately, was nothing more than an agreeable interlude, not something that lasted and kept on dropping pennies into her bank. She had to look for something more substantial, but she did not find it in the little piece called *Jonesy* from the pens of Anne Morrison and John Peter Toohey. It had been dangled tantalizingly before her eyes for months, on again, off again, and she must often have thought of the Biblical adage anent hope deferred. To make matters worse, she had another bad cold that left her inconveniently hoarse and deaf. At last, however, after innumerable postponements, Jed Harris summoned her to the first reading rehearsal. It was the same old story—*Jonesy* opened and shut like a jack-in-the-box, in Brooklyn. When it eventually opened on Broadway, Josephine was not in the cast. At this stage of her career she did not have the Midas touch—nor did Jed Harris.

Then came a comedy by Kenyon Nicholson called at this time *Babes in the Woods*. It was nothing new; nearly a year before she had been dispatched to Philadelphia to see it at a matinee and "look over part for next season." After the temporary closing of *Jonesy*, she agreed to try her luck with *Before You're Twenty-five*, as the piece was now called. But her luck had not changed one whit for the better, and after May 4 she was back exactly where she had been before—in the doldrums.

Despite the uncertainty of her financial situation, she decided loyally that she must be on hand for the great Radcliffe Sesquicentennial. To have missed it would have been akin to blasphemy. So off she went to Cambridge, and no one there was allowed to suspect that all was not well with her particular world.

The celebrations began on May 31 under the approving eye of Leland Stanford's most illustrious alumna, Mrs. Herbert Hoover. There were reunions with "heaps of friends," a buffet luncheon, and a concert in Symphony Hall, where Mabel

Daniels had a "fine ode performed." The next day was even more thrilling.

> To college for birthday party,—parade of alumnae, balloons, songs, cake, check, etc. . . . To Castle Sq. for performance of Rad. Revue, to 2200 audience. Our "Minuet" went well. Aunts G. & N. & Russell there. Flowers.

Minuet was a sentimental little one-act play in which she not only acted, but danced as well. The salvos of applause sent tingles down her spine, but she would have known even greater joy could she have heard the comment of a freshman who sat behind Mrs. Van Buren Moody: "Isn't she wonderful? If I could have a figure like hers when I had been out of college thirty years, I could die happy!"

Josephine's next job carried her far afield, back to Chicago, where she took over the part of Mrs. Barton in *The Nut Farm* by John C. Brownell. The visit to her old haunts had many pleasures. One of the members of the cast was Wally Ford, and she quickly found that he, his wife, and his little girl Patricia, were the kind of people she liked to be with. "Josie," says Ford, "very few people she would permit to call her 'Josie'—will never be forgotten in our family—ever." They all shared one very gratifying experience on July 11, not long after her arrival.

> Up early, to theater. The co. were driven out to Mooseheart, the orphan settlement; luncheon in Alaska Hall there & gave our play in street clothes for the children in P. M. Wonderful.

Josephine always responded warmly to children; perhaps there was a little poignancy in her enjoyment of them because she had been denied any of her own. So the chance to bring pleasure to these underprivileged youngsters gave her peculiar satisfaction.

There were other pleasures too. When she reached Chicago,

she found Katie Grey there, supporting Otis Skinner in *A Hundred Years Old,* and they had a joyous reunion. Grant Mitchell also was in town, and he gave Josephine, the Fords, and Sam Coit a beautiful luncheon at the exclusive Indian Hills Country Club at Winnetka. Among the other guests were Dean Ralph Dennis and Professor Garret Leverton of Northwestern University, and Mrs. Ben Marshall, a wealthy woman whose "magnificent, unique home" they were invited to inspect before they returned to their labors.

Chicago had a soberer appeal for her too, and she could not ignore the places associated with the first days of her marriage. She got someone to drive her out past the Windermere Hotel, and also made a pilgrimage to St. Paul's Chapel, "for a little prayer, & read the marriage service alone there. . . . Had a little weep when I got home."

Then something went awry, and suddenly she signed off. "Why she left us at the Cort Theater," says Ford, "only Josie knows." There was some sort of trouble between Lambert, the manager, and Dave Burns, a member of the cast, and the latter evidently received his notice. She promptly turned in her own, whether out of sympathy for him or for other reasons; as Ford says, she alone knows. Later when she saw the play during its New York run, she wrote in the diary, "Assured I was right in not staying," a statement which completely baffles her friend. Sam Coit put her on the train to New York.

If she had entertained any hopes of finding something better there, she was in for a painful disillusionment. Absolutely nothing came her way, at least nothing she would touch. (She turned down one offer six times.) She did have her radio work, and that was probably what kept the wolf at the foot of the stairs, for her weekly lessons at St. Agatha's were not especially remunerative. She kept busy in one way or another, finding many odd jobs to do at home, such as painting the kitchen and sawing wood for the fireplace. Apparently she had given up composing, possibly because the rather naïve little numbers she produced no longer sold.

Her friends, whether suspicious or not of the real state of

her affairs, were assiduous in their attentions. George dropped in frequently and often took her out to one of her favorite restaurants or to the theater. Eugene Bonner, a talented young musician of whom she had grown fond, escorted her to the opera. She played a great deal of bridge with Callie, Jess Busley, Gladys Hanson, and occasionally Julie. From time to time Mary "ran in," Josephine's euphemism for toiling up her three flights of stairs. So matters continued, and the actress-out-of-work perforce had to practice all the little economies she could to make ends meet.

There were, however, two old Boston friends, who not only grasped the situation, but determined to do something about it. Betty and Percival Merritt, returning from one of their frequent trips to Europe, stopped off in New York on their way home and immediately sought her out. Whether Betty wrung some true confessions out of Josephine or simply saw for herself how the land lay, she decided that drastic action was called for and proceeded to take it. She and Percival intended to return to Europe in the spring, and insisted that Josephine go with them. On New Year's Day there arrived in 56th Street, by special delivery, a "wonderful letter and check." Betty generously celebrated her seventieth birthday by giving her friend new and inspiring hopes and glamorous anticipations. Once again Josephine looked out on a rose-tinted world.

Ironically, just at this time she received another offer and, even though it was a bit galling to her pride, she did not hesitate very long. She would need pocket money for new clothes and little purchases not covered by the Merritt check, and that was worth a little humiliation. The new play was *Those We Love*, by George Abbott, and the company included, besides the author himself, Armina Marshall and Charles Waldron. So much was to the good. The trouble was that her role was "a poor little one" in the first act only. In Josephine's opinion this was definitely not good for her prestige, a commodity even more important to actors than good hard cash. She could not permit herself to become identified with bit parts; nevertheless, she made up her mind to take the risk just this once. There was another risk too. Suppose the play was a success and ran on and on. Of course she would have to withdraw—it was not exactly consoling to think she would not be missed—but May was a long way off, and not for years had she been in a play that had lasted four months. *Those We Love* proved no exception. Another serious discussion of marriage on the order of Philip Barry's *Paris Bound*, it failed to duplicate the success of the earlier play, and after seventy-seven performances it closed in plenty of time for Josephine to put her house in order.

CHAPTER FOURTEEN

OLD WORLDS AND NEW

BETTY'S "CURE" BEGAN TO TAKE EFFECT with the first trip to Cook's office. When Josephine emerged with her passage on the *Vulcania* safely booked, she was in a state of exaltation such as she had not known in years. Before she knew what was happening, May 14 was upon her.

> George & his man Jo took me, trunk & baggage to the Vulcania & went all over her. George gave me a wonderful dinner (9) at the Biltmore & everyone saw me off. Sailed at 12.15,—friends, gifts.

She was installed in a "chintzy" little cabin with all the latest gadgets and a plate-glass window instead of the usual porthole, and she proceeded to give it a homelike character with family pictures and various personal trinkets. The Gang had seen to it that it was full of flowers. In the upper regions of the ship the Merritts occupied de luxe quarters with a private deck. There they stayed until noon, coming out just in time for the elaborate luncheons that were de rigueur on such luxury liners.

This left Josephine time to stretch out in her deck chair, chat with Helen Moore and her friend, Mrs. Trier, and watch the operatic celebrities as they took their constitutionals. Above all, she could fill her lungs with the salt air she loved, and feast her eyes on the ocean. Nothing could have done her more good.

At noon, with the emergence of her hosts, there came a change. Grateful as Josephine was for their kindness, she found herself daily facing certain embarrassing complications. Before leaving home, she had undergone a thorough physical examination, and Thompson had decreed one of his diets. This she was conscientiously trying to follow, but with the Merritts at the same table, how could she? Never in her life had she encountered anyone to whom food was such a dominating interest. Near the end of the summer, she confided to the aunts that she sometimes suspected that Percival lived to eat. Although on rare occasions compelled to do violence to his principles by submitting briefly to a diet, he considered dieting the invention of Satan himself and resented being reminded that anything so obnoxious even existed. "Percival was so outraged if I wanted water instead of wine, I had to have it sent to my room surreptitiously! I'd burst if I had to live that way. So it took much toying with food to disguise my failing to keep up, after one or two attempts." Yet, she said, both the Merritts were as thin as rails.

On the morning of the twenty-second she had to pinch herself to realize that it was she, Josephine Sherwood Hull, who was gazing at the Rock of Gibraltar and the Pillars of Hercules. After that thrill her days were given over to ecstasy. She first set foot on European soil during a brief stop at Marseilles. After another stop at Naples, the *Vulcania* rounded the Italian boot and turned up the Adriatic. At Trieste she and the Merritts disembarked, and Josephine began with zest the sightseeing that was to occupy her days for the next four months. After Trieste came Venice, which she said she was incapable of describing, and then the Merritts departed for Constantinople, leaving her to visit on her own the usual cities and sights from the Blue Grotto at Capri to the Sacristy at Milan, as scheduled for her by Cook.

Even the enervating heat in Rome—and she hated heat—could not keep her from walking from one end of the Seven Hills to the other. A Monsignore Ugolino, to whom she had a letter of introduction, arranged an audience with the Pope, and she was careful to take with her rosaries to be blessed for Mary and Margaret. Yet she had a still more important project to carry out. Two days before her Shelley's birthday, she made a pilgrimage out to the Protestant Cemetery on the Appian Way. There, with her arms full of carnations, cornflowers, and marguerites, she followed the paths that led to the graves of the two young English poets resting there. "I put most of my flowers by Shelley, but could not leave Keats without a few when there were so many."

When she left Rome for the South, she was pleased to be able to report that she had robbed the Eternal City of only two of its population of fleas, really one of her major achievements in Italy. For her explorations of Naples and the Surrentine Peninsula she enjoyed, thanks to the prestige of the Merritts, the services of the "star courier of the whole Cook organization, the one they give important visitors like Lloyd George, the Rockefellers and even royalty." He happened to be free because he wished to stay near his little son, who was recuperating from a serious illness. "So they put him in charge of me. I never was so beautifully taken care of before, and he was such a superior and charming person it was soon like having a friend along too." Signor Boccia in his turn was completely captivated by her. Of course she had to go out to his home to meet his wife and see the little boy. Knowing Josephine, we can be sure that she was all smiles and that her arms were full of goodies.

The end of June found her ensconed in the beautiful Villa Serbelloni at Bellagio, where amid the riotously growing flowers she settled down to watch the sunlight sparkling on the waves of Lake Como, and await the coming of her hosts.

I'm glad to stay quiet for a while. But I feel so well, and look so well. All the exercise, climbing and going around, galleries, ruins, mountains, catacombs, churches—has put me in fine physical trim, and I eat and love the food, and drink a glass of the good light wine at lunch and dinner, and it agrees with me—and I'm so well I no longer need sleep; the days are long,—I go to bed by eleven and am wide awake by six or earlier just as I used to be years ago. Thompson said this would restore vitality, and it certainly has, and I'm so happy and grateful—and I think much less heavy—at least in fit condition.

In a few days the Merritts came, and for the time being her relaxation was at an end. Percival was a sick man, really sicker than he knew, for, in addition to his obvious ailments, he had a heart condition that he had wisely not been told about. Why a man in his condition should want to drag himself all over Europe, he may perhaps have known, but his reasons were a mystery to his guest. He should have known better, for he was a man of brains, a scholar—he was an authority on the life of Mrs. Piozzi—and a writer. But travel he would, and did until he died at Monte Carlo, two years later. Probably he was pursuing the will-o'-the-wisp of health, and had convinced himself that the farther he got away from his own Boston back yard the more likely he was to find it. It was Josephine's secret conviction that he could have found it in one of the diets he abhorred. The cold damp weather in Constantinople had aggravated his discomfort. By the time he reached Bellagio he was worse than usual, consumed with self-pity, and alternating between spells of irritability and of weeping. Patiently his wife sought by every means she could invent to make him comfortable and soothe his feelings, but there was little she or anyone else could do. Josephine, eager to help, tried to radiate her usual good cheer, but there were times when she could not fail to see that, attached as he was to her, she was merely getting on his nerves. There were moments when she could scarcely contain herself and yet suffered from pangs of conscience because of the great debt of gratitude she owed these

unhappy people. When she felt her feelings getting the better
of her, she took refuge in solitary walks on the paths above
the lake.

Much as she adored Bellagio, she was glad when the time
came to leave it, hoping that a change of scene would restore
Percival's spirits, if not his health. Their destination was Vitz-
nau, a small town on the shore of Lake Lucerne where the
Merritts often made lengthy stays. Thither they headed by way
of Lugano, driven by their own chauffeur, over the St. Gott-
hard Pass. The trip was not so enjoyable as it might have been
if Percival had not suffered a temporary relapse, but they
reached it at last, and there, deeply moved with pity, Josephine
left them in the pouring rain, and took herself off with a guilty
sensation of relief to Lucerne, Geneva, and ultimately Paris.
The question of her rejoining them later was left up in the
air. As it turned out, Percival's doctors decreed that he should
be left alone with Betty, and she did not see them again until
after they returned home in the fall.

Her four weeks in the French capital were the climax of her
summer. She encountered not a single disappointment or disillusionment. Everything was even more wonderful than her
happiest anticipations. "I love prowling thro' the narrow, old
streets and hunting out the houses where historic, romantic and
literary echoes of the past still linger." If she missed any of
them, it does not appear from her diary or letters.

Those letters! They must have been written in the watches
of the night, for surely there was no time for them by day. They
went on for pages and pages, on assorted pieces of stationery
purloined from the various hotels that sheltered her, sometimes as many as four different kinds in one epistle, written
criss-cross and in no consistent sequence. She wrote well, for
she had an observing eye for interesting detail, and the gift
for words that had delighted Copey years before. Mr. Baedeker, if still alive, might have found her a useful addition
to his staff.

Paris, of course, was full of Americans, and she was forever
running into friends from home, whom she sometimes joined

for excursions to Versailles, Fontainebleau, and Chartres. Her small feet ached from hours of traipsing through the galleries of the great museums; she dedicated one whole morning to rapturous contemplation of the Venus de Milo in the Louvre. An enchanting visit to the Luxembourg with Mildred Morris was followed by one of the happiest experiences of her vacation.

> We went to a nice little place, the 'Comet,' for lunch,—and there sat Dicky Le Gallienne at a table close by. He moved right over with us, remembering me—and we jabbered fast all thro' luncheon, and nothing must do but we must go to his workshop just a few doors away. Which we did, and he made coffee for us there, and we had the most delightful sort of time. He works up many flights of stairs in a top floor apt. looking over most of Paris, and has a little roof garden and a lovely Siamese cat. Irma, his wife, was at their home and they have no telephone. So he couldn't get hold of her, but planned a meeting soon. And he was at his most charming and lovable, not changed a bit, except that his hair is white.

Later Irma came to call, and they all had dinner together at the Tour d'Argent. He also sent her a beautifully inscribed copy of his latest book. All in all, it was a pleasant second chapter to the days at Roycroft Inn long years ago.

Of course Josephine did not forget that there were theaters in Paris. By the time she reached London, her supply of ready cash was so short that she had to forego treats that a few months before she could not have thought of missing, but in Paris she was still able to put money in her purse and betake herself to the *Comédie Française* and, yes, to the *Folies Bergères*, where she saw more nakedness than she had ever seen before in her life. She contemplated it, however, without swooning, for she was always able to put her Puritan upbringing on the shelf when she thought she had a good reason. After all, she had not gone to the *Folies* for Racine. The *Opéra Comique* and the *Grand Opéra* she enjoyed to the full, but is was at the *Comédie*, to which she found her way four times, that she was lifted above this world. Once she was taken there by the Cowards, friends from the Comedy Club at home, and found Helen Westley sitting near her. The bill that evening was composed of De Musset's *Caprices de Marianne* and Molière's *Le Malade Imaginaire*.

My goodness, how they can act! Every young actor should be led there, to watch that technique and listen to that diction. And this is a session when understudies are apt to be on, too. But there is not a member of the large co., which I have seen three times now, who does not know his or her business—the older members are marvellous, the younger ones make ours at home look like amateurs.

But time was passing, and she could not go home without seeing London. Thither she went at the end of July, and found that it was indeed no anticlimax. She stayed there more than three weeks, and explored highway and byway with the same zeal as in Paris. But, for reasons cited above, she saw no plays.

After all her professional disappointments, she was reassured to learn during her trip that she had not acquired the reputation of an untouchable Jonah, but was still wanted by important people. The realization was excellent medicine. While in Sorrento she had received a cable from John Golden imploring her to drop everything and hurry home for a fine part he had for her. Such a course was unthinkable. Give up her Grand Tour when it had barely started! She cabled him two very adamant no's. Marc Connelly, too, wrote her about a play for the next season, but it never materialized.

Whatever lay ahead of her in New York, she realized that it must be faced and that, much as she hated to leave London, it was time for her to get down to business. "My N. E. Conscience is pricking me,—time to be back at work again after such a *wonderful* vacation. . . . Honestly I don't believe I could *hold* much more sightseeing. I go and go, but begin to get groggy."

On September 17 she boarded the boat train for Plymouth,

and after some delay caused by bad weather, was transported through driving rain to where the huge bulk of the *Paris* was waiting outside the harbor. Even on shipboard, the flow of letters from her pen was not arrested. She knew she still would not see the aunts for some time, and they must be deprived of no joyous circumstance.

> I think some old Tewksbury or Sherwood or Brainerd must have been a sea-captain or a Viking or a British tar or someone-or-other maritime, for it seems to me there's almost no ecstasy like being on the ocean. . . . I'm blissfully happy and feeling so well, and shall sleep, rest, walk, and get all in mental shape to attack the work ahead with vigor such as I haven't had for a good while.

But, as she confessed the next time she felt like taking up her pen, she learned once more the truth of the old proverb about pride and falls. The *Paris* had scarcely reached the open sea when she ran head on into a terrific storm. The descendant of the Vikings was elated. Now she could show the stuff she was made of. In the salon she airily began her dinner. Then she began to notice that the atmosphere was decidedly close. After downing two courses, she felt that it would be the part of wisdom to get some fresh air, and, still with her head in the air, haughtily made an effective exit. "But when I went down finally to bed, I lost those two courses, so my proud record is broken, and the old British tar went back on me." She was some-what consoled to learn later that the next day at lunch only three persons had the hardihood to brave the celebrated French cuisine, and that the captain himself was sick. Eventually the storm wore itself out, and she was able to return to a chair and gaze out at the heaving waves through the spray-dashed glass. At eight o'clock on the evening of the twenty-third, the bat-tered *Paris* was eased into her dock. The great vacation was over.

Docked at 11 P. M. Frances, Nat & George met me, saw

me thro' customs. Jess & Rosalie too, all brought me home
late, & to Childs' for supper. Bed after 3. Home all safe.

She had been home only a few weeks when the Merritts returned. When Josephine went to the Gotham to see them, she
found poor Percival in a deplorable condition, practically helpless. She paid almost daily duty calls, sometimes bearing delicacies she had prepared herself, eager to show her gratitude
in every possible way, but knowing full well that everything
she did was futile. Yet the next May they were off again on
another tour, this time accompanied by a nurse.

Meanwhile she plunged into radio work, which brought her
a sporadic income. Most of her broadcasts were done for the
Radio Guild, and to her gratification, in plays really worth
doing, some of them classics like *Macbeth* and *The School for
Scandal,* and some good plays by modern authors. She greatly
enjoyed reading Auntie Austin in *Craig's Wife* and Mrs. Fisher in *The Show-Off,* although the later required much hard
work, inasmuch as that delightful but sharp-tongued lady required her to accomplish something of a metamorphosis. It was
a pleasure too to do the Duchess of Berwick in *Lady Windermere's Fan* to Mary's Mrs. Erlynne. In spite of all the rehearsals these broadcasts involved, Josephine had time to do some
coaching at St. Agatha's, and to go regularly with Callie Emmet to the Philharmonic concerts in Carnegie Hall, sitting
right up under the lofty roof.

The radio, all right in its way, was after all only a stopgap.
It was good news, then, that the Guild was interested in en-
gaging her for a new play by Claire and Paul Sifton, at first
called *In the Meantime,* but eventually *Midnight.* This proved
to be a very minor Guild offering, so minor in fact that Lawrence Langner wastes no words on it in his *Magic Curtain.*
Philip Moeller, one of the most accomplished directors around,
wrestled with it during hectic rehearsals and out-of-town tryouts—all to no purpose. Josephine was very soon again dependent on N.B.C.

Whether because, thanks to all her frustrations, she was not feeling fit or because she was uneasy over the very obvious tendency of her figure to revert to the Tewksbury type, she was soon making pilgrimages to Thompson's office for tests and examinations, with the result that she found herself on an every-other-day buttermilk diet. Years later a newspaper man declared that Josephine Hull was one actress who did not pray for "this too, too solid flesh to melt," but that time had not yet come. In the past Shelley had fought to keep clear of the matinee idol category. Now she was struggling to escape being typed as a plump little lady of the motherly kind, the dire fate that Howard Lindsay thinks was overtaking her. It was a battle, for she had to fight heredity, as well as her own very strong inclinations.

She was unfortunately in no position to refuse undesirable parts when they were offered her. She had to accept them willynilly. Just such a one now presented itself in *Unexpected Husband,* an unimportant comedy by Barry Conners. From the first this ill-starred little piece was in trouble. There was illness in the cast, and one difficulty succeeded another. The weatherman joined its enemies, and on opening night, June 2, the temperature became so "piping hot" that Josephine did not blame people for staying away. This public show of indifference had a very undesirable result—her pay check bounced. Day after day the diary reports "No salary yet." Since she was not playing Mrs. Egbert Busby for love or glory, she saw no reason for keeping on, and at the first opportunity followed Hugh Cameron and Robert Middlemiss through the exit.

Matters had now reached such a pass that Josephine realized more drastic economies were unavoidable. One was a move to a smaller apartment. Although the aunts were helping with the rent (on the excuse that they used her apartment during their rather infrequent visits), it was still—in more than one way— "too high." Margaret Davis had been retired because of age, and now even Julia, her replacement, became a luxury Josephine could not afford. She was herself a strenuous house cleaner, but the walk-up under the eaves took more scrubbing and polishing than she could manage, even in pursuit of slimness.

After a little hunting, she rented a tiny place in the Gainsborough Studios on Fifty-ninth Street. Since it had no place for her dining room table, she put it in storage; she simply could not bring herself to sell it. "When shall I see it again?" All this upheaval was hard on her disposition, nor did the diet tend to make her more placid. Like most people in similar situations, she had to find a scapegoat, and she picked out Stern's, which was not making its deliveries as promptly as she thought it should. So she descended upon that establishment and "blew up various dept. about linoleum, chintz shades, etc.," no doubt to the exquisite terror of the clerks and floorwalkers. Having visited her rage on these cringing culprits, she felt better. Ordinarily she would have heaped reproaches on her own head and apologies on those of the offenders, but, if she did, she has left behind her no evidence of any such contrition. After all, even dear Josephine had a right to get mad every now and then, especially when on a buttermilk diet.

Her wonted sunny disposition was restored when she was engaged by John Golden for a play she really liked, *After Tomorrow*, on which he had collaborated with Hugh Stange. It is "nice and sentimental," and she accepted another middle-aged role and a decidedly unsympathetic one—"a dreadful old cat, but I loved her." For some reason her contract was to run for only four weeks. The stipulation may well have been her own, for by this time she again had other irons in the fire. Yet when, after her withdrawal, she went back to see it, she was homesick.

Her nostalgia was of very short duration. She was by no means through with *After Tomorrow*. One of the irons she had in the fire was the possibility of her making a picture of it. Fox Films was tempting her to go to Hollywood, and, after a series of tests, eminently satisfactory, she put her signature to the contract laid before her. Then came a flying trip to Newton and the cemetery, and the hasty packing of her effects. She "had a scene" with Jess Busley, who wanted to sublet her apartment, but Mother E. had priority on that, and Josephine would not yield. On November 19, almost before she knew what was happening to her, she was on the Western Express.

To her surprise, she was met in Los Angeles with a flourish that was decidedly morale-lifting. To her well wishers back East, she dispatched a day by day, play by play account of her first days on the coast. After that she was too busy for extended correspondence.

Waiting on the platform were (1) yet another Passenger Agent, (2) Camera-man all set to shoot, (3, 4) Two Fox publicity genties. Pictures were taken of arriving character actress with arms full of coat, umbrella, handbag, books, boxes, etc.

Passenger agent, reassured as to perfect well being and satisfaction of passenger, faded out of picture.

Camera man did his worst and also faded.

Asst. pub. man took hasty resume of life-history and a few pertinent observations, likewise faded away. (Note: the picture turned out to be "awful," and the life-history faulty.)

Head pub. man proved to be a perfect dear and personally conducted me all day. First to this hotel in Hollywood—where he inspected my rooms with me, admired the chrysanthemums and little begonia plants with which darling Louise Hale had bedecked each one, looked over my shoulder at her note, which explained that she had left at dawn for work on the new Arliss picture, but would meet me at dinner-time, saw my bags safely bestowed, and took me on to the Fox studio on Western Avenue. There is this huge tract of offices, shops, theatres and studios, and then there is their great Fox Hills plant out near Beverly Hills, which I haven't yet seen. I believe "After To-morrow" is to be taken out there.

Although her contract did not take effect until the last day of the month, she was kept busy all day. There was constant testing with Willie Collier, Sr., who was taking over the part played on Broadway by Donald Meek. Then too, her reputation as a teacher had preceded her, and she was assigned to coach the several girls who were being considered for parts.

But her Sundays and evenings were her own and were made delightful by the presence of Louise and Grant, who showed her about the clustering towns and introduced her to the Brown Derby, Ivar House, and other choice eating places. Usually, though, she and Louise had dinner quietly in the hotel, either in one of their rooms or "downstairs." The near approach of Christmas entailed frequent explorations of the delectable shops nearby and many visits to the post office. One evening the two of them drove about "to see Christmas trees lighted up in homes in Beverly—outdoor illuminations." Then they watched each other open their gifts, and "we drank to our dear ones." Christmas Eve Josephine had dinner with Don Marquis and a friend in the hotel dining room, and listened while a vested choir sang carols about the gaily decorated tree, and a string quartet also made music. It was all very charming and heart-warming, but still "Christmas Day 'way out here!'" Nostalgically she went through the annual ceremony of opening in bed the stocking faithfully sent by Aunt Anne, and then called up Newton to say "Merry Christmas!"

At first the new medium terrified her—at least so she said—but the daily rehearsals under Frank Borzage met with her very positive approval. He was "confidence-inspiring," and kept a strong hand on everyone and everything, a director after her own heart. There were none of the spats or ructions that had upset her digestion at home. When the actual shooting began on the day after Christmas, he had all phases under control and ready to go without the slightest fuss. She also liked her fellow actors, Collier, Charles Farrell, and Minna Gombel. Once more she enjoyed full peace of mind.

On January 11 she finished her scenes in *After Tomorrow.* Her work had not passed unobserved, and she was at once signed up for another film, *Widow's Might,* starring Joan Bennett and John Boles. This kept her going to and from Fox Hills till the twentieth, and the shooting proved to be another happy experience. One scene in a country railroad station awoke old memories of her trouping days and of the cold morning when she and Shelley had watched the sun rise over the Mississippi at Davenport. It was not that cold here, but the weather was the coldest southern California had known in fifty-four years. This, however, was better than the dreadful heat of the past summer.

There were many VIP's in town, and she got no little satisfaction from seeing the Lunts and the Arlisses, for she had the most profound respect for greatness that knew how to behave itself. Beulah Dix was there too, with her husband George Flebbe, and together they opened wide the doors of reminiscence. There was, however, one sad note. Her old friend of Portland days, Frank Sylvester, died suddenly shortly after she and Louise had dinner near him and Clara in the hotel. She lost no time in going to the widow to help her as best she could.

To pay off some of her social debts, Josephine gave a grand dinner party for Grant, Louise, and others, in the Los Angeles Biltmore. Afterward they went in a body to see, of all things, *Sherlock Holmes!* After the performance they went backstage to pay their respects to Gillette. Josephine might well have told him that, if he ever needed an understudy on short notice, she would be prepared to step in without a rehearsal, for she had been watching him play that part for thirty years.

Then, on February 4, her California sojourn was over and she was free to go home—or so she thought.

> All packed, bags downstairs, Grant here to take me to the Grand Canyon Limt. train. Fox Studio phoned I must stay over for re-take of a scene, putting me on salary again today. Much bustling to cancel train reservation & get trunks back—they are held at San Bernardino, having gone ahead.

Four days later, the unsatisfactory scene having been put to rights, she was given an O. K. and this time Grant succeeded in getting her on the train.

CHAPTER FIFTEEN

FUTILITY, FUTILITY

IT WOULD BE WEARISOME to detail at length the dreary succession of failures that, during the next four years, harried Josephine's spirits and progressively lightened her pocketbook. It is the same story over and over again, with only minor variations, a story of exhausting rehearsals, upsetting quarrels, out-of-town tryouts, and then short shrift on Broadway—if that mecca was gained at all.

First came *A Thousand Summers,* by Arch Selwyn and Shephard Traube. Even the beauteous Jane Cowl, effusing glamor, while a Cornell boy named Franchot Tone gazed at her adoringly could not supply enough oxygen, and, if a Cleveland manager had not seen the play through rose-tinted glasses, it would have expired forthwith. As it was, the city marshal was so rude as to cart away the furniture, and they had to get through the last two performances with hastily gathered makeshifts. Then all but Tone, who was replaced by young John Griggs went to Cleveland. There Josephine sought out the dining room of the Hollenden Hotel and at a table as near as she could get to the one where Shelley had proposed to her, she sought comfort from his unseen presence. When John asked if he might join her, she politely shooed him away. Later in her room he was dazzled by the knowing discussion of the occult carried on by her and Miss Cowl. Next desperate measures were tried—*Camille*—but the public was no more enthalled by Dumas than by Selwyn.

Even before these two attractions—if they can be so designated—had been disposed of, Arthur Hopkins was angling for Josephine for a play about opera singers, at that time called *Encore*, written by a young man named Victor Wittgenstein. Ethel Barrymore was to be the prima donna—thereby insuring good business—and Hopkins wanted Josephine for the part of a German contralto. The first rehearsal pleased her, but before long she again had misgivings. For one thing, she had more than a little trouble with the required accent and deep chest tones, and that among other reasons led her to apply for a release. She had other offers but Hopkins had what he wanted and would not let her go. Her worst fears were realized at the opening in Wilmington, November 18, "nightmare performance, Ethel not knowing her lines." A few evenings later, at a performance in New Haven, Josephine was encouraged by the attentions of Mrs. George Pierce Baker and other Radcliffe cronies, but the next day it was announced that Miss Barrymore had the grippe, and the jig was up—for the time being.

Only for the time being. The following spring Hopkins, having rechristened the piece *The Amazing Career*, took the script from the shelf, dusted it off, and had another go at it. At that time the depression was at its depth—so far as her diary shows this had escaped Josephine's attention—and not even Miss Barrymore could attract people into the theater. She herself describes the play in *Memories*, as "a very amusing comedy about an opera singer who gets progressively younger as the play goes on, and marries and marries and marries." She concludes, "There was nothing funny about the depression in which we were doing it. . . . Finally, when we were in Chicago, and the Government ordered all the banks to close, there wasn't any money at all, and although the play had been doing very well indeed, we had to close it."

This explanation is inaccurate, aside from the fact that the diary reports that business was not good, in that the play did not close until May 20, long after the banks had been reopened. That Josephine did not fancy F.D.R. was no secret, but the collapse of *An Amazing Career* was one calamity for which she did not hold him responsible. Instead, she took or threatened to take legal action against Miss Barrymore, and eventually, thanks to the diligence of Rebecca Brownstein, collected at least part of what she considered her due. "Hooray!"

Sandwiched between the two versions of the Wittgenstein play was another that was clearly not to her taste. She was a very sentimentally patriotic individual, and anything that reflected unfavorably on the American people rubbed her the wrong way. George O'Neil's *American Dream* did precisely that. With conditions what they were during the winter of 1932–33, the young playwright can scarcely be blamed for a somewhat cynical outlook upon our national life, past as well as present, but that did not make his play palatable to Josephine, or, for that matter, to her friends. That it had real merit was beside the point. Even the fact that it was a Guild production directed by Philip Moeller could not reconcile her to it. Her judgment was confirmed by the reactions of the Morrisons and of Harriet Sterling, and the first matinee audience "hated it." So after a week she handed in her two-weeks notice.

Fortunately for her, the depression had not stifled the summer circuit, and she was able to get away from the city heat for two weeks at Dennis and Cohasset, where Alexander Dean was trying out a new play, *Tourists Accommodated*. Her enjoyment was tempered by the shocking news of the sudden death of Louise Hale. Five years before, when Ethellyn Defoe died, Louise had written her, "Please live on. I am growing a little lonesome." Josephine must have remembered these words while she sat on the beach that afternoon. And Louise was not her only loss. Some weeks before Aunt Fanny had fallen and broken her hip. In September she too died. Although Aunt Fanny had never been as close as her sisters, Josephine nevertheless felt the first break in the circle of the aunts.

When she returned to New York from the funeral, she yielded to the importunities of John Golden and agreed to play a small part in a new venture of his, *Divine Drudge*, which he had adapted from the German of Vicki Baum, and was now using to launch the American career of Mady Christians. From the very first Josephine heartily wished herself a long way from the Royale Theater, for she hated her part, Frau Klapstuhl. By dint of will power, and because she needed every penny she could honestly come by, she managed to hold out through the rehearsals and the twelve performances, and was relieved when those twelve were disposed of.

The next play in which she appeared was *By Your Leave*, a very trivial comedy by Gladys Hurlbut and Emma Wells. The names listed, one below the other, on the program might have been expected to insure that it would run on merrily for months. How could theater-lovers in their right minds resist such an aggregation of "names" as Dorothy Gish, Howard Lindsay, Kenneth MacKenna, and Ernest Glendinning, to say nothing of Josephine Hull? The trouble was that at least some of these were not yet "names," and the public's resistance was too much for them; after a month, they all gave up. By this time Josephine's spirits were at rock bottom.

Her next play, however, was another story and a much longer one, for it left wounds that were a long time healing. This was Ivor Novello's comedy *Fresh Fields*, a very expert and entertaining piece of craftsmanship. The Century of Progress was in full swing in Chicago, and Leslie Casey and James Littell thought they saw a way of getting a slice of the pie by presenting Margaret Anglin there in what looked like a sure-fire hit. Miss Anglin, for her part, was more than willing, and as early as March, plans were shaping up. There was an excellent role for Josephine and she too was happy to be a participant, even though she had to turn down offers for summer work from Alexander Dean. After much telephoning back and forth, in June rehearsals finally got under way. There were many fittings for costumes and many visits to Thompson's office for last checkups. She had followed a new regimen for some time, and both were gratified when the scale tipped eighteen pounds less than it had on her last visit. Her blood pressure was not ideal, but not dangerous either. So by July 3 all was ready, and the sisters-in-law set out gaily for Chicago. They spent the morning of the Fourth going over their lines in the Pullman, and then registered at the Blackstone, next door to their theater.

So far the sailing was smooth. But it did not remain so for long—sailing was seldom smooth when Mary was in the boat. By the sixth the diary was reporting "ructions," then more "ructions and conferences." Nevertheless, the opening three evenings later was a triumph.

> Opened at night, lovely audience, orchids from Mary, roses from the mgr.

Next day the notices were all they could wish, although the *Tribune* did not mention Josephine.

So the two actresses proceeded to enjoy themselves. Of course, they could not overlook the fair, and their first free Sunday they spent on the grounds.

> Mary & I & Emmy went to the Fair (Century of Progress). Llama Temple, Switzerland Village (lunch), Hall of Science, rode round grounds, to Eng. Village & Globe Theater (All's Well). Black Forest & ice skating, dinner at Old Heidelburg, fountains & fireworks. Home at eleven.

They moved from the Blackstone to the less expensive Whitehall, where they had kitchenettes and could get their own meals. Fortunately Josephine's room was on the twenty-first floor, so that she could get the benefit of any stray breezes that were blowing. The temperature rose to a record-breaking 105 degrees. As soon as it dropped, she betook herself once more to the fair, where she enjoyed Frank Buck's animals and a Mexican orchestra.

All this was too good to last. Business slumped and the friction began again. So did her stomach pains. Two days later it was "tiresome ructions, discouraging, management here & Mary." She says nothing about threatened salary cuts, but it is possible to read between the lines that they were in the air.

> Mary & I had a confab, more complications about the play.
> Ev'g performance & ructions. Miss Carlisle sent mss. to Novello's agent behind Mary's back. Disgusting.

On September 1, after a benefit performance, Mary informed the management that she was withdrawing, a telling blow inasmuch as she was the star. Howard came on from New York and took his place beside his wife. Meanwhile a hurried call was dispatched to Gladys Hanson to come and take over the role of Lady Mary.

> I was rushed from my vacation in Atlanta to Chicago—and with three days rehearsal—tossed into Miss Anglin's part. Of course, blessed Jo Hull stood by, offering more helping hands than were ever possessed by any heathen god. The rest of the company were equally helpful, but I had walked in upon a completely unhappy & disrupted group. Several had made up their minds to send in their notices. Miss Anglin was most charming to me—upon the several times I saw her in my rehearsals.

It was clear, Miss Hanson adds, that things had been falling apart for some time, and she soon realized she had taken all her trouble for nothing.

Here endeth the first chapter of the tale of *Fresh Fields*. The second was still in the future, and meanwhile Josephine had to live. Mary, still eager to appear as Lady Mary on Broadway, embarked on a series of negotiations, but for Josephine marking time was out of the question and she did her best to find work. Not until Leighton Rollins engaged her to direct a Christmas miracle play to be given by the students of

his drama school did anything come her way. From this undertaking she made a little in a material way and for short periods
kept her mind off her worries.

Her Christmas, which would otherwise have been dreary,
was cheered by an offer from Lawrence Langner of a part in
his new *On to Fortune*. With Armina Marshall, Ilka Chase,
and Glenn Anders also in the cast, Josephine foresaw agreeable
and prosperous times ahead. They proved agreeable enough,
but hardly prosperous, for after a month of rehearsals and
the usual out-of-town tryouts, the play closed with only four
days in New York to its credit. Fortunately Miss Chase does
have one entertaining memory of Josephine and her performance.

> About the only thing I remember of it was Josephine's cross
> from stage right out the French window stage left. She played
> my aunt and was supposedly going into the garden to sunbathe,
> a fairly beguiling concept in itself. She wore a sort of rich sienna
> terry cloth bathrobe, and her head was done up in yellow tulle
> with an enormous bow over the brow. She carried a very large
> knitting bag and during the run in Washington and our one
> week's appearance in New York brought joy to my heart,
> otherwise depressed by the fact that I was in a flop.

Miss Chase was not the only one who was depressed. Two
weeks after the collapse Josephine made the first of her trips
to the Empire Gold Buying Company and sold some little
"gold & silver pieces." This transaction must have been a hu-
miliating blow to her pride, and she kept it strictly to herself.
A few days later Guthrie McClintic sounded her out about a
part in a new play by John Van Druten. She was of course
more than interested, but in an evil moment she was persuaded
to hold out for *Fresh Fields*, which seemed about to make the
grade. When it was too late for her to accept the McClintic
offer, on March 27, "Mary telephoned play is off again."

By this time she was entirely dependent on her radio jobs.
She was invited to be in The Players' *Seven Keys to Baldpate*,

and was delighted to have something to occupy her too many
idle moments, although it brought her no cash. The production was fun, and so was the party at 16 Gramercy Square that
followed the last performance. She arrived home, escorted by
Helen and Percy Moore, at a quarter of five in the morning.
All things considered, a little jollification, no matter how late
the hour, did not come amiss.

The summer season came to her rescue with two short engagements, as Lady Wishfort in *The Way of the World* with
Rollins' company at Bar Harbor, and *The Torchbearers* and
The Bishop Misbehaves under Alexander Dean at Cohasset.
The Congreve comedy, a delight, left Josephine "nearly dead
with the stairs, heavy costumes, changes & work." At the Kelly
farce the audience laughed uproariously, but she found Mme.
Pampanelli heavy sledding. In the house one evening was one
of her old friends of New Orleans days who had not seen her
for thirty years, David Perkins who had been enamored of the
dainty ingénue in the days of his callow youth.

> I was intrigued by the voice. I knew it, but could not identify
> it. Looking at the program, I saw the name, Josephine Hull,
> but it struck no responsive chord. This actress was plump and
> rolypoly, but when I got a profile view, I realized it was Jose-
> phine Sherwood.

Even before she had sailed off to Maine, *Fresh Fields* put
her in a state of exasperation and she turned, as she was prone
to do, to her devoted mother-in-law. Mary had now made up
her mind that she would tackle the summer circuit herself,
and she was eager to have Josephine with her. She knew that
nowhere else was she likely to find so good a Lottie, and undoubtedly, knowing the straits she was in, wished to help her.
Unfortunately, however, she did not consult Josephine first,
but went ahead and arranged dates which were out of the question for her "Of course," the latter wrote Mother E., "Mary
may not go through with the Dennis thing, & if she does even
then it may not be done in N. Y. I will never count on that

again, nor give up anything for it—it nearly ruined me waiting for it this year."

A week later Mrs. Hull, Sr. received another bulletin on the conflict between her daughters-in-law:

> Mary really has arranged to do "Fresh Fields" in Dennis,— the very two weeks I'll be in Bar Harbor. Moore called to offer me my part but of course I am tied up and unavailable. Then she has also got Leighton Rollins to let her do it in Bar Harbor the last of August when I will be in Cohasset. She wanted me, but it is neither her fault nor mine that I have two other jobs which interfere, and I am apt to have a more *peaceful* job each time, also to be the important member of the cast, featured in both places, as I should not be if she were the star. If her play goes on here next season, maybe I can do my part again. But I shall never sacrifice anything for her again on a chance.

Apparently Mary took offense, believing that her attempt to be helpful had been ungratefully rejected, and preserved an injured silence. Josephine, for her part, declared feelingly, "I will not break a contract to oblige anyone." The great silence persisted despite a peace offering from Josephine in the form of a silver basket containing orange-blossom perfume. Mary at last succeeded in getting *Fresh Fields* to Broadway in February, 1936, but there was another Lottie, and Josephine was deeply hurt, so much so that weeks passed before she "summoned up courage & saw Mary in 'Fresh Fields.' " There was no backstage visit. Not until October was the breach healed with a dinner and a reunion. This was fortunate, for within the year Howard was dead, and, whatever the circumstances, Josephine would never have ceased to reproach herself had there been no reconciliation.

During the summer of 1935 she had reached the unwelcome conclusion that she would have to give up even her small apartment in the Gainsborough, store what was left of her furniture, and take a room in some inexpensive hotel. After that, if her bad luck persisted, she might have to resort to paying extensive visits to loving friends and relatives. At the same time, "I tell myself I will not worry over my own crisis—somehow it will resolve itself." When she got back to New York the crisis showed no sign whatsoever of resolving itself. She moved to a room in Harperly Hall but postponed the visits, with their mortifying implications. Meanwhile she sought out manager after manager. In a way it was like her first days in the city, and yet it was not the same at all, for then she had been young, strong, confident; now she was tired, half sick, and bitterly discouraged. On the other hand, now the managers knew and wanted to help her. When a play Philip Dunning had been discussing with her was called off, he sent her a bottle of whiskey as a "consolation prize."

The one small part she managed to get—in Hugh Strange's *Night in the House,* based on Hugh Walpole's *The Old Ladies* —lasted little more than a week. A backstage visit from kindly Maud and Otis Skinner was comforting, but it did not keep "this lovely play" alive. "Packing up disconsolately and coming home very late." Only the radio—the Radio Guild, Gang Busters, and Warden Lawes—stood between her and real want —and her trips to the studios had to be made afoot because she could not afford the dubious luxury of the subway. Years later she confided to her friend Helen Moore that she was down to "one dress and one nightie." Everything else had been worn out or sold. The nadir of her fortunes was reached early in January, when she again sought out the Empire Gold Buying Company, and sold her mother's watch and ring. Only absolute desperation could have made her do that.

Mrs. Wallace Morrison (Helen Moore) said that none of her friends had any suspicion of the true state of her affairs. With chin well up, she attended meetings of the Executive Council of Equity, presided as hostess at the weekly gatherings of the Episcopal Actors' Guild in the Guild Hall upstairs at the Little Church Around the Corner, and rehearsed her broadcasts, with no one the wiser. Just how much the aunts in New Ipswich knew of all this, it is impossible to say, but they had their suspicions, and in April they sent her a "wonderful check" that acted like a dose of adrenalin, and she was able to treat herself to a few modest pleasures.

Although she was denied the comfort of knowing it, this was for Josephine the classic dark hour before dawn. She was to have her troubles in the years to come, plenty of them, but never again were her fortunes to plumb so deep an abyss. The eleven long years of frustration, hardship, and humiliation would soon fade into a memory, and eventually she would be able to dismiss them as just had luck. At the moment she found little to cheer her except Helen Hayes in *Victoria Regina*.

CHAPTER SIXTEEN

THE TRIUMPH OF ILLOGIC

You Can't Take It With You

JUNE 29. To Sam Harris office for appointment. Kaufman-Hart play, new.

This laconic note in the diary she did not amplify. Too many similar visits had led her up blind alleys, and she did not permit this one to build up hopes that might be false. Yet Sam Harris, George Kaufman, and Moss Hart were not precisely run of the mill, and, as she was soon to discover, feelers from them were not to be taken casually. The first thing she knew, she was writing her signature on a beguiling contract, and, presto, the mirage was transmogrified into something substantial.

In August they sent her the script and her delight in it helped fortify her against the "horrible landslide for Roosevelt"; even so, she dutifully devoted hours to moping over the awful New Deal victory. It was a case of *noblesse oblige*. Once she was able to immerse herself in rehearsals, she put these futile lamentations behind her. If the Sycamores didn't worry, why should she? She capitulated without reservation, spoken or unspoken, to the play, the cast, and the director.

Among those who studied her admiringly as she built up the

224

character of Penelope Sycamore was Miss Abby Lewis, who had been engaged as general understudy for all the women's parts.

It was my privilege to watch her from early in rehearsal— to see how she invented & contributed. Mr. Kaufman & Mr. Hart are indebted to her for many pieces of stage business. I remember one piece in particular. "Miss Wellington" (played by that lovely musical comedy actress Mitzi Hajos) had had too much to drink & was asleep on the sofa—had her face turned to the wall—her back to "Penny." Mrs. Hull noticed that "Miss Wellington's" buttocks were not supported by the sofa—were, in fact, suspended in midair, so "Penny" in passing lifted one knee & shoved hard, thereby depositing "Miss Wellington" more securely on the sofa.

This invention of Mrs. Hull's was kept in the show and never failed to delight the audience. Such a dear little lady doing such a practical but "vulgar" piece of business.

It was in "You Can't Take It with You" that Mrs. Hull's role said early in the play: "What time is it?" And on one night a gentleman in the front row answered her: "9:15." He was never aware he had spoken—so much was the audience with Mrs. Hull—and she was not startled & answered "Thank you" and went right on with the play.

The first tryout performance was given in the McCarter Theater at Princeton and "went pretty well." In an interview with an emissary from *Theatre Arts* years later she gleefully reminisced about an experience that had further heightened her enjoyment of an already delectable evening.

I had never met our producer, Max Gordon, but just before we opened in Princeton, New Jersey, he had sent me a nice little note, and I wanted to thank him. After the show we all crowded into cars to go to the station. There were not enough cars so a number of men, including Moss Hart, squeezed into the car with us and sat on our knees. I mentioned to Mr. Hart that Max Gordon had sent me this note and said I would like to thank him for it.

"Now's your chance," Hart said dryly. "He's sitting on your lap."[1]

On December 14, after two weeks at the Chestnut Street in Philadelphia, *You Can't Take It with You* opened hilariously and triumphantly at the Booth. "Very big house & wonderful."

Enthusiastic friends were hard put to it to squeeze themselves in among the flowers and piles of telegrams in her dressing room. She was exclaimed over, embraced, and kissed until she scarcely knew what was going on. For once the ecstatic congratulations did not have to cover up any mental reservations.

The state of the world in December, 1936, was so depressing and ominous that the public was glad to seek forgetfulness in Grandpa Vanderhof's living room just around the corner from Columbia University. "The every-man-for-himself room would be more like it. For here meals are eaten, plays are written, snakes collected, ballet steps practiced, xylophones played, printing presses operated—if there were room enough there would probably be ice skating." Grandpa, his brood of Sycamores, and their nondescript satellites are oblivious to all the stresses outside, ostriches perhaps, but happy ones.

"There is not a single ounce of rational thinking or acting in the lot of them" says Edith Isaacs in *Theatre Arts* "and yet they are all made to seem more sane, during the time of the play, than those of us who go hard about daily tasks and fight our neighbors for the right to work longer and more fiercely than they do." (Times have changed since 1936. Have we all become Sycamores?)

When the curtain rose, Josephine had the stage to herself.

At the moment, GRANDPA VANDERHOF'S daughter, MRS. PENELOPE SYCAMORE, is doing what she likes best in the world. She is writing a play—her eleventh. Comfortably ensconced in what is known as Mother's Corner,

---

[1] Gordon was a silent partner.

she is pounding away on a typewriter perched precariously on a rickety card table. Also on the table is one of those plaster-paris skulls ordinarily used as an ash tray, but which serves PENE-LOPE as a candy jar. And, because PENNY likes companionship, there are two kittens on the table lapping at a saucer of milk.

Penny, whose previous forte had been painting, had switched to her present form of aesthetic self-expression, when someone had providentially left a typewriter at the door by mistake. The setting of her current opus is a monastery. As she logically observes, "You know, with forty monks and one girl, something ought to happen."

You Can't Take It with You is one of the funniest plays ever written, as Brooks Atkinson declared, "the perfect idiot's delight of the season." It tells again the age-old story of Romeo and Juliet, but with the feuding Capulets and Montagues metamorphosed through the genius of its authors into the zany Sycamores and the snobbish Kirbys, and the tragic ending changed through Grandpa's irrefutable illogic into as happy an ending as any sob-sister could ask. The dialogue is inspired humor compounded with dazzling skill. Before the audience could catch its breath after one laugh, it was convulsed by another. Josephine declared that one woman became so hysterical that she fell from her seat into the aisle, and one old man knocked himself out beating his head on the balcony railing.

To squeeze the last ounce of fun out of this triumph of unreason, Kaufman and Hart had the co-operation of a perfect cast. Critical applause was practically unanimous, especially for Henry Travers as the benign patriarch. Brooks Atkinson said of Josephine that her "homely comedy is in a related key, gasping, fluttery, egregiously middle class." Nearly everyone was the recipient of a verbal bouquet. Josephine loved them all, and it was well that she did, for they were to be a long time together. As for the audiences responsible for this happy result, she was extremely broad-minded. She might write "Curses!" in her diary when Herbert Lehman was elected governor, but it was quite all right with her if he brought his family to see the play on Christmas evening.

The play and its success played havoc with her annual Christmas preparations, but not with her unfailing thoughtfulness, as Miss Lewis testifies.

> During those "You Can't Take It With You" days I was unmarried & alone in the city. Mrs. Hull knew that & gave me her holidays. She knew my Christmases & Thanksgivings would be just like all my other days unless she made them different for me. She did. I was her guest at Sardi's (the restaurant in the theater district so famous). We had champagne & all at our feasts. When I think of all the fine company she could have had & yet preferred to care for a lonely girl—I know why everyone loved Mrs. Hull.

In addition when Miss Lewis was called upon to substitute for someone, Josephine lent her the competent maid she had as a dresser.

Among the casualties of the season had been her Christmas present to Jane O'Reilly, usually a "must." On January 18 she at last found time to write her chum a penitent letter.

> It is still a matter of daily miracle to be in a *hit!!* And I am so thankful it keeps me pinching myself to be sure it's all true. The play is very gay and foolish, and we are sold out for weeks ahead—with from thirty to sixty standees at each performance. It is so good to hear people laugh a whole evening—and refreshes one even while it absorbs vitality. I find I can do little else but my job; but on Sundays, whenever possible, I go up into Connecticut to be with Mother Hull, who nearly died just before Christmas when I was in Philadelphia for our opening fortnight. She is in a precarious condition—it hardly seems she can outlive the winter—practically blind, very feeble and very flighty—yet her vitality is amazing and courage ditto—so there is no telling. Henry and Howard go up Sundays too if they can. Christmas Eve I was able to join Henry's family here in town for a midnight Christmas tree and supper.

By this time she was beginning to find herself a minor celebrity, one of those whom *Time* calls "the near-great." She was
the guest of honor and sometimes the speaker at one affair after
another—the League of Political Education, the Town Hall
Club, and the Episcopal Actors' Guild. When news came that
the play had won the Pulitzer Prize, Josephine was the one
chosen to go before the curtain and make the announcement.

She could now afford certain comforts and luxuries she had
been obliged to do without for some time. For one thing, she
replenished her depleted wardrobe, taking especial pride in a
new Bendel gown. She also left her cramped quarters in Harperly Hall, moving first into "a lovely suite" at the Gotham and
then a year later, to Hampshire House. When the second
season opened in the fall, her weekly salary was raised to three
hundred dollars.

Prosperity, although we may not like to admit it, has pen-
alties as well as rewards. This truth was brought home to her
all too soon, and by March, 1938, she was "so tired & 'put upon'
in spite of my beloved work." Her soft heart was not exactly
a well-kept secret, and inevitably she was fair prey for would-
be borrowers. She had always been ready to share her goods
with anyone who could persuade her that his need was greater
than hers, and now, after her recent long-drawn-out ordeal, she
was more vulnerable than ever. It was only too easy to put
herself in the petitioner's place. Refusing help made her mind
a battleground for doubts and self-reproach, and yet the hard
years had taught her that, however generous her inclinations,
she must not run the risk of finding herself again among the
"genteel poor."

Death too struck close to her. In August of that first year
Howard died—"Poor Mary!" The next Christmas was sad-
dened by the death of lovely Maud Skinner, and Priestly Morrison's a few days later severed yet another precious tie with
Shelley. From these sorrows she found relief in Grandpa's
living room among the kittens, the snakes, the fireworks, and
the happy-go-lucky Sycamores. When Hallowe'en came round,
she put orange bows on the current generation of kittens. On

the first anniversary "Harris, Kaufman, & Hart gave us a lovely supper party & gifts," and warm-hearted Mr. Sardi treated her to her New Year's dinner. But Thompson Sweeny gave her something else, "a course of sprouts," because of "blood pressure, overweight, bad knee & everything."

You Can't Take it With You ran two years in New York. The original Broadway cast never was called upon to face the rigors of the road. These were left to the so-called Chicago and Boston companies. It remained intact until the withdrawal of Henry Travers in May, 1938. The following fall, business at last began to dwindle, and the handwriting was seen on the wall. The production was shunted to the Imperial Theater, and then to the Ambassador, which she hated—"Awful hole & dump. Dressing-room ditto." Then, finally, on December 3, 1938, "Our last performance of this wonderful engagement. Many curtain calls—Geo. Kaufman in—Goodbyes."

The next two years were for Josephine little more than an interval between memorable successes. Far from idle, she was on the go day and night, and many things happened to her, good and bad. Sometimes she was convinced that more bad came her way than she deserved, and gave herself over briefly to gloom. Once, when Thompson was dosing her for a cold, she called herself "just a worn out old wreck," but she always bounced back up out of the depths.

She was not, certainly, without legitimate causes for distress. Six weeks after the play closed, Mother Elinor slept away peacefully. Although Josephine knew this was for the best, the passing of one who had for many years been so close to her brought a pang. At Christmas time, a year later, Aunt Anne suffered a heart attack, and after lingering on for five months finally died in May. Then too the war news grew worse and worse. Almost as hard to bear, the repeated triumphs of the nefarious Democrats elicited such plaints as "The returns make me sick," "Nauseating," and "Curses!" It was hard to be a stern and rock-bound Republican in those dreadful days. Less serious, but galling just the same, were the misdeeds of the labor unions. She wanted very much to move to a different apartment in the Hampshire, but she was halted in her tracks by a strike, and called down imprecations on the heads of the union leaders. Quite forgotten were the days, twenty years before, when she had gloried in the name of *striker*. It all depends on whose ox is being gored.

Her life had many agreeable phases too. One of the pleasantest was in 1939, a brief engagement to give the summer residents of Nantucket a taste of her Penny, under the aegis of Morgan Farley, who had been her rebellious son in *Fata Morgana* long ago. This was at Siasconset on the south shore of the island, and the sea air, despite some fog, had its unfailing restorative effect on her. How delightful it was to have a tower room at the Beach House, to fill her lungs with good salt breezes, and to find pansies on her breakfast tray! " 'Sconset was at it loveliest, roses & sea & sun—we did make her happy & comfortable, and the co. adored her. A memory without a blemish."

On the other hand, she had to endure two professional fiascos. Early in January, 1939, she was engaged by Auriol Lee and Al Lewis to support Ruth Chatterton in a piece called *Farewell Appearance*. At first full of blissful anticipations, she was within a few days "very unsettled in my mind."

> Rehearsed at Ruth C's (Pierre's) & so unhappy, gave up
> my part after rehearsal, hopeless muddle. Nice talk with Auriol
> & Ruth. Wrote Al Lewis & left note at hotel. Relieved but
> sorry. First time I gave up.

She suffered so many pangs of conscience that she could not sleep.

The other setback did not involve her conscience. This was Vincent Sheean's *International Incident* in which she again tried her luck with Ethel Barrymore, who apparently bore her no ill will in spite of their earlier financial hassle. This time the director was Guthrie McClintic. The play was being tried out in Boston, and she was summoned up to study the performances. When it opened, appropriately, at the Ethel Barrymore in New York, on April 2, she was on hand in the dual roles of Mrs. Wuthering Blackett (of New York) and Mrs. G. Hiram Tracy (of Detroit). "But," says Miss Barrymore, "it was a light play, quite different from the serious one that the title and the author's name and the state of the world led people to expect, and it had only a short run." Fifteen performances. Josephine loved it, but the public did not.

She had, however, other things to occupy her time and attention, and they were not light. Josephine, like most of the women in her profession, was dismayed by the fearful course of events in Europe. They were quite incapable of sitting by with hands folded in their laps; they had vivid memories of their war work a generation before and were eager to make such contributions as they could. So on January 15, at a meeting called by Rachel Crothers at Antoinette Perry's apartment, the American Theater Wing for British and French Relief Funds (as it was later called) was formally organized. The roster resembled a roll call of the great on the distaff side. Miss Crothers, a born leader, was elected president as before, and again Josephine was chosen treasurer, with Ilka Chase as her assistant. Through the co-operation of Winthrop Aldrich and Mrs. Louis F. Slade, suitable quarters were put at their disposal in Rockefeller Center. There were a number of rooms which could serve as offices, and a small stage, which could be used for entertainment if so desired. The women wasted no time on non-essential preparations, but rolled up their sleeves at once. Miss Chase's account in *Free Admission* makes very entertaining reading and is enlightening for those who still are convinced that actresses are frivolous beings bent only on self-exploitation. "We opened a workroom, and cues by the dozen were missed along Broadway as actresses, from stars to character bits, knitted and snipped with a will, making long white seamen's socks for British sailors and flannel nightgowns for the British sailors' babies.

Someone donated a knitting machine to the workroom, but

no one liked it much; it was intricate of operation and possessed
a cold mechanical personality. Owing, possibly, to the lack of
a sympathetic touch, it dropped more stitches than we did, and
Josephine Hull used to regard it with mistrust and mutter balefully, "Look at it, that *thing*." Aided by it, if ungratefully, and
by hundreds of hardworking volunteers, we relieved first the
Allies, then the British, and, after Pearl Harbor, the Americans.

Avoiding the soulless *thing*, Josephine embarked in her own
way on the knitting of sweaters. After the seventh, she stopped
counting, but she very definitely did not stop knitting. Occupied with her needles and her funds, she had little time to give
to other phases of the Wing's work, including the famous Stage
Door Canteen, nor could she entirely neglect the finances of
Josephine Hull. She had become a radio personality and was
in great demand, especially for serials like *Meet Miss Julia*
(which was pre-recorded), *One of the Finest*, *The O'Neills*,
and *Echoes of New York*. She had no colds or stomach upsets.

Then Joseph Kesselring, heretofore a not very conspicuous
dramatist who aspired to write a farce, thought of his grandmother. As incongruity is the basis of farce, he tried to decide
what, of all things, she would be most unlikely to do. What
would be most completely out of character? He weighed and
ruled out several suppositions, and finally came to murder.
There he stopped to consider. He wanted to write a farce, and
murder is not funny. At least, *one* murder isn't. But how about
murders by the dozen? They could be made so preposterous as
to remove them from all reality, and so, if he played his cards
right, could be made amusing. Yes, he would have a go at it.
Sir Philip Sidney's Muse is reported on good authority to have
said to him, "Fool, look in thy heart and write." Although
Kesselring was no fool, he made up his mind to follow the
advice anyway. His Muse was so flattered that she inspired him
with humor, inventiveness, and all the other qualities that go
into the making of the kind of play he had set his heart on.

"ARSENIC AND OLD LACE" established Josephine among the immortals in Broadway's Hall of Fame. If she had never played another part, she would have been secure in the possession of her niche. She had been, like Frank Bacon before he wrote and acted in *Lightnin'*, well known and highly esteemed in the profession, but to the public at large almost unknown. Penelope Sycamore had given her status in New York, but she had never gone with her on the road, and someone else took over in the motion picture. With Abby Brewster, however, it was very different. She not only appeared hundreds of times in Manhattan, first at the Fulton and then at the Hudson, but she twice traveled the highways and byways from the Atlantic to the Pacific, and people who had missed her in person could—can still today —see her in the movie. She also did the part on the radio. Although others have appeared as Aunt Abby, for those who saw Josephine, she was *she*.

There is no evidence she ever had the slightest inkling that such glory awaited her. The diary is very matter of fact. She read the play, and on November 28, 1940, taking time out

234

from broadcasts of *The Girl Interne,* she went to the Empire Theater and signed the contract with Howard Lindsay and Russel Crouse. And that was that.

Once the contracts were in order, the producers lost no time. The first reading rehearsal was held a week later, and the out-of-town opening occurred in Baltimore, at the Maryland Theater, the evening after Christmas. Both before and after the opening, rehearsals were held daily, usually under Bretaigne Windust—Josephine's darling "Windy"—occasionally under the critical gaze of Lindsay or Crouse. These rehearsals were grueling and exhausting, but there were no complaints from Josephine. She was a perfectionist, and no amount of work that contributed to perfection ever drew a protest from her.

She resolutely set about mastering the part of Aunt Abby. That meant first understanding it, and then finding ways to make the character clear to her audiences. The reason behind every gesture, every inflection, every timing must be grasped, and then, no matter how long it took, no matter how tired or ill she was, projection had to be perfected too. No one ever understood what made her "tick" better than the late Bretaigne Windust, and fortunately he has left us his analysis.

> Her little round figure dominated by beautiful snapping black eyes, and a small head, carried slightly forward as if in the constant habit of keeping a well groomed bun on the nape of her neck and at the same time trying to look up to a particularly engaging tall man, suggested that at one time in her younger days she had been very well proportioned, for a then popular cuddly type. Everything about her suggested warmth and pleasantry, and softness. But actually she was a woman of very decided opinions about many things. And when once she had understood and digested a point of view in any direction, it was almost impossible to shake. Had she not been so intelligent and so well educated these strong opinions would probably have been murderous prejudices.
>
> In addition to all these assets and characteristics, Miss Hull was a first class actress. She had a completely split personality

in the theater, at her work. She could stand off to the side, as it were, and observe Josephine Hull at work. She knew when to do and what to do and how to do all the accepted things which a well trained and gifted performer has at her disposal to keep an audience aware of her, and of the character she is portraying. Once she had decided on a course of action, and felt that she had the complete confidence of the audience she varied less than almost anyone I have ever known.

For what he called a "slight schizo-phrenia" Windust had an interesting explanation.

In ARSENIC AND OLD LACE she was required to be slightly insane. This insanity took the form it often does, and necessitated a character which could either ignore or otherwise eliminate certain aspects of reality. Miss Hull understood this completely from the very beginning, and never had any trouble convincing an audience. I have always felt that this was due to the fact, in part at least, that she was borrowing from one side of her life and upbringing. After all, a strict finishing school —college for girls—type upbringing was pretty incongruous for a woman in the Theater when she started. What's more she married an actor, and a leading man at that. These things are not as opposed now as they were then, but at the time she must have been a person riding on two horses, and I don't believe that she ever found it very difficult.

About one thing, however, Windust was mistaken. This was about her manner of locomotion. Knowing her inventiveness, he did not believe she got "that little trot" from anyone in particular. "She just felt her size, and as she stood in the back of the theater watching herself on the stage, she added that in. She may have seen another actress run across the stage, but the way she did it was entirely her own." Josephine gives her own explanation of it.

I got the notion from an old actress whom I never saw— Mrs. Vincent, the famous character woman and comedienne of the Boston Museum stock company. My aunt, who saw her play, once told me of a funny scene in which Mrs. Vincent trotted across a room holding a teakettle. She bounced as she went, and with every step the water splashed out of the spout. So I borrowed from Mrs. Vincent, but I don't have a tea-kettle. The white stockings were Windust's idea. He thought there was something comic about my feet when I scurried along. So he had me wear ankle-length dresses, instead of skirts touching the floor like Martha's. The white stockings make my feet more noticeable.

One of the sacrifices she made for her art was her corsets, a very important item to Josephine. They had a way of getting themselves into her diary among the other oddments for which it served as a repository—time and again before going to bed she recorded for posterity the fact that she had washed them. These garments, she thought, did not belong on Aunt Abby, because, for all her sweetness and light, she had a rather sloppy figure, or at least ought to have. So, while she and Josephine were together on the stage of the Fulton, the corsets stayed at home in the closet.

Abby is not the only aunt in *Arsenic*. There is also Martha, who is just as "batty," but a bit more timid. For this part the producers engaged Jean Adair, and Josephine would have been the first to say they never did her a greater favor. The two "sisters" had never happened to meet, but they soon realized they were kindred spirits, and remained devoted friends to the end.

In order to add further *éclat* to the production someone was inspired to lure Boris Karloff on from Hollywood to play the fiendish Jonathan, who has had his private plastic surgeon make his face over into the likeness of—Boris Karloff. The whole scheme frightened the bogey man of the screen.

When Lindsay and Crouse suggested to me that I come to New York for Arsenic, I confided my reservations to them about my first appearance on Broadway and made it a condition that I would come if there were two parts in the play better than mine to carry the load. Little did I dream at the time that I would be in the capable, generous hands of those two darlings, Josephine Hull and Jean Adair.

Needless to say, I was really terrified at the prospect, and Josephine's unfailing kindness and understanding of my problem gave me the measure of confidence I needed. After I had found my feet a little, I found that my main problem lay in getting her to be upstage of me at the climax of the third act, when with her usual generosity she tried to insist on giving the advantage to me.

Amid all the hurly-burly of rehearsals, visits to the wigmaker, costume fittings at Helene Pons's, and dress parades on the stage, Josephine could not forget the old aunts up in New Hampshire—only two of them now—facing a lonely Christmas among the snows at the foot of Mount Monadnock. She sent for them to join her in Baltimore, and they accepted the invitation with alacrity. As it turned out, they caught only fleeting glimpses of Josephine on Christmas, because the whole day was given over to last-minute rehearsals, but they were on hand for the opening next evening. Although it went off brilliantly, there still remained much tinkering to be done, and for the next fortnight Baltimoreans were privileged to check on the merits and demerits of the additions and subtractions that were displayed on the stage of the Maryland Theater.

Back in New York Josephine was confronted with a domestic problem. As she wrote Jane, "My new apartment was filled with aunts and their civilized hours of living, so with the press of opening I moved to a hotel till the strain was over." The difficulty was that the old ladies, all agog with the excitements of a new world—a world at which they had once been wont to shudder—forgot all about their "civilized hours." They simply would not go to bed at the usual time, but insisted on waiting up until Josephine, tired out and wanting nothing but peaceful relaxation, came home and then sitting on the edges of their chairs to hear full accounts of each day's proceedings.

"But Aunt Nellie soon went back to Boston, so Aunt Gertrude and I hold the fort till they both go to New Hampshire in April." This experience taught her a lesson, and after that, she always parked Aunt Nellie in a hotel for her brief visits, and kept Aunt Gertrude with her till spring. She could cope with one at a time.

On January 10, 1941, *Arsenic and Old Lace* exploded before the eyes of those happy New Yorkers who were lucky enough to see history made that evening in the Fulton Theater. As Stark Young put it, they "screeched and roared" in delight. Backstage, Josephine was hugged and wept over by emotional aunts, cousins, and friends, and when she joined the crowd at Sardi's to wait for the morning papers, everyone in the restaurant rose to his feet and cheered in an ovation for which history had set no precedent. Then the throng settled down to kill time in the traditional Sardi fashion. Yet there was one departure from the normal. This time there were no fears of the big bad wolves of the dramatic pages. Kesselring's play was a house of brick and stone, not one of straw and hay, or sticks and twigs. When the papers came, there was a rush and the verdicts were read aloud with excitement.

> Let's not exaggerate. At some time there may have been a funnier murder charade than "Arsenic and Old Lace." . . . But the supposition is purely academic. For Joseph Kesselring has written one so funny that none of us will ever forget it, and Bretaigne Windust has directed it like a man inspired. (Atkinson.)
>
> The theater which is several thousand years old, has never produced anything quite like "Arsenic and Old Lace." (Louis Kronenberger.)
>
> The audience howled itself red in the face. (Burns Mantle.)

In the center of all this enthusiasm was Josephine. Thanks to the modesty of Karloff, the star, she was propelled, willynilly, into the rays of the spotlight, hand in hand with Jean Adair. "It is hard to remember," said Richard Lockridge "when acting more delightful has come along than that contributed by Josephine Hull and Jean Adair as the maiden murderers, Miss Hull, particularly, is without recent parallel in comedy." John Mason Brown was entranced by everything, but especially by "the chirrupy Miss Hull with her wondrous waddle and her sly comedy." It was a great night.

The yarn born of Joe Kesselring's grandmother has become a modern classic of the stage. No one exposed to it, as Atkinson says, is likely ever to forget it. According to Lockridge, the play, "starting from a preposterous premise, goes off so comically in so many directions that the mind boggles even when in direct contact."

A homey old house next door to a Brooklyn cemetery has sheltered for as long as anyone can remember a family that has, we may say, its own conceptions. It is now the domicile of two gentle maiden ladies, the last survivors of the older generation, and a nephew who thrives on the conviction that he is Teddy Roosevelt and that the front stairs are the embattled slopes of San Juan Hill. His aunts have such a reputation as ministering angels that not a policeman in Flatbush could ever be persuaded that they could be induced to look harshly at a fly. True, but their benevolence does lead them into strange ways. They are so moved with compassion for lonely old men who have no families to love them that they are sure the kindest thing to do is to put them peacefully to sleep with the aid of a few sips of elderberry wine, artfully doctored in the kitchen by Martha. Then after suitable funeral services—they are always careful to determine beforehand the faiths of their gentlemen callers—at which the two mourners appear swathed in yards of black crepe, Teddy lays them to rest in the locks of the "Panama Canal," which happen conveniently to be in the basement. All would be well but for the untimely return of the black sheep of the family, a nephew with sadistic tendencies who, thanks to the ministrations of his private plastic surgeon, has been made over to resemble Boris Karloff. Jonathan also has helped a goodly number of his fellow creatures to pass on to a better world, not, however, inspired by philanthropy. Now he has returned to make the old family home his headquarters, but must first dispose of a supposed brother, who has the misfortune to be a dramatic critic. For a while things look pretty black for Mortimer, and the gentle aunts are outraged because Jonathan is in open competition with them. Despite the obtuseness of the best-hearted policemen Brooklyn ever saw, Mortimer is saved from the cruel fate plotted by Jonathan. Having stumbled on the secrets of Panama, he arranges to have his two aunts—fairy-storywise, they turn out to be neither kith nor kin—placed quietly in a nursing home and Teddy conveyed to a sanatorium. Just before the gentle sisters are removed, they succeed in scoring a final victory over that "mean boy" Jonathan, by hospitably persuading the melancholy emissary of that institution to take "just a little sip" of their own peculiar brand of home brew. "Delicious!" he exclaims, and expires. Now their score is thirteen to their nephew's twelve, and the curtain falls on their happy smiles.

In the telling, *Arsenic and Old Lace* sounds as if it had come right out of the Grand Guignol, and would freeze horrified audiences to their seats like the dogs sticking to the sidewalks in the arctic temperatures of *The Skin of Our Teeth*. It did nothing of the sort—the audiences screeched and roared. The answer is that it is just a numbers game—thirteen to twelve—and, except when Jonathan-Karloff is whetting his knives, "an incredible air of sweetness hangs about this farcical melodramatic insanity." Anyway, who could resist Josephine when, confronted with the body of one of Jonathan's victims in the window box where she had recently deposited a Mr. Hoskins, she exclaimed in outrage, "That man is an imposter!"

The initial excitement having abated, play and actors settled down together for no one knew how long. *Arsenic* ran for 1444 performances in New York alone, though not, like *You Can't Take It With You*, with practically the same cast. There were illnesses and one death, and two were drafted. Some of the old originals were sent for a time to Hollywood to make a movie, and then to tour the country in addition to still another company. For Josephine the next four years were probably physically the hardest of her life. She was getting no younger, and her health was very far from good. Often it was only her grit that carried her through. The late Jane Oaker once said that her seven years in *Lightnin'* became a nightmare for her. After saying the same words over and over again, thousands of times, she became possessed with the terror that she would forget them. She knew that, if she were to try to think what she was to say next, she would "dry up" completely. So she sent her mind wandering off to far places and went through her part mechanically. There is no record that Josephine ever found herself in such a plight, but, having worked everything out in detail to her complete satisfaction, she varied her perform-ances not an iota. Exhausted and ill as she often was, if she had relied on the inspiration of the moment, all would have been irretrievably lost. Under such circumstances many actors go stale, but she never did. By some innate magic she managed, as Karloff says, "to make her thousandth performance as fresh and new as her first. She always knew precisely what she was doing. Even when her voice was completely gone offstage, the moment she emerged from the wings, the lovely tones were back and not even close friends were the wiser.

Responding to the approach of spring, John Anderson, dra-matic critic of the *Journal American*, had a happy inspiration. Wouldn't it be wonderful if *Arsenic* could be taken up to West Point as an Easter present for the boys? That such a thing had never been done before was no reason it shouldn't be done now, especially in war time. When he broached the idea to Lindsay and Crouse, "two of the kindest men on Broadway," they felt in with the plan immediately and ordered full steam ahead. Easter morning found Josephine, not in St. George's or the Little Church Around the Corner, but on a bus headed up the Hudson Valley, munching on apples provided by a member of the cast.

Although a bit tiring, it proved to be a wonderful adventure. More than two thousand cadets, officers, wives, and sweethearts jammed the Department Theater, and no previous audience had ever roared quite so loud. The stage displayed a replica of

242

Raymond Sovey's set, constructed down to the last detail by the cadets themselves. The furniture's rather grim associations made it singularly appropriate to the matters in hand. It had been the property of none other than General Custer himself, stowed away in academy warehouses ever since the Little Big Horn.

The single-throated roar that went up at the antics of Boris Karloff, Josephine Hull, Jean Adair, Allyn Joslyn and John Alexander, in Kesselring's cock-eyed thriller, suggested that the Army cracked more ribs in the theater than it ever had on the football field. I don't suppose the Hudson Valley has echoed to such a thunderous rumble of amusement since Washington Irving's legendary bowlers played nine-pins.

So Anderson, modest as he was about it, had every reason to be pleased with his inspiration. And probably no one derived more gratification from the afternoon than Howard Lindsay, who, incredible as it may seem, had never seen the play before. As Father Day in *Life With Father*, he had been busy elsewhere. "This seems to be a very funny play, something like a mixture of 'The Bat' and 'Charley's Aunt.' Maybe we ought to keep it open."

If the actors were not wined, at least they were dined, and the three ladies were weighted down with bouquets handed up over the footlights, as in Josephine's Radcliffe days. When at the end of the afternoon they sped away in their bus, followed by the cheers of the cadets, they left behind them just one unhappy man. An enlisted soldier had scheduled a christening ceremony for a regimental donkey. No one had come.

John Anderson was not the only one to have ideas. Out in California Frank Capra had them too, and one was to do a picture of *Arsenic* with as many of the original cast as he could kidnap from the Fulton, especially Josephine and Jean. Such a venture would involve a pretty violent wrench for a lot of people. On the other hand, the play had a lot of backers, and a cut of the movie profits would mean money in many pockets.

There was not too much trouble in reaching an agreement, although the two little ladies themselves had to be content with less than they had at first stipulated.

Capra's first inspiration had been to get none other than Bob Hope for Mortimer, but this daydream dissolved before his eyes; he settled for Cary Grant, who was probably much better in the part than the master of the wisecrack would have been. The producers balked at releasing Karloff, but fortunately Raymond Massey was available for the part, and after a good deal of struggling with various makeups, he was made over into a reasonably convincing double of the original Jonathan. Lindsay and Crouse did agree to let Capra have John Alexander, to charge up the Hollywood version of San Juan Hill, when they could find a substitute for him, as they succeeded in doing before the time came for him to go.

On October 17, after nine months on the stage of the Fulton, Josephine and Jean, having turned over the Brewster sisters to Patricia Collinge and Minnie Dupree, boarded the Golden Arrow, along with John and Genevieve Alexander—who celebrated their silver wedding anniversary en route—and Selena, Josephine's dresser. The long train trip fortunately allowed them to get much-needed rests, for once in Hollywood they were to be plunged into extremely strenuous routines. "Time for nothing but work out here," groaned Josephine. Usually she had to rise from her bed in the beautiful Chateau Elysée at five-thirty in order to be on the Warner lot for makeup, body makeup, and hairdo before the shooting started at nine. She was not frightened as she had been the first time, but she set about learning all she could. "After a few days," says Massey, she knew as much as any of us, for, on and off stage, she was a perfect listener." They all worked till six, and not till half-past seven were they back at the hotel. One of her greatest satisfactions came from the addition to the cast of Grant Mitchell, who was to be Dr. Witherspoon, the last of her winebibbers.

Despite her touching plaint, if there really was no time for anything but work, she manufactured it. She had some free days, and these she spent for the most part in bed, resting or

JOSEPHINE HULL, FRANK FAY, JESSE WHITE, FRED
IRVING LEWIS, AND JANE VAN DUSER
in a scene from the stage production of *Harvey*

JAMES STEWART WITH JOSEPHINE HULL
in *Harvey*

dosing one of her "hard" colds. But, no matter how she felt by day, an evening party was a party, and she could seldom summon up the resolution to say, "Get thee behind me, Satan." Hollywood is one of the "partyest" communities in the world, and it was full of her friends, all of them vying with each other in seeing that her nonexistent leisure did not hang heavy on her hands. There were the Nashes—Florence, Mary, and their attractive mother—Gene and Kathleen Lockhart, Edith Wynne Matthison and her husband, Charles Rann Kennedy, Beulah Dix Flebbe, and of course all the Stewarts, to name but a few. Grant Mitchell put his chauffeur at her disposal, and she reveled in luxury. But there were two sad notes. This time there was no Louise to welcome her home after her day's stint, and in the Pottenger Sanatorium "dear Thompson," who had given her so many courses of sprouts, was himself a patient. She returned from a visit to him with gloomy forebodings which were realized all too soon.

There were earthquakes too, that she found rather interesting. On December 7 the Japanese bombed Pearl Harbor. The cast halted work long enough to listen to Roosevelt's address to Congress, and then settled down again to the tasks before them. At last, on December 13, Josephine was through.

> Our last day on the picture of Arsenic & Old Lace at Warner's. Gifts—bedroom scene, poison recipe re-take, & a few others. Jean & I gave party to all on the set—fun.

The Jimmy Gleasons gave a big party as a send-off. Then, having sent boxes of fruit to everyone in the cast, she packed up and went home.

Life on the home front was not tranquil. The truants were welcomed back, but had to go through endless rehearsals, very inconvenient just before Christmas, in order to get back into harness. With the advent of the holidays came "the darlings" from New Hampshire as eager-eyed as ever. This time, having learned her lesson, she managed to keep her household under control.

The entry of the United States into the War of course gave new impetus to the activities of the Theater Wing, of which Josephine was still treasurer, and, now something of a celebrity, she found herself in demand as a speaker at rallies and luncheons. There were air warden meetings on the stage, and the Red Cross sent over emissaries to train the actors in the techniques of first aid. The cast itself was disrupted, for two members, Carl Fisher and Tony Ross, were drafted, and Jean had the first of a series of heart attacks which were to keep her on the sick list off and on to the end of the run. All this meant more rehearsals to break in the replacements and understudies.

The bad news from Europe depressed Josephine, all the more because the two Hull boys were now in service. It was therefore with a feeling of personal involvement that she carried her pound of sugar to the new Stage Door Canteen, and it was with a special feeling of appreciation that she found her dressing room brightened with flowers from Mrs. Sardi's garden—roses, irises, and peonies.

A welcome vacation began on June 28 and lasted until August 9. Perhaps, "vacation" is not the most appropriate term to apply to that period, for there was no letup in her extracurricular pursuits, and she had, besides, once more to break up her apartment. She was not to return to the Fulton, where Laura Hope Crews was now abetting Jean in her personal brand of "lonely hearts" operations, but was to start on a tour that was to take her into the hinterlands for no one knew how long. She found time, however, to go up to Lyme on July 14 for the lovely garden wedding of Henry's daughter Joan, to young Charles Turner. The bride's two brothers had been able to get off for the occasion, and among the guests she found her old associate of *A Thousand Summers*, John Griggs, whom she and Jane Cowl had so bewildered with their discussions of the occult.

With the end of her vacation came the beginning of a tour that was to keep her on the move for a year. Not since the days of *Jerry* had she been through anything like it. Yet there were differences. For one thing, it was wartime, and traveling conditions were far from luxurious or even comfortable. The trains were crowded to capacity with servicemen and their families. "I think," says Ilka Chase, "in the weeks I toured I never saw a fresh face or a clean train." Furthermore, the *Arsenic* cast could not count on fixed salaries. Everything depended on the box office and no one could forsee how, in such unpropitious circumstances, the public would behave.

Clear across the country they went, all the way to Los Angeles. When they reached the Biltmore, there, waiting to welcome them, was Karloff, who had gone on ahead.

The very day we arrived, Boris and some of his friends called for us in the afternoon, and drove the entire company out to his beautiful place in Beverly Hills. Such a charming spot, a rambling old California house and a garden that went up and down on stone steps with the most beautiful trees and shrubs and mossy nooks—and a beautiful blue swimming pool— around which we sat while the boys went in for a swim, and were served all sorts of delicious mouthfuls and cocktails in the afternoon sunlight, visiting excitingly and happily all the afternoon. Numerous friends dropped in and the party prolonged itself into a supper. In fact, poor old Josephine had to excuse herself and take an hour's nap in order to last through, accompanied, by the way, by the most beautiful white Persian cat.

The opening was so brilliant that everyone was blissful, and "top salaries" were forthcoming. One party followed another, but most exciting of all was a Heifetz concert in the Hollywood Bowl to which Grant, mindful of her love of music, treated her. "So wonderful in the evening air with the night closing down over us."

Three weeks in San Francisco were as glorious in their own way; spirits were high and salaries still "tops." Then the management made a mistake—it sent them back to Los Angeles. Unfortunately there had been a change. "War rationing of gas has Los A. in the jitters." They found themselves playing to empty seats, and the experience was not a pleasant one, either for the actors or for Messrs. Lindsay and Crouse.

That was not all. Josephine was beginning to realize more acutely every day that all was not well within her. "Not pleased with own condition, trying to be sensible." Being sensible meant turning down at least a few enticing invitations. Matters were made worse by the fact that Jean's heart was giving her a great deal of trouble, and Josephine had to take over some of her business. But they both stuck to their guns, and business began to pick up.

After two weeks the company returned to San Francisco for a fortnight, and then started East, through Oakland, Sacramento, Salt Lake City, and Denver, to St. Louis. Wherever they stopped, they were greeted by huge audiences and shrieks of merriment. In St. Louis for the first time Josephine had to decline Jane's hospitality—although she went to a party there that she enjoyed in spite of her obvious weariness. She stayed at the Mayfair down near the theater, a change that brought her one experience that did her no end of good. As one of her friends says, "If Josephine had a weakness, it was a craving for popularity and recognition." Those were the days of taxi-sharing. A passenger did not just climb in and ride off in solitary grandeur. One evening after a performance she had a young serviceman as a fellow passenger. He had seen the play and, thinking her one of the audience, expatiated on its delights. "I liked Aunt Abby best of all." As he politely handed her out of the cab at the Mayfair, he got a good look, and gave an audible gasp. Aunt Abby went up to her room in a glow.

In Chicago the glow, if it still endured, faded out. The Windy City had already seen another company and did not feel overinclined to compare its merits with this one even though the newcomer could boast of the "original Broadway cast." Worse still, the people who did come were not invariably polite. She complained once that they were "icy," another time that they were "low brow." The houses later improved both in quantity and quality, but she was getting desperately tired and more and more concerned about herself.

When she reached Cincinnati on December 3, she was in the dumps. "Terrible trip on dirty old day coach, no water—jammed all the way, only escape to diner, reached Cincinnati 1½ hours late. Hotel Netherland-Plaza, unpacked bags & fell into bed." Pittsburgh, which was next on the agenda, was almost too much for her, with its smoke and indifference. Just before Christmas after more hectic days en route, *Arsenic* reached good old Boston. Even the Touraine Hotel had grown shabby, but, after all, Boston was Boston, and she could spend the holidays surrounded by solicitous relatives and friends.

She was, however, reaching the end of her rope. When the weary company pulled into Philadelphia, after a hasty trip to Washington and Richmond plus three one-night stands, she knew the jig was up. She would have to break the record of which she was so proud, and ask the management for time off to go to Johns Hopkins for a checkup. She was humiliated, but she had no choice. Karloff says her friends in the company knew she often went on when she should have been in bed. "But, no matter how she felt, it was always opening night to her." Her request was granted as soon as made, and a month after Christmas she was flat on her back in the famous Baltimore hospital. As soon as she was able, she wrote Jane to explain why she would have to remain in seclusion at the Mayfair during a forthcoming stop in St. Louis.

When I learned that, instead of closing Feb. 6th, our tour was to turn right round and take me out to the West coast again, lasting at least till June—well, I had stuck it out till then, but just had to tell our managers I must have time out for a check-up at Johns Hopkins. (We were in Philadelphia.) They were so nice about it, for Jean Adair had had a heart attack on New Year's Day in Washington, and hasn't played since. So our understudy was doing her part—they sent for Cissie Loftus for mine, as she had played it in Canada.

No wonder I had been feeling meaner and meaner. I had diabetes—but it is controllable, and after two weeks in the hospital I feel like a different creature. I rejoined the co. in

Buffalo last Thursday, and shall be all right. Only of course I am under strictest orders as to diet and as to getting sufficient rest. It is going to be a terrific tour, but I am ready for it, and have taken my vows as to obeying my Dr's. orders.

Just before leaving the hospital Josephine learned of the death of Betty Merritt, but could not grieve, because the poor woman had been exhausted by her selfless care of Percival during his protracted illness. Still mindful of Josephine, she left her a legacy that was a help and a reminder.

Josephine was right; the tour was "terrific." The company backtracked to St. Louis and Milwaukee, *not* to Chicago, and after a week in the Twin Cities, journeyed across North Dakota and Montana in bitter March weather with five one-night stands in crude, drafty old theatres. In Fargo they fought their way through a blizzard to a tiny stage—"6 of us in upstairs change room at once." At Great Falls the first performance had to be canceled because half the company had stalled in the snow. Helena, among its beautiful snow-covered mountains, was dreary with ruins left from an earthquake eight years before. "Marlow Theater, S. R. O. Manager gave us baskets of fruit. Bad night in horrid room—roaring drunks."

The winds might howl and the snow might swirl, but in almost every town the theaters were filled. Many of the spectators were enjoying a novel experience, and the sight of real live actors present in the flesh and not just images on a screen was somewhat baffling. In one town the stage manager, treating himself to a bite to eat in a small café near the theater, overheard one of the waitresses regaling another with an account of what she had seen. "Have you seen this new picture at the Mayfair, the one with Boris Karloff? You ought to go. I never saw a picture in the flesh before."

At last they reached the welcome warmth of the coast—and everything changed. San Francisco almost succeeded in outdoing the enthusiasm of its previous welcomes, and even Los Angeles, recovered from its jitters, opened its arms to them.

Then back again to Seattle, where Josephine wrote at the end of a happy evening:

> Our last day of this wonderful, fearful tour. We closed with 2 sold-out performances. Boris gave me a mastodon ivory pin —Jean a satin bedjacket. Victor [Sundberg] & Linda a corsage. Goodbyes, telegrams, tears & laughter. Packed.

Whatever she may have thought at the time, she was not bidding a final farewell to Aunt Abby, not by any means. Lindsay and Crouse knew she was too precious a commodity to be allowed to escape as long as there were any signs of life in *Arsenic*. But before they tackled her again, Josephine had a long enough respite to establish herself again in Hampshire House, spend a few weeks in New Ipswich, and just to play safe, submit to another inspection at Johns Hopkins. Then, back at the Fulton again, she found that things were not the same. The producers were busy playing musical chairs with their actors, and scattering their blessings over the smiling land. Josephine's old confreres were being sent out to do the scattering, while in New York she and two others—and the old men in the cellar—were the only survivors of the original cast. Boris had been succeeded long since by Erich von Stroheim, and in Jean's place was Effie Shannon, the same Effie Shannon who had played opposite Shelley in *Under Orders*.

It might well be taken for granted that everything would be easy, that it would involve no effort for her to slip quietly back into her old part. Perhaps to her surprise, it proved to be quite the reverse. It took all her will power and the frequent ministrations of Dr. Sydney Kanev to see her through the ordeal, which lasted from August 9 until June 17 of the following year. Only when the last curtain had fallen did she, to her great mortification, get around to thanking Jane for her Christmas present.

> But, oh, Jane, playing my old murderess with a new (to me)

251

cast—all year in New York was a terrible task, and nearly laid me low for keeps,—so that literally *all* I could do was theater and resting up for the next performance. We moved to the Hudson Theatre, where I had the very same dressing-room Shelley had had in "The Cinderella Man"—that was a happy happening. But we were put on a schedule of two Sunday performances added to the two on Saturday, because of the war-time crowds, jamming everything on week-ends. [She doesn't say so, but they usually had Tuesdays off.] And as the Hudson rooms were all up a long winding iron stairway, my Saturday-Sundays gave me forty-four dashes up and down, on stage and off. I didn't think much about it at first, but it got me finally—so when we finally closed *I* was close—to a wreck! No excuse for not writing you, dear, but I was nothing but a *lump* between performances.

Josephine was not always the soul of accuracy, and when she told Jane that she literally did nothing but rest between performances, she was indulging in poetic license. It was true that she curtailed her party-going, but she could not think of turning down all the demands made on her for broadcasts and meetings that had to do with war work.

The high spot of the year's run came in March when she, Effie Shannon, Russel Crouse, and Walter Wagner took part in an Atlantic Spotlight radio program, with three members of the London company. "With ear-phones on, Effie Shannon and I did a scene with the London nephew Norton Wayne—and Dame Lillian Braithwaite and Mary Jerrold over there did one with *our* nephew. It was given there from the stage of the Strand Theater with the audience in front, and, believe me, one of the 'kicks' of my life was to say a line in the N. Y. radio and hear the London audience laugh!"

That was the last thrilling adventure Josephine had with *Arsenic and Old Lace*. On June 12 the final curtain fell. With 1444 performances they had broken the record of *Lightnin'*, but *Life With Father* was still—or rather, again—"packing 'em in." She gathered up her effects, including the "dear little picture from the set," which the managers bestowed on her, bade goodbye to Selena, and took to the hills.

After the play closed I went to Baltimore for a check-up. The old trouble is *completely* under control (a reward of virtue!), but the year's strain had caused blood pressure and tired heart muscles, so I am ordered *much* rest, which just suits me. It isn't really restful here with my aunts in one way, for "Help" is non-existent and I just couldn't let my two dear eighty-year olds do the work when I'm around,—but it is green and cool, —and so quiet one can do nothing but the house-and-garden sort of thing,—and much family visiting. My dear little older aunt is wasting away, gradually, and may do so indefinitely, but her spirit is unbeatable, and we have what might be called a good time together,—at least a comforting time.

I turn my back on play and radio offers, and don't want to think of work till just the right play comes along.

CHAPTER EIGHTEEN

RABBITS, RABBITS EVERYWHERE

SHE DIDN'T HAVE VERY LONG TO WAIT. On August 28 Brock Pemberton handed her the script of Mary Chase's *The Pooka*, better known to the world as *Harvey*, and then and there the course of her life for the next four years was settled. The producer had been so preoccupied in trying to find the right man for the role of Elwood P. Dowd, the amiable "lush" whose vagaries start the chain reaction of events in the play that, he admitted, he had given little thought to casting Elwood's sister, Mrs. Veta Louise Simmons. Then someone volunteered that the perfect person to play the poor woman was Josephine Hull. "I felt foolish," he told the students of the Yale Drama School, "because the only person to play Louise is Josephine Hull."

"I took the play to her," he continued. "We located her that evening. We found that she was at a broadcast of N. B. C. and we went there and waited from nine to ten, I think. With the script under my arm, I waited outside the door, and when she came out, I thrust it at her. She said, as actors always do, that she had several other things brewing. However, she said she would be glad to take it home and read it. And the next morning she rang up and was enthusiastic with joy."

He did not exaggerate, for she had fallen in love with Veta Louise the moment they met. She could just see and hear herself in the part, and knew that she would be "a riot." The unhappy lady is sure fire in her appeal. Men laugh at her because they find her uproariously funny in her perplexities, but they see her only from the outside. Women have an altogether different point of view, and she gives them a splurge of empathy. It is easy for them to imagine themselves in her place. They would scarcely wish to do that with the nitwit Penny Sycamore, and certainly not with that *femme fatale,* Abby Brewster, however benevolent her intentions, but the plight of the ultrarespectable Mrs. Simmons is very different. With a marriageable daughter on her hands, she finds herself daily embarrassed by the eccentricities of her gently bibulous brother and his buddy, an invisible six-foot rabbit whom he persists in introducing to her society friends. The ladies can also understand how she feels when, attempting to stow Elwood safely away in a rabbit-proof sanitarium, she is herself mistaken for the patient and dumped, protesting, into a hydrobath. No wonder she gets so upset that she sometimes thinks she sees Harvey herself! That could happen to anybody. All these truths Josephine grasped while she was reading the script, and no matter how many things were brewing, she wouldn't for anything have let Veta slip from her grasp.

While she was waiting for rehearsals to start, the movie of *Arsenic and Old Lace* opened at the Strand, and she hied herself over to the theater. She was not the only one who wanted to see it, and she discovered that to get in she had to stand in line on the sidewalk. Did anyone recognize her? Probably not, for it is unlikely that it would occur to anyone that she, of all people, would have to queue up. Probably too she was a bit let down, for she was noncommittal in her reactions to the picture. But there were compensations, and that evening she wrote: "An important day for me, with that and the news in the papers of my new engagement & featured in the Celebrities Service Sheet as 'Celebrity of the Day.'" Later she returned to the Strand, and enjoyed the film considerably more. Moreover, the enthusiasm with which it was greeted was very flattering.

Rehearsals, which soon started under Antoinette Perry, proved to be delightful. She took to her fellow actors—as she almost invariably did—and watched with admiration as Frank Fay developed his exquisitely underplayed Elwood. To make matters even better, the out-of-town tryout was scheduled for Boston. Although by this time she had more friends in New York, the old ones, most of them, lived in Cambridge or near the Common, and she wanted them to see her first. The reception of *Harvey* proved to be more wonderful than even their most sanguine anticipations, except at one performance when an experiment was tried that burned their fingers. Just that one audience caught a glimpse of Harvey in the flesh, or rather in a six-hundred-dollar rabbit suit. Now Pookas, like all fairy spirits, are most potent when invisible, and so it proved with Elwood's pal. He was never seen again, nor was the bunny suit.

In Boston Josephine and her confreres got the first taste of the rabbit fare which was to be their portion for years. At a luncheon given in their honor the table was gaily decorated with unusually beautiful carrots and lettuce, and, as an extra-special feature, there was a huge live rabbit arrayed in his own fur, which had not cost him or anybody else six hundred dollars. From that day on she was haunted by rabbits in every shape and form that nature or human ingenuity could invent, and unlike Harvey they were not invisible.

The New York opening at the Forty-eighth Street Theater on November 1 bore out all the promise of Boston. She found herself in another smash hit. "Oh, how fortunate I am & thankful!" While critical attention was naturally centered on the gentle Elwood, who declares, "I wrestled with reality for over forty years, and I am happy to say I finally won out over it," Veta Louise was by no means overlooked by the public, the critics, or those with whom and for whom she worked.

Mrs. Chase wrote her: "You have a quality—all your own—in your comedy which enraptures them." She went on to tell her about a boy whose mother had almost had to remove him bodily from the theater when Veta, coming on stage in a state of distraction, had exclaimed with relief, "Good! Nobody here but people." His rapture had very nearly wrecked the performance. No one else in the world could put into that simple ejaculation what Josephine did. But what pleased Pemberton above all else was the adroit and selfless way in which she worked on the team, as eager for the success of others as for her own.

> It is her presence, her technique, it is her delightful charming comedy that lays the scene for Mr. Fay to come in and mop up. I don't say that Mr. Fay is not magnificent, because he is, but that she is so successful in giving the background of this family and establishing the credibility of it, that what happens does happen.

Once more she found herself enmeshed in the consequences of being in a hit, the endless demands for autographs, the requests for appearances here and there, and the tormenting appeals for help. With the rest of the cast she was photographed for *Life* and *Vogue*, and interviewed for *Colliers*. Business boomed so that there was no avoiding extra performances. During the Christmas holidays there were so many that she cried out that it was "like a 2-a-day stock week." With Selena ministering to her, she snatched what rest she could in her dressing room, which Pemberton had decorated with a soft russet carpet and with wall paper displaying pink rabbits. But after she went home she sat up until four or five o'clock in the morning addressing cards and wrapping up presents until Christmas put an end to that. She lighted the candles beneath Shelley's picture, and sent her annual New Year's message to The Players.

A few months after *Harvey* opened, her old friend Walter Prichard Eaton, now on the faculty of the Yale School of

Drama, asked her to come to New Haven and talk to the students. She needed no second invitation, but had to wait until Dr. Kanev coaxed her voice back. She was always willing to help young people entering her profession to learn how to master its complexities, that is, provided they were serious and not mere dilettantes. Phoebe Foster, Sylvia Field, and Abby Lewis, among others, have spoken feelingly of her sympathetic interest when they were girls. While Kendall Clark was a young novice, he had the good fortune to be a member of a summer stock company with which she played an engagement, and he still remembers how she used to stay after tiring rehearsals to help him solve his problems. For years too she had taken a deep interest in Leighton Rollins' Theater School, and had been deeply touched when annual scholarships were given in her name. So the talk at Yale fitted perfectly into her scheme of things.

On a rainy morning in May, her vocal cords restored, she went, accompanied by Pemberton, up to New Haven, and gave the dramatic students a talk they were not likely soon to forget. She had an easy, natural platform manner, and spoke without a trace of the elocutionary style that sometimes passes for public speaking. There was much more of practical advice than of abstract theory, and all was lightened with appropriate reminiscences and touches of humor. Although they may not have realized it, she was giving them her own artistic credo.

Harvey ran gaily on through 1945 and attracted innumerable celebrities to Forty-eighth Street. Mrs. Roosevelt came, a few days before the President's death, and after the performance went backstage to congratulate the cast. Josephine was able to separate the person from the politics that were anathema to her. (It is not without significance that Josephine kept in her private archives several copies of "My Day" in which her Aunt Abby was praised. Then there were the other Roosevelts, the Republican ones, Mrs. T. R., Jr., and her daughter, who came to her dressing room bearing bouquets, Chief Justice Hughes, Governor Landon, Mayor La Guardia, the Duke and Duchess of Windsor, and Eddie Cantor. Whenever she was told that so-and-so was out front, she scurried about, spreading the good news, and always added "Wasn't it nice of him to come?"

Of great importance were the special performances at army and navy hospitals, where the actors brought laughter to the wounded boys. These moved Josephine deeply and left her thoughtful. At the same time they reinforced her almost religious faith in the spiritual mission of her profession.

There were honors in plenty, too, including the Pulitzer Prize. The winner of this of course was Mary Chase, but the actors had their days too, especially on July 5, 1946, when the Donaldson Awards were given to Josephine and Frank from *Harvey*, and Laurette Taylor, Julie Haydon, Eddie Dowling, and Tony Ross from *The Glass Menagerie*. At that time, Josephine had not yet seen the Williams play; she went in October with Mary Morrison, and wrote: "Laurette wonderful, exquisite play & performance." One of the best features of the award afternoon was that the gold keys and scrolls were handed out by Bert Lytell, old friend of New Orleans days, forty years before.

On May 19 Josephine took "poor Mary Hull" to the Stage Relief benefit performance of *Born Yesterday*, which, surprisingly, she pronounced "very vulgar." Why that particular play should have shocked her is not clear. She had taken many others with risqué lines in her stride, for in spite of her upbringing she was no prude and when she adopted the stage as a profession, she did so with her eyes open. She knew she would encounter many things of which she could not approve, but she had no intention of sitting in judgment. If a script was submitted for her consideration that she found offensive, she simply returned it. "Not for me." And, once she had agreed to appear in a play, even though there were passages she did not like, she felt that she had no right to demur. She simply ignored them.

Nor was she so unwise as to demand that all her acquaintances conform to her personal standards of conduct. She was an actress, not a reformer. She chose for her intimate friends those who shared her principles. Not that she hesitated to make her views known. She blew up from time to time, in a not very terrifying way, or, if deeply angered, she merely looked the guilty party coldly in the eye, and said, very quietly, "Mr. Brown." She was not the one to drop her eyes first. Thereafter, no matter how prominent the offender, she treated him with chilly formality.

Perhaps she took *Born Yesterday* too seriously because she was getting tired. Pemberton was perceptive enough to realize that people no longer in the prime of life need occasional breathing spells. So he began to mete out vacations. Josephine got hers first, six whole weeks beginning in June. She went at once down to Baltimore for another checkup, and then to Portland for a lazy time at the Eastland. She took the Casco Bay boat out to Peaks Island two or three times. The old Gem was gone, but she enjoyed the flowers. Once she was called back to New York by the death of "Tony" Perry, and went by plane, staying only long enough for the services. On her return, the flight from Boston to Portland was canceled and she had to go by the train, which she now found annoyingly "poky." Vacation ended with a visit to New Ipswich, and on July 20 she ensconced herself in the parquet for the novel experience of watching *Harvey* from out front. After studying Veta anew, she reopened two evenings later. "Fine houses, still turning 'em away." Then Fay took his turn, his part filled during his absence by Bert Wheeler.

The year 1947 had its ups and downs, among the former a complimentary comment by John Mason Brown in the *Saturday Review of Literature*, and her election as an honorary member of Phi Beta Kappa. Both were very cheering, but when May came around again, she was ready for another vacation. She permitted herself no more than two weeks at the Eastland, for she was needed in New Ipswich, where Aunt Nellie had begun the slow process of "slipping away." When she returned to Forty-eighth Street, it was to welcome Jimmy Stewart, whom an astute management had engaged to fill in for Frank Fay. This arrangement was a master stroke. The theater was besieged by such eager crowds that squad cars were required

JUNE LOCKHART, TOM EWELL, AND JOSEPHINE HULL
in *Kin Hubbard*

JOSEPHINE HULL AND LORING SMITH
in *The Solid Gold Cadillac*

to keep them under control. "Of course, Frank Fay was the ideal Elwood," she commented later, "but Jimmy Stewart is a terribly sweet boy and much more part of the family." She hated to see him leave when his engagement was over, and sent him off with a pair of cuff links. Reciprocating, he presented her with a "wonderful Sheffield pen and ink set." Happily, they were to meet again.

Meantime, in spite of booming business and continued honors, there was much to prey on her mind. The unhappiness of Mary Anglin, now retired, distressed her, and conditions at New Ipswich haunted her constantly. And she had other anxieties. Once more she suspected that all was not well with her health.

Relieved of her fears about the diabetes, she had relaxed her discipline. She took her insulin dutifully every morning, but otherwise she let down her guard. After the evening performances she and Frederica Going, her closest friend in the cast, would take a Seventh Avenue bus up to Hampshire House. The trouble was that she did not go directly to her apartment as she should have, but, despite all Freddie's protests, betook herself to a corner drugstore, where she perched herself on a high stool in plain view of all admirers, and indulged her passion for ice-cream sodas. She loved too to entertain friends, usually at Sardi's. Invariably she insisted that they order dessert, and then of course the tenets of Emily Post required her to take one too. Whatever Mrs. Post might have decreed, these pleasant practices were not approved by Josephine's doctors.

By fall, however, she had to face the fact that something was wrong—very wrong. One evening in the sanatarium scene she failed to rise from her chair when she was supposed to, and her dismayed fellow actors realized that she could not. Somehow they got her to her feet, supported her through what was left of the scene, and then steered her out through an exit. Nobody knew what would happen next. What happened was that when the curtain rose again, she marched out onto the set and played to the end as if nothing had happened.

Nevertheless, for all her determination, she could no longer

261

let nature take its course. In a few days she wrote: "Feeling very queer, all my left side. Ev'g performance holding onto things." The next day she gave in and summoned her doctors.

> Had Dr. Webster & Dr. Kanev, both at home & theater. Selena bro't little dinner to me in dressing-room. Left side is numb. They decided I must not play this week.

Much as she hated to surrender, she had to turn Veta over to Dora Clement. But the doctors didn't tell her that she mustn't have dinner with Callie and Bill Bement, and go with them to *Finian's Rainbow*. Probably she just forgot to mention this little project in their presence. After that sortie she stayed more or less docilely at home until November 1. That was the third anniversary of *Harvey's* opening, and it was unthinkable that she should miss that and the inevitable party at Sardi's that followed. Somehow she browbeat her doctors into letting her go, although the canny Dr. Kanev went along to keep an eye on her. A few days later she returned to Baltimore, where she received her usual royal treatment while undergoing tests. Back in New York again, she settled down once more with Veta, but heeded the advice she had received and cut down the number of her offstage activities. Meanwhile Pemberton guarded his valuable piece of property by protecting her as much as she would let him. He had a large chair placed in the wings, reserved for her exclusive use, and, at the suggestion of Helen Moore, he also provided a limousine to take her back to Hampshire House after the performance. For a basically unassuming person she could at times take a surprising amount of satisfaction in a little grandeur, and she did enjoy sitting back luxuriously in that limousine and sometimes sharing its comfort with less fortunate friends.

In January she emerged from her semiretirement in order to take part with Jean Adair, Howard Lindsay, John Alexander, and Edgar Stehli in a broadcast of *Arsenic* on the Ford Hour. She loved it and once more the public could hear her say as no one else could, "Now, I wonder who that can be?" as she studied the deceased stranger in the window seat. Jimmy Stewart came back for a final fling at Elwood and business soared. As soon as he left and Jack Buchanan took his place, it was once again "Minimum salary this week." After thinking the matter over and taking stock of the situation, Josephine decided that the time had come for her to say goodby to Veta and Harvey, and she asked Pemberton to find a replacement for her. His first impulse was to close the whole production, but he changed his mind and kept it open. Josephine's role was taken over this time by Frances Lawrence, in private life Mrs. John Feist, a friend of the O'Reillys, who had taught dramatics at the University of Kansas, and played with great success at the Little Theater of St. Louis.

Tired as she was, she could still summon up a surprising amount of strength when the occasion demanded it. On her next to last evening as Veta, Jane's youngest son, Elliott, brought his bride to see the play, and she entertained them with a late supper at Sardi's. The place was so jam-packed that a less indomitable person might have hesitated to make the plunge. Not Josephine! She just lowered her head and, with the newlyweds in tow, went through the crowd like a football end.

Of course she could not be permitted to quit *Harvey* without befitting ceremonies. No one knew that better than she did herself.

My last day in "Harvey." . . . Such flowers & gifts. Brock a gold bracelet, inscribed co., crew, musicians. Clarence & Tom a silver coffee set, cake and coffee at night for everyone. Telegrams, love, farewells.

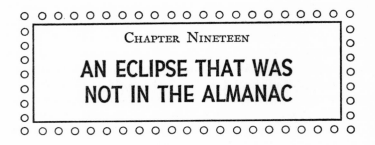

CHAPTER NINETEEN

AN ECLIPSE THAT WAS NOT IN THE ALMANAC

JOSEPHINE WAS WELL AWARE that she needed a long rest, but she did not intend it to exceed what she considered reasonable limits. She was not prepared to climb on any shelf; she never was. Long before her parting with *Harvey*, she had begun to lay the groundwork for her next venture. In February John Gassner had sent her a script to read that fascinated her. It was a gentle little Welsh fantasy called by its author, Richard Hughes, "a comedy of good and evil." So completely was Josephine taken with it that she not only contracted to act in it—she bought herself a share. Furthermore, she was to be starred. Gassner says he would not have given it without her. It seemed certain that it had the makings of her third hit in a row.

Minnie and Mr. Williams tells the story of a virtuous Welsh clergyman and his wife, who unfortunately has a wooden leg. For comfort in her difficulties she has one simple want—a cat named "Gladys." She gets Gladys all right, who, although feline enough, is really a little fiend in human form, dispatched to Wales by the Devil to ensnare the guileless soul of John Williams. Having a sportive nature, she loves to play pranks, of which Minnie is sometimes the victim. One thing Gladys does is to get Minnie a flesh-and-blood limb adorned with a very inappropriate red slipper, and then proceed to conjure it into all sorts of pranks that are very embarrassing to its new owner. All turns out for the best because Gladys succumbs to kindness and maneuvers poor John into heaven when he dies, instead of consigning him to hell as she was sent to do.

Gassner and his partner, David Dietz, like Josephine had complete faith in the play and assembled for it a cast of the first order. Eddie Dowling, fresh from his great success with *The Glass Menagerie,* was engaged both to direct it and to costar with Josephine. Elizabeth Ross was slated for Gladys, and there were also Clarence Derwent, Geoffrey Lumb, and Gwilym Williams, who tutored Josephine in the required Welsh dialect.

There were troubles almost from the first. At a rehearsal somebody spilled red paint all over Josephine's good coat. Then, there was that leg. Dowling says it was a plastic device equipped with a spring and a button by means of which Josephine could make it do unbecomingly obstreperous things. In one scene Minnie plays hymn tunes on an organ, and he had the inspiration that she could bring down the house if she were to jazz them up a bit and at the same time kick the devil-possessed leg out in unreasonable directions. To the pious Josephine this smacked painfully of sacrilege. Her credo required implicit obedience to her director, as she had preached eloquently to the students at Yale. But this was something different, and there were protests and tears. These so moved Dowling that he offered to forget the whole thing. Whereupon she executed a complete about-face. Those laughs would be too good to miss. "After all," she said to him with her eyes twinkling, "I think God has a sense of humor." She believed she would be forgiven just a tiny sacrilege. After a tryout in Boston, where *Harvey* had fared so well, the future of the play did not look so rosy as it had, and it was with misgivings that the producers took the play to New York, to open at "the dear old Morosco" on October 26.

"It was not, however," said John Beaufort, "a play to withstand the harsh autumnal blasts of Broadway." Burns Mantle, one of the few to see good in it, wrote: "One might say it should never have come to Broadway in the first place—but where else could it go?" His brethren so enthusiastically damned the fragile little piece that after two evenings the notice was posted, "Close Saturday."

"We hardly got started," complains Dowling, "before the trucks were back to cart us away, to the Golgotha of the theater, the dump where they burn the scenery—the one thing the critics and audiences can never defeat." Josephine herself had fared well enough, for everybody had liked her, and the errant limb had got its laughs. She had also reaped a harvest of no less than ninety telegrams and gifts. Yet there was blood rather than tears in her eye. She never forgot or really forgave the malicious-hearted critics, and there were times when her friends were hard put to it to keep her from telling them so in the most positive terms she was capable of. It is too bad that so innocuous a little comedy should have left such bitterness behind it.

Surprisingly after the unmerited demise of *Minnie and Mr. Williams*, Josephine became almost a stranger to the Broadway stage. It did not see her again for two years. In fact, for five years she was dangerously near to becoming in that garishly lighted district just a memory—albeit a pleasant one. During that half decade she was seen exactly forty-nine times. Forty-nine times in five years for the heroine of *Arsenic and Old Lace* and *Harvey!*

These few appearances were made in two comedies that were soon as lost in oblivion as the rejects of Shakespeare's Globe. The first was an expertly carpentered affair called *The Golden State*, written by Samuel Spewack and produced by his wife, Bella, at the Fulton on November 25, 1950, which held out for twenty-five performances, a long run compared to that enjoyed by poor *Minnie,* but certainly nothing to celebrate. Josephine did have the satisfaction of again seeing her name in electric lights above the door, but it was not exactly flattering to have it disappear after a few nights. Not even Josephine as a daffy old woman who thinks that she owns most of Beverly Hills could lure paying customers in any appreciable numbers. And that hurt.

Furthermore, her performance got her one of the few really uncomplimentary reviews she was ever called upon to digest. George Jean Nathan said she was tiresome. In his *Theatre Annual* he declared that in whatever role she appeared, she was always the same. This was one of the more-crabbed-than-accurate observations of Mr. Nathan. By way of contrast, Brooks Atkinson wrote a review so acute that it is worth quoting at length.

> There must be a lot of acting in her performance somewhere. But THE TIMES' hired theatergoer is unable to detect it. Churning with many emotions and bewildered by all the decisions that have to be made at once, she gives the impression of always being interrupted in something she intended to do but has forgotten. The personality seems tentative. Life just swarms all around her, and most of it is good. She is not cynical or bored. She is perplexed, perhaps. Little shadows of unhappiness hurry across her face when she hears something unpleasant. But she is an eager person who is overjoyed by little things.
>
> In another actress these qualities might be sentimental. But they seem true when Mrs. Hull expresses them. They seem sound and genuine and uncontrived. Although Mrs. Hull is not a sentimental actress, she induces plenty of sentiment in the audience. New York is crowded by men and women who will see that no harm ever comes to her.

"Too bad," he concluded, " 'The Golden State' isn't a more sprightly comedy."

When her next vehicle folded, again after a lapse of two

years, very few tears were shed even by the star, who heaved
a sigh of relief when she and Selena packed up her costumes
and makeup for the last time. Nevertheless, again she held the
gentlemen of the press responsible and spoke of them with
tearful resentment.

This play by Robert Finch went by the provocative name of
Whistler's Grandmother, but the resemblance to the famous
portrait stopped short with the title. "It was a lovely part. I
played an old woman who came into a saloon to get out of the
rain and sat there getting tipsy on beer. I guess people don't
like to see me get tipsy. They'd rather have me poison old
men."

She got tipsy in the President Theater, which was described
by one of her outraged friends as "an old barn of a place without heat." It was so cold that between acts Josephine had to
crouch over a heater in the forlorn dressing room at the back
of the stage. Luckily she wasn't called on to shiver very long,
for *Whistler's Grandmother* fell one short of its predecessor's
score of twenty-five.

Her absence from the Broadway stage did not by any means
result in inactivity. Quite the reverse. Indeed, there was too
much activity, and ultimately it led to no good. Only a woman
of extraordinary determination and stamina could have survived this pace at her age. Her doctors had to be constantly on
the alert, and there were frequent flights to Baltimore, where,
as always, she was on the most affectionate terms with her
physicians, their wives, the nurses, and the various members
of the staff. Through all this she remained outwardly blithe.

At least there were none of the financial anxieties that used
to plague her between engagements. She was in constant demand for radio and television engagements, and she no longer
had to trudge on foot to the studios. One day, catching her
breath for a few minutes, she sat down and wrote Jane another
belated acknowledgment of a Christmas present.

Honestly, Jane—such a life, hardly *human!* This season
plans constantly misfired, and I took to television plus radio,

a hodge-podge program, much more tiresome than a play—
but interesting medium, though exhausting to this old trouper.

The airwaves carried her face and her voice to even more
people than the theater, and she was recognized wherever she
went. She reveled in this celebrity and never made the slightest
attempt to dodge recognition. In fact, she exasperated her
friends by stopping on the sidewalk to write autographs for
all who asked for them. She beamed upon the world. It had
taken her a long time and lots of hard work to reach her present
eminence, and she had not the slightest intention of foregoing
any of its pleasant-tasting fruits.

In the midst of everything she had to move again. When
Hampshire House went co-operative in 1948, she transferred
her chattels to two expensively elegant rooms at nearby Essex
House. Among the decorations were two portraits of herself, one done years before by Henry Rittenberg, the other a
"lovely head" by Callie's husband, Bill Bement, which they
had brought her as a birthday present. The two rooms were
all she needed, for the old aunts were no longer able to visit
her, but kept her shuttling back and forth between New York
and New Ipswich.

The highlight of this period of her life was the picture of
Harvey for which she was engaged by Universal-International
to support Jimmy Stewart. The invitation brought her under-
standable exultation. She signed the contracts only after she
had, as usual, scrutinized them carefully under the eye of her
agent, Herman Bernstein. That done to the satisfaction of them
both, she was ready to go in March, 1951. "Henry sent his car
to take me to Grand Central," and, accompanied by Selena,
she was off again to the West Coast. But her happiness was
qualified by the deaths of two good friends, Brock Pemberton,
the producer of *Harvey*, and "dear Katie Grey."

In Hollywood she was greeted as usual by Rosalie and her
brother, and the Chateau Elysée outdid itself to make her comfortable. On the lot she found that Jimmy Stewart had turned
over his luxurious cottage-dressing room to her, a generous

gesture that puzzled the local bystanders. Why should Jimmy put himself out, literally and figuratively, for the likes of her? Who was Josephine Hull anyway? She was not a celebrity on the lots of Hollywood.

Her cheerful frame of mind continued until she saw the results of the first test shots the cameramen made of her. Then it vanished into thin air. "Dreadful! Conferences!" Retakes were so bad that all she could write in her diary was "Disgusted!" Further experimentation, with new makeup and new hairdo's, placated her, and she was ready for Veta. When she saw the finished shots just before going home six weeks later, the misdeeds of the cameramen were not mentioned.

At this point she would have liked nothing better than to be allowed to sink down among her possessions in Essex House and catch her breath. Such relaxation was not to be, for word came that Aunt Nellie was ill and she was needed in New Ipswich. There she stayed a month, helping the nurses and doing the housework, for there was a limit to what Aunt Gertrude, now nearing ninety, could do. Just when she was about ready to start home, Aunt Nellie fell at the head of the stairs, but, praying for the best, Josephine left anyway. Plans for *The Golden State* were brewing, and she had had all the "vacation" she could afford.

The Spewack comedy was no sooner deposited in its grave than a call came from Rosalie's brother, Stuart, who told her that Universal-International wanted her again, this time for a film to be known as *The Lady from Texas*. She had never been a cowgirl, and she found the prospect intriguing. Conditions in New Hampshire were worse than ever, but, as she put it, the "wherewithal" was necessary, and reluctantly she agreed to go.

This visit to Hollywood coincided with the big event of the year, the ceremonial bestowal of the Motion Picture Academy Awards. She was excited and a bit flustered at the prospect of being part of the grandiose affair. Was she suspicious that one of the Oscars might come her way? Or afraid that it mightn't? Whatever she felt, she knew one thing, and that was that she must appear at her best. Accordingly she spent the morning in the hands of a beautician. Tightly curled and decked out in a mink stole borrowed from the costume department, she was ready for whatever happened.

> Stuart took me (orchid) to Pantages to the Academy awards —most exciting. I recd. an Oscar for best supporting actress in "Harvey." Spoke. Saw Ethel Barrymore, Helen Hayes, Ruth Chatterton.

The next day she proudly bore her trophy to the lot, where she was given a luncheon with an impressive cake on the table, and gorgeous roses from Jimmy. "Returned mink stole to wardrobe." By now she was a celebrity in Hollywood too.

Her happiness was short-lived, however, for the inevitable happened in New Ipswich. During a rehearsal, she received a call from Mrs. Luhtala, Aunt Nellie's nurse, who told her that the old lady had died. There had been four old aunts, and now there was only one. There was nothing to do but return to the set, and, later, telephone Aunt Gertrude, order flowers, and drop in at St. Stephen's Church "for a little prayer." Sympathetically Rosalie and Beulah Bondi saw that her spare moments were filled with activity.

As soon as *The Lady from Texas* was successfully shot, Josephine hurried back East, depleted physically and emotionally. Wisely she stayed at home for two weeks, summoning up strength to face the ordeal ahead. Then she went to Aunt Gertrude. Probably excited by her arrival, the old lady promptly fell down and broke her arm. That meant Mrs. Luhtala again, fortunately an affectionate and capable nurse. It meant too that practically all the household chores landed squarely on Josephine's shoulders. She had to do the cooking, keep the house decently "redded up," carry the garbage out to the little nook in the stone wall at the back of the place, and, when the June weather turned wintry, bring up the firewood from the basement. It helped that some of the meals were brought in from the Maynard's across the street, but still she had plenty to do in addition to carrying on the voluminous correspondence that followed her north, and studying play and television scripts. When, to everyone's amazement Aunt Gertrude was discharged by her doctor, Josephine took herself off to the Essex, where she fell on her bed and slept ten hours in a row.

One of the scripts Josephine had read was *Kin Hubbard*, a comedy about the late Indiana journalist, that the Langners wanted her to do at their summer playhouse in Westport. Tom Ewell telephoned her about it, and she thought it at least worth considering. The play involved her in one of the adventures of her life, but she was not in a particularly adventurous mood, and, except that it served later as a conversation piece, she would have been satisfied to dispense with it.

The Westport Country Playhouse is an old barn which Lawrence Langner and Armina Marshall had converted into an attractive theater in which they could experiment with plays that interested them. Now at the tag end of its twentieth season, their son, Philip, wanted to see what was in this new script by Lawrence Riley. In addition to Josephine and Ewell, he engaged June Lockhart, Queenie Smith, Fred Lewis, and John Alexander to put it across.

Josephine settled comfortably in a pleasant room at the Inn, which had what seemed at the moment a great advantage, a quiet remoteness from all other human habitation. There was a tang of autumn in the breezes that blew down from the Berkshires, and she was all set for a refreshing interlude between responsibilities.

On September 4, after a day devoted almost uninterruptedly to last-minute rehearsals, she was tired. The play opened brilliantly in the presence of enthusiastic friends, including Mrs. Hubbard herself. Josephine was elated when the last applause was stilled and she could head for her waiting couch. The grateful Rileys volunteered to drive her the short distance back to the Inn, and with a sigh of relief and happy anticipation she climbed into their car. The Rileys, however, were not at home in that part of Connecticut, nor familiar with the roads about Westport. They took off gaily in the wrong direction, and went on till they were brought up short by the lights of New Haven. That meant reverse action and further exploration. Two hours after leaving the Playhouse, they pulled up at the door of the Inn, deposited their passenger on the threshold, bade her an apologetic good night, and drove off. The Inn was as silent as Juliet's Tomb before Romeo and Paris crossed swords at its gates. What happened next June Lockhart got at first hand from the lady herself.

When she got in, she found that her key was locked up behind the desk in a cage-like affair. She could see the key, but couldn't reach it. The telephone was also behind the cage, so she couldn't summon help that way either. She went upstairs and tried her door—it was locked.

After some investigation she found that she was the only guest in the place, and the manager had gone somewhere else to spend the night! The Inn was actually closed, because we were doing the show *after* Labor Day, and practically everything in Westport shuts down after the first Monday in September. The Inn was located far out in the country, and she couldn't even walk to a neighbor's for help.

There wasn't a lobby for Mrs. Hull to sit in, no heat in the building, so she went to the kitchen because it was the warmest room. There was a large table in the huge New England kitchen and one chair. She put her little satchel and her script down and tried to make herself comfortable.

But that was not easy. Mrs. Hull was a very tiny woman, and, no matter what chair she sat in, her feet never touched the floor. (As a matter of fact, on stage in "Kin Hubbard" there was one chair which was "hers" to sit on; it was dead center and had the legs cut off, so that they were about 6″ long. This made her seem and look very comfortable, but was preposterously funny when other actors sat in that chair with their chins on their knees. I know, because Tom Ewell and I did it!

Time passed and still no one came to let her into her room. She kept her coat and hat on, and I can imagine must have been a very pathetic little figure, sitting there in the glare of one

273

light bulb, with the wind whistling outside the kitchen windows.

Some time after four a.m. she was aware of a dripping noise from behind what seemed to be a closed pantry door. It continued for some time, and then she noticed, seeping out from under the door, a puddle of blood! She stared at it—this star of "Arsenic and Old Lace"—and was too horrified to look behind the door. She had nowhere else to go. So she decided to ignore it.

It was five minutes after seven when the cook arrived for work, gave her the key, made her a cup of tea, and Mrs. Hull finally went to bed.

The blood? The cook explained that it was meat thawing. And, as it thawed, it dripped.

Mrs. Hull never could sleep well during the daytime, she said; so she had only a little nap that morning. At 12 noon she was at the theater, bright as a button, regaling us with her night's adventure, and ready to do a matinee and evening performance.

The next night she moved to Mrs. Kellie's on Main Street.

Returning to New York by late train after the last performance, she sat down to take stock of her situation. She was not, however, allowed much leisure for cogitation, for she was immediately overwhelmed by overtures and demands of various sorts, most of them professional, but many social. One invitation moved her deeply. Ever since Shelley's death The Players had held a unique place in her affections. Not once through the thirty-two years had she failed to send the members her New Year's greetings, and never when she could help herself had she missed a Ladies' Day on Shakespeare's birthday. So it was with deep emotion that she learned that she was to be guest of honor at the annual luncheon on the birthday of Edwin Booth. Seated at the head table, she was introduced by the president, Walter Hampden, and "spoke to Shelley's beloved club." Then with the members present she crossed the street into Gramercy Park, where a wreath was laid at the foot of Edmond Quinn's statue of the Prince of Players.

Among the scores of scripts she studied she hoped to come

across one of a play that would suit her, but she found none that she would touch. Radio and television were different, and she passed the season, as it were, on the airwaves. Summer, of course, brought more pilgrimmages to New Ipswich.

As we have seen, the season of 1952–53 opened in melancholy fashion with *Whistler's Grandmother*. At the end of January there came a hurried call from New Ipswich, where Aunt Gertrude was near death. To save her, the doctors wanted to amputate a limb, but she told Josephine that she intended to take out of the world everything she had brought into it. And she did.

For the first time in her life Josephine was free of family responsibilities. For as long as she could remember, the "darling aunts" had been on her mind, and in everything she did had to be taken into account. Even when she went her own way, instead of the one they would have chosen, she had to assuage their feelings and soothe their apprehensions. Into this scheme of things Shelley had entered gallantly. Yet the reassurances worked both ways, for, whatever happened to her, she always knew that they were standing by to help her in any way they could. Letters, cards, and presents crossed each other in the mail. Every Saturday evening precisely at six, she telephoned them to check on their individual healths and to compare their solutions of the "jumbled word puzzles" in the *Times*. Her diary is witness to her constant preoccupation with their well being. Now the load was lifted, almost but not quite, for death does not solve all problems.

There still remained the house in New Ipswich, with all its accumulations. Nellie had left it to Gertrude, and now it was all Josephine's—heirlooms, antiques, books, Aunt Fanny's watercolors, and a thousand useless trifles. The thrifty old ladies had never thrown anything away. All this assortment had to be disposed of in one way or another. But it would have to wait. She was busy. And she was not well.

On her way home from a matinee of *Dial M for Murder* she had what she called "a gasping fit." Two nights later she had another. She called her doctor, and was told to keep quiet.

As usual she interpreted that instruction in her own way. She stayed at home all day, but in the evening went with Beulah Bondi to see *Midsummer Night's Dream*. "Bad, but we enjoyed our visit." After a few days she underwent a number of tests, including an electrocardiogram administered by a very nice young lady-doctor. Then she received the verdict. "I've had 'walking pneumonia.' Knew I was sick."

There were other things to weigh her down too. Mary was in a nursing home, and visits to her were sad. And Jean Adair, "sweet friend," was dying. She went to see her too, and kept in touch with her nurse. When the end came, she went with Mary Morrison and the Kesselrings to the funeral. Her usually buoyant spirits were having a hard time these days.

Two weeks later, early in June, she braced herself for the task ahead and went up to New Ipswich for the last time. She had decided to sell the house and everything in it except the few articles she could not bring herself to part with. With Mrs. Luhtala to help her, she put on old clothes and went to work. It took them weeks to sort things out. Then came the sale, which proved to be a civic event of the first order. It was not every day that one could see a famous actress and movie star auction off her heirlooms. Neighbors and tourists swarmed all over the lawn and crowded the house. One day Henry and Julie drove up from Lyme to lend their support. The ladies of the Congregational Church served refreshments. In the midst of it all, torn to bits inside, was Josephine. "I saw the old things marching out the door like my life marching out."

When at last it was over and the doors were locked on the empty rooms, she took refuge at the Eastland and went into seclusion.

CHAPTER TWENTY

"TO-NIGHT JOSEPHINE"

This is a fairy story—the story of Cinderella and the four ugly corporation directors. Once upon a time, not so long ago, Cinderella went down to Wall Street, not in a gold coach drawn by six white horses, but in the I.R.T. subway.

THIS IS WHAT THE VOICE OF FRED ALLEN SAID over the loud speaker in the Belasco Theater about Mrs. Laura Partridge, ex-actress. And Laura Partridge was Josephine Hull, or vice versa. So far as Josephine *in propria persona* was concerned, there were a few inaccuracies in Mr. Allen's remarks. In the first place, she was not an *ex*-actress; not if she knew it, she wasn't. Then she went, not to Wall Street, but to Forty-fourth Street (where the Belasco is), and, instead of four ugly corporation directors, there were three very kind and solicitous gentlemen, two of them authors, Messrs. Howard Teichmann and George S. Kaufman, and a producer, Mr. Max Gordon. (It is true that Mr. Kaufman was also a director, of the Broadway, not the Wall Street variety.) Otherwise Mr. Allen was not too far wrong, except that her means of transportation was neither a glass coach nor a subway, but a Cadillac limousine.

This particular fairy story first got really under way in very unpleasant times, shortly after Aunt Gertrude's death, when Josephine was perambulating about with walking pneumonia

277

and badly needed something to brace her morale. So the news that Kaufman and Teichmann were actually completing the comedy they had threatened her with when she was in Hollywood was well calculated to cheer her. Of course she observed the convention referred to by Pemberton, and said that she "had several things brewing"—she did—but she would not have missed this chance for anything. She lost no time in consulting Bernstein, who gave her "good advice." That advice obviously was to seize the delectable goods proffered her, for he shortly returned with Kaufman and a few days later Josephine signed the contract. Her pleasure in the new prospect gave her strength to face New Ipswich and the auction. On August 7, refreshed by the sea breezes of Portland, she was back in New York, and ready to climb into her new vehicle.

The Solid Gold Cadillac had its own ways of going about its business, not the stereotyped ones of the ordinary Broadway play. For one thing, it made liberal use of a public address system (and Mr. Allen), and, for another, of motion picture cameras placed in such strategic spots as airports and courthouse steps, where Josephine went in her limousine, to have her picture taken with Loring Smith, her costar. She also journeyed out to Mineola for studio shots and sound dubbing. Besides all that, there was much ado about costumes. The first inspiration was to have her dazzle the ugly corporation directors by presenting herself at the stockholders' meeting in a flaming red dress, but after some experimentation that garment was stowed away in the closet.

Then there was a discussion about her status. "Actually," says Teichmann, "she had to be urged to accept star billing. Being the modest woman she was, she was ready—even eager— to accept feature billing. That is billing under the title of the play"—not Josephine Hull in *The Solid Gold Cadillac*, but *The Solid Gold Cadillac* with Josephine Hull. But, if they insisted on starring her, she didn't mind a bit, and anyway Loring Smith was to share the honor.

One of the things that practically overwhelmed her author was the modesty he refers to.

During rehearsals Mrs. Hull was the model of what every actress should be. She was never late, she never questioned or quibbled about a line; she never complained of the heat, the length of the rehearsal, or the hours set for these rehearsals. There was one time on the road, however, when she was five or ten minutes late. To my utter surprise, she came in, went directly to George Kaufman and apologized personally to him, came over to me, apologized, and then apologized to every member of the company before allowing the rehearsal to begin. It's the only time I have ever seen anyone in the theater behave with such great courtesy and such thoughtfulness.

One thing bothering her, though not too seriously, was her memory. "Having trouble with lines—darn it!" She had had such trouble before, without coming to grief, and this part was shorter than many she had played. Ann Noyes came in to cue her. Josephine seemed to think nothing should be wasted, for if she dropped a line in one scene, she usually managed to stick it in later.

Cadillac opened on September 28 in Hartford and "Everything went well, considering." Knowing that others would probably be nervous, Josephine sent Mrs. Teichmann a box of flowers. "I know what it's like to be a wife in the theater on opening night." Hartford was cordiality itself, and sped the parting guest on to Washington with doubts comfortingly laid to rest. The capital opening was a nightmare. Teichmann still recalls that evening with a shudder.

Actors forgot lines, the bulb in a lamp hanging center stage exploded, sending a shower of sparks to the floor, the curtain was fouled once or twice, the electrical system which ran the public address system so that the audience could hear the narratives in between scenes went out of whack completely.

Whatever anyone else may have felt, the star seems not to have been fazed for all she recorded in her line-a-day was the imposing list of the VIP's on hand. William Douglas might have been a bit surprised to find himself promoted to the chief justiceship of the United States. She went to sleep and forgot the whole matter.

The next morning, however, she was subjected to one of the cruelest blows she ever had to suffer. One critic, not content with tearing the play to shreds, wrote that Josephine Hull had "the body of an old coal barge and the face of an ugly English pug."

The company was aghast. "I saw Mrs. Hull cry for the first and last time," says Teichmann. "She told me that there was very little she could do about her body at this stage of her life, and the same went for her face. If he had criticized her acting, it would have been one thing, but to criticize an old lady's physical qualities was something else."

The Washington debacle was followed by much rewriting and endless rehearsals; the play the Quaker City saw was a substantially different one. The reviews were suitably replete with brotherly love, and everyone read them aloud to Josephine. "What a joy it was to see her face! Finally she was unable to contain herself. She burst out into that wonderful smile and did a little dance around the sofa." Actors, playwrights, stage hands, Selena, and everyone else flattered themselves that the malicious gremlins had been chased away for good. But gremlins, as everyone should have known, are notoriously persistent and very hard to exorcise.

The night before the opening in New York there was a paid preview, and that night was worse, if possible, than anything that had happened in Washington. Not only did the mechanical aspects of the play go wrong—the worst being that the stagehand who pulled the curtain at the end of the play sent said curtain, not down onto the stage floor, but high up into the grid, leaving the actors stranded helpless before the audience—but also, it was the night when Mrs. Hull forgot more than just one line. She came on, spoke a few lines, and then inexplicably skipped some fifteen minutes of exposition and characterization to the end of the scene. Chaos reigned. Everyone knew we were doomed.

No—one person knew no such thing. Perhaps she was unaware of what had happened. "Went well."

The next evening, an hour or so before curtain time, three frightened men, huddled together in the empty auditorium, sat staring at the bare stage. Out of the wings came a little old lady in her dressing-grown, "a pathetically small, frail, and helpless figure." She stood there a few minutes looking out over the house. Then she turned and made her way slowly into the wings.

She always reached the theater long before anyone else, for putting on her makeup was a very slow process, and she did the whole job herself. Even Selena was not allowed to do more than hand her what she required. "She used the old style of mascara, a candle burning, a bar of mascara melted over it, and a match-stick to pick up the melted mascara and apply it to her eyelashes." Her hands shook, but she managed everything herself, except that she allowed the maid to adjust her "wiglet."

Just before she left her dressing room, she was handed a telegram. It was from Howard Lindsay, and it contained just two words: "To-night, Josephine."

At twenty minutes to nine on November 5, 1953, the curtains opened on "Josephine Hull in *The Solid Gold Cadillac*." Draperies concealed all but the center of the stage. Through the opening the audience could see, in their accustomed places, the four ugly corporation directors nefariously conducting a stockholders' meeting. One brief glimpse was enough to show everyone in the crowded Belasco that they were up to no good. Being up to no good, they were in very high spirits. Little did they know that behind the curtain that hid her from those out front sat their nemesis, her tiny feet scarcely reaching to the floor. Then the curtains were pulled wide apart, and, as one spectator put it, the audience nearly jumped out of their seats with a roar that shook the old theater.

*A dumpy little woman has got to her feet. A real charmer,
but tough. Having got up, she is really never going to sit down
again till the show is over.*

When the show is over—almost, not quite—and she does sit
down again, the ugly four have fled, and she and her Prince
Charming are seated in their chairs. We fear, maybe, that they
also are not up to too much good. Just as at the beginning a little old lady rises to her feet and comes forward with a question.

"Oh no. That's how I got my start! The meeting is ad-
journed." And Laura bangs down her gavel so hard that the
curtain man hears it and this time does exactly what he is supposed to do.

Josephine had forgotten not a word, a line, or the minutest
bit of business. It was incredible. "She was magnificent."

"Josephine Hull is the nearest thing to a human plum pud-
ding there is." Evidently the theater was crammed with devotees of that succulent dish, for the applause was deafening,
and it went on and on, while the actors bowed to the audience,
bowed to each other, and bowed to the little lady in their midst
while she beamed upon what was for the moment her world.
What that world had been privileged to participate in was the
culmination of a long career. It had seen some superlative comedy acting, often so subtle that, as Atkinson had said, you
couldn't put your finger on it. For instance, there was the not
so innocent innocence with which she had faced the evildoers,
the appalled expression as she watched Smith declaiming
"Spartacus to the Gladiators," and, best of all, the inimitable
emptying of her desk after she had been dismissed by the directors—before she had them on her still well-padded hip with
her proxies. Richard Rodgers said that if she had not found
that second galosh, he'd have stayed in his seat till morning.
"I'm always addled in my plays, but in a smart way."

When the tumult had subsided and she could edge her way
out of her dressing room, she departed in her Cadillac—not le-
gally hers, just chivalrously when she needed it. This time, in-

stead of going to a party at Sardi's, she gathered relatives and friends about her, and took them home for a modest celebration there. Then she went to bed "shut up in measureless content."

Next day the reviews were a chorus of praise. Every two minutes the telephone bell jangled, and one florist boy trod so fast upon the heels of another that it seemed all the flower shops must be depleted of their wares. Best of all, on the first snowy day of winter, a line extended from the box office through the lobby, out into Forty-fourth Street, and almost down to Sixth Avenue. At last Josephine Hull was the star of a Broadway hit of the first magnitude.

Once again the great sought her out to do her homage. One evening no less a personage than former President Truman, with Margaret smiling at his side, came knocking at her dressing room door. There was no denying that he was a Democrat, but politics stopped at the footlights. She was thrilled and asked him to sign her guest book. He did and that, she had to admit, was more than any Republican President had ever done. What is more, she had her picture taken with him.

There were other unprecedented results of her triumph. No one pestered her now about elderberry wine or invisible rabbits—they wanted tips on the stock market. The Chase Manhattan Bank ran an advertisement proclaiming to the world that she had carried an account there for years. Robert R. Young was inspired to run one too, a whole page, announcing that she was backing him in his fight for control of the New York Central, but she, along with other minority stockholders, squelched that scheme a-borning. How silly can people be? And how nice!

It was all wonderful. Too bad it couldn't last.

In December she began again to feel unwell. Her eyes bothered her, and she lost her breath when she walked. And Christmas was coming up with "1000 things to do." The doctors laid down the law. She must take care of herself. "So far behind in everything, & told to rest, not worry, let things slide." Visitors to her dressing room at the theater saw a large bathtub, installed years before by Belasco for the benefit of Lenore Ulrich, who had to use body makeup in one of her roles. Now the three solicitous gentlemen who at least tried to look after her while she was on the premises found another, an unorthodox, use for it. They transformed it into a couch on which Josephine reposed between afternoon and evening performances and occasionally at other times. She was growing uneasy about her work, and anxiously questioned callers to find out if they had detected any slackening. Of course they all reassured her.

To the pages of her diary, for over fifty years, she had confided everything, big or little, that had made up her life. But now when she got home she was too tired. On Sunday, December 20, she wrote:

> Callie & Bill called, she ill, cannot go to perf. of Teahouse of the August Moon. Dr. Webster called up, glad to go. We have Ziegfeld car both ways—beautiful performance, Wayne, Forsythe, splendid co. Enchanting play.

Then she put her line-a-day away for good.

She did not become a recluse. She continued to have a few friends in for tea and small sandwiches, and to go to a few public affairs. On May 4, at a luncheon at the Hotel Pierre, she was given the Delia Austrian Medal Award, which is given annually by the Drama League of New York. "It was," says Teichmann, "a joyous occasion for her, naturally. However, it required her to appear Tuesday afternoon, Tuesday evening, Wednesday afternoon, Wednesday evening. Thursday she had off during the day, played a performance Thursday night. Then came that awful Friday evening."

She was obviously in no condition to go on stage, but one thing not affected was her grim determination, and on she would go. Had she grasped the truth, she might have yielded, especially if she could have foreseen the results. However, on she went, not only that evening, but twice the next day. The performances were nightmares. She had great difficulty in walking, her speech was thick, and she was often at sea in her lines. Smith and the others never knew when they would be called upon to pick up cues from *Arsenic*, *Harvey*, or any of the other plays she had been in. Of course the audience saw that something was wrong, and not a few, drawing the most deplorable conclusions, went to the box office and demanded their money back.

On Monday Teichmann, who had been out of town, found her waiting to try again. "I had had a grandfather who had suffered a stroke, and Mrs. Hull gave every evidence of similar symptoms." It was impossible to pretend any longer that she had just a bad cold. She was hurried to the New York Hospital, and Ruth McDevitt took over as Laura.

Yet Josephine had not the slightest intention of crying quits. After her release from the hospital, she betook herself to the Eastland, shut herself up, and set about preparing for her return. For one thing, she had to learn to speak again, for there were times when it was almost beyond her power to make herself understood. She persisted doggedly and was at least partially successful. Walking, also, was a problem, and one eye had to be held open by an annoying wire contraption. At last she decided that she was ready, and notified the management that she would be back on the job on August 1.

Teichmann had taken over the direction while Kaufman was abroad.

I found her in the star's dressing room, surrounded by the cast, and with two canes. I had the stage manager call the company on stage and began the rehearsal. I saw Selena help Mrs. Hull into the wings stage left. I saw Mrs. Hull stand there held by her canes and by her maid, and then, when her cue was given, she put aside the canes, gently shook herself loose from Selena, and somehow, God knows how, she made her entrance. It was one of the bravest moments I have ever seen on the stage. She was able to walk four steps to the chair where she was to sit, and there, holding the back in her hands, she began her lines. I had re-staged the play so that at no time was she out of reach of a chair or a table or some support. The one time when she had to make an exit away from any furniture, an actor was detailed to assist her offstage.

Since no one had any idea what to expect, there was no public announcement that she was about to make a comeback. When the astonished and delighted audience recognized her, there was a salvo of applause that made her struggles worth while. In one way or another she contrived to get through and so did the rest of the cast, although on tenterhooks, for three weeks.

Early in the morning on August 24, she fell over a table in her room, and could not, try as she would, get back on her feet. For a few minutes she lay there, until she managed to crawl to a small table and reach the telephone. She called the office downstairs. Would the clerk please be so kind as to send a bellboy up to 607? Whatever else may have happened to her, one thing was unchanged—her sense of propriety. After all, she was a new England lady, and she was in her nightgown. So she added: "Be sure to send a married bellboy."

The doctor found that she had broken a rib, taped her up, and dosed her with codeine. The next evening, her lips locked on her secret, she presented herself as usual at the Music Box. When the curtain rose, there she was in her familiar chair. The "whim of iron" died hard. But it was plain to see that something was amiss, something even worse than before. Ruth McDevitt was summoned and stationed in the wings, ready to go on when the inevitable collapse came at last.

I shall never forget the agony of her last performance. She was so dopey with pain and codeine she couldn't remember her lines, and was afraid to move. I had to leave the wings in tears.

"I have often wondered," concludes Mrs. McDevitt, "if she realized it was to be her last time on the stage." She did not,

not then or later. Evening after evening she returned, was made up, and waited for the entrance that was never to be hers again. No, she did not realize it. But Josephine Hull's long career had closed.

CHAPTER TWENTY-ONE

"THE HOUSE WENT CLEAN"

JOSEPHINE WOULD PROBABLY HAVE CHOSEN to go suddenly and unconsciously, in the hour of her triumph. Instead, she lived on for over two years, always hoping that she could return to her great love. "If only somebody will write a play about an old lady in a wheel-chair, I'll be back." Without the theater, of which she had for so long been a part, there was no real life for her.

She did manage two or three television appearances, but they involved many difficulties. For *The Meanest Man in the World* on the United States Steel Hour (in July), she had to be completely wired for sound. Paula Trueman, who stood by in case of an emergency, has told how this arrangement was managed.

On her head, well disguised among the curls and waves of the hair-do she used for the part, was a pair of ear-phones such as telephone switchboard operators use. These were connected with a battery fastened to her belt in back where it never showed. Thus there was a direct line to Sidney Lumet, the director of the show, in the control room. He read the speeches to her if she faltered and was uncertain of her next line, and she in turn spoke them.

She managed beautifully, and no one was the wiser. But that was the last time.

When she was able, she went to watch others doing what she wanted so badly to do herself. Loyal friends stood by to take her to plays, concerts, and broadcasts when she wanted to go. Once she made up her mind to go under her own steam. Frederica Going wanted to call for her, but she said very positively that she would meet her *at the theater*. The play was *The Rain Maker* with Geraldine Page. "Freddie" waited in the lobby, but there was no Josephine. Loiterers about the box office went inside, the houselights were extinguished, and the curtain went up. Still no Josephine. Really alarmed now, Frederica went to the telephone and called the Essex. Mrs. Hull had gone out.

Frederica went out onto the sidewalk just in time to see the missing person tumble out of a cab, her arms full of packages. She stopped to pay her fare, plus an exorbitant tip, and reached the sidewalk sadly short of breath. She was sorry to be late, but she had had to stop and buy some presents for heaven knows whom.

At last Frederica got her inside and, chaperoned by an usher with a flashlight, they proceeded uncertainly down the aisle to a row near the footlights. "Do you think she'll make it?" the usher asked nervously. People turned and stared. That was quite all right with Josephine. Far more than when she was on the stage, she relished a grand entrance. Finally reaching the proper row, she pushed herself in and sank down into a seat behind Charles Coburn, tripping over the feet of Brooks Atkinson, who was on the aisle. Clutching those of her bundles she had not dropped, she settled down to enjoy Miss Page.

"I can't hear a word she says!" Freddie tried to hush her, but Coburn turned around and told her she was right.

"What's the matter with her? I can't understand a word she says!"

Somehow Miss Page managed to carry on despite these distracting interruptions. If Josephine had only recalled her own preachments, she would have noticed how superbly the young actress "listened," but all she could think about was her "bad diction."

Then came April 23, Shakespeare's birthday and Ladies Day at The Players. Josephine could not think of missing one of her favorite occasions. There Sylvia Field Truex saw her for the last time.

> It was after her illness and I wouldn't have known her—
> so thin and tiny. I had greeted her, and then someone said Mrs.
> Hull wanted to leave. I helped her down the stairs and into a
> taxi—then I wept.

At Essex House matters were rapidly getting out of hand. Books and letters were strewn about the place. Even under the bed were stacks of unopened envelopes and unpaid bills. Officials at the bank were becoming increasingly perturbed. The signatures on her checks were often indecipherable and could not be honored. What would happen if she could not write at all? When relatives attempted to intervene, Josephine was adamant. She would brook no interference—she could manage her own affairs, and she WOULD. At last Callie Bement, one person Josephine would listen to, decided that the time for temporizing had passed. Through her friend, Mary Ward Crawley, she learned of a competent colored woman who was looking for a position. She told Josephine that she simply had to have a maid and she was sending one. That is how Mabel Carter came to the Essex.

One day in September she presented herself at the door of Room 607. Josephine received her with gracious cordiality, asked her to be seated, and settled down for a formal call. When Mabel asked if she wished to employ her, Josephine seemed surprised, as if she thought the whole matter had been arranged. She asked Mabel to come three days a week; later friends saw to it that she came every day.

Although at first Mabel was cautioned to touch nothing, after she had won Josephine's complete confidence, she got permission to do some straightening up, and the apartment took on an appearance of orderliness it had not known for months. This was a good thing, because many visitors dropped in. They were enthusiastically welcomed. The hostess wanted to talk shop; she was hungry for the smallest crumb of theater gossip. With Mabel to chaperon her, she also got about more. Sometimes they would go to Callie's for supper. It was understood that Mabel, like Margaret and Selena before her, was strictly a member of the family, to be treated accordingly. There was to be no nonsense about that. As Christmas approached, a great deal of shopping had to be done. Josephine's gifts became more and more prodigal. At the shops floorwalkers and clerks made a great fuss over her, installing her in comfortable chairs and spreading their wares before her. The amounts she spent caused her friends what used to be known as "conniption fits," but they had to do their worrying in silence, at least when she was within earshot.

Sometimes in the evening, after Mabel had gone home, she would call Frederica, and with her go cruising about the theater district gazing at the bright lights and resplendent marquees.

Once, years before, after having dinner with her, Archer O'Reilly, Jr., and his wife Mary, hurrying to make their train, had been compelled to let Josephine out of a cab near Times Square. They were perturbed, but not she. "These are my people," she had said, indicating the Broadway crowd, and tripped off confidently into the throng. But "her people" had sometimes come a long way to reach Times Square. One evening in August, venturing out alone, she fell on Fifty-seventh Street. Close at hand, some young soldiers on leave who were seeing the sights of the city, played good Samaritans. Rather awed to discover whom they were rescuing, they hustled her into a cab and took her home. There, a few days later, she received a solicitous letter from one of them, a boy named William Burke, who had seen her in *Harvey* and who now was anxious to know how she was getting along. She thought again, "How nice people are!" Her people. But her sorties became steadily less frequent. Usually she stayed at home, reading or watching television. She loved baseball, which reminded her of the Harvard-Yale games of her girlhood. Often she and Mabel would sing as they watched. Generally she was cheerful, laughing at little things that amused her, and regaling her maid with entertaining reminiscences.

Things went along after this fashion until April, 1956, when a serious stomach upset precipitated by corn beef and cabbage sent her back to the hospital, where she had another stroke. It was a slight one that didn't detain her long, and soon she was back in 607.

By this time she was ready to concede that she must let someone take charge of her affairs. She chose Joan's husband, Charles Turner, whose alfresco wedding in the garden at Lyme she had enjoyed fourteen years before, and signed the necessary papers to give him power of attorney. It took him months to plow through all the accumulated bills, uncashed checks, and letters—which were still pouring in. One day he brought a projector and showed her the movie of *Harvey*, and she enjoyed hearing the familiar lines again. His kindness and thoughtfulness won her deep affection and entire confidence. Much as she had hated the idea of surrendering her independence, now that it had been done, she felt great relief and peace of mind.

In May she suffered the last great sorrow she was to know. Jane O'Reilly died in St. Louis. They had been intimate friends for over fifty years, and she couldn't speak of her without tears. "I've lost my best friend—my sister."

Of all things Josephine dreaded most being shut up in a nursing home, and Charles promised he would never send her to one without her consent. She did, however, agree to a short stay in a place by the sea in beautiful Easthampton so that Mabel and the nurse might have much-needed vacations. On her return to the Essex, she suffered a distressing spell of melancholy, that she seemed to be unable to shake off. One Sunday she was driven up to the Turner's place at Westport, and they offered to fit up a cottage for her on their property, where she could stay with Mabel and the nurse. But she couldn't bear to be out of sight of Central Park, near which she had lived for so long. Contrary to the impression of some of her friends, there was no immediate financial problem, now that her affairs had been untangled. But she required round-the-clock nursing, and her expenses were mounting to frightening figures. For the present these could be met, but uncertain as was her hold on life, the doctors could not foresee how long conditions would remain unchanged. Some economies, therefore, had become imperative. Although the nurses could not be dispensed with, the spacious suite at the Essex was no longer needed. Luckily Charles found in the Berkeley a bright, cheerful apartment, that, in addition to a living room and a bedroom, had a terrace on which Josephine could sit and enjoy fresh air and a pleasant view. She liked it so much that she told him to rent it, and early in October, with the aid of Shelley and a friend, he moved her and her possessions into it. Immediately her natural cheerfulness reasserted itself and she seemed to be contented.

In less than two weeks, however, another stroke sent her back to the hospital, with Mabel going along to keep her company. The bond between the two had become so close that without her Josephine was bewildered and lost. She was wholly dependent on the selfless devotion of her friend, and Mabel was at her side during all her waking hours.

This was fortunate, for one day a strange man walked uninvited into the room. Claiming that his wife was Josephine's goddaughter, he said he had come for the Oscar, which he seemed to know they had brought with them. When Mabel's protests had no effect, she threatened to call the police. At that he fled.

In February the doctors said that there was no longer any hope of improvement, and that Josephine should be moved to a hospital for incurables. She was taken to St. Barnabas, to a large, sunny room, newly redecorated. Most of the time these days her mind was in faraway places, but when she was lifted from the ambulance and saw the little park that surrounded the hospital, she looked about with obvious pleasure and murmured that she hoped to sit out in it in her wheelchair.

The doctors said repeatedly that an average constitution would have succumbed long before this to the series of strokes she had suffered, and that she might live on for some time. But very soon a change set in, and it was clear that the end was not far off.

On March 12 she died very quietly.

Of course she must be buried beside Shelley in Newtonville. She had survived him thirty-eight years. First, however, there was a service in her church, the Church of the Transfiguration, and for a day she reposed in the Chapel of St. Joseph. A silent line filed past her, professional friends, and strangers who had known her only across the footlights, truck drivers in their working clothes and bellhops in their uniforms. All her life she had projected warmth and love. Now they were returned to her.

Upstairs in the Guild Hall some of the members were rehearsing a play. Suddenly someone stopped short. "Oh, we forgot! Mrs. Hull is downstairs."

"Keep right on," said Helen Morrison. "She'd love it."

If it may be said that anyone could enjoy his own funeral, Josephine must have liked hers. It was on a clear, sunny day, and there was not an empty seat in the Little Church Around the Corner. As the box office men say in the theater—

"The house went clean."

BIBLIOGRAPHY

MOST OF THE MATERIAL for this book was obtained from miscellaneous unpublished sources and from conferences and correspondence with friends and associates of Josephine Hull. It would be impossible to mention all of them in detail.

In her diaries Josephine Hull left a complete record of her life for over half a century, from 1897 through 1953, with only two periods omitted. She did not keep the diary in 1898, nor from April to December of 1899. The last entry was on December 20, 1953, less than four years before her death. Each diary was jotted down in a small line-a-day that admitted of no embellishment. Although most entries seem to have been written when they say they were, there were times, as on the death of her husband, when they had to be filled in a few days later.

In the practice of her profession, Josephine Hull was meticulously methodical, but her private life was pursued in a delightfully haphazard manner. In keeping her diaries she bothered not to separate the wheat from the chaff. She did not distinguish between the important and the trivial. Her various successes, Shelley's proposal, and her marriage are given little or no more space than the cleaning out of closets and the washing of her corsets. She was given to filling any left-over space with exclamations of delight or of grief.

In addition to the diaries, there was available a collection of scrapbooks containing programs, reviews, and feature articles relating to her own career and that of Shelley Hull. By no means all the newspaper articles are identified. There are also letters to and from relatives and friends.

The items named above are in the possession of Mrs. Hull's nephew and executor, Mr. Charles L. Turner of Westport, Connecticut.

Another collection of letters and cards, written by Mrs. Hull to Mrs. J. Archer O'Reilly of St. Louis, is now in the possession of the author.

About two hundred letters were received by the author from Mrs. Hull's friends and colleagues, and from various libraries to which he applied for information.

PUBLICATIONS OF RADCLIFFE COLLEGE
(Chronologically Arranged)

Radcliffe College, "Class of Ninety-nine." *Yearbook.*

Stevens, Elizabeth. "Radcliffe Dramatics, a Five Year Retrospect," *Radcliffe Magazine*, March, 1901.

"Decennial History, Radcliffe College, Class of 1899." 1909.

"Thirty-fifth Anniversary Report on the Class of '99, Radcliffe College, 1899–1934."

Cannon, Cornelia James. "In Memoriam, Josephine Hull," *Radcliffe Quarterly*, August, 1957.

McCord, David. *An Acre for Education.* 1958.

"Half a Hundred Radcliffe Women." Undated.

MISCELLANEOUS PUBLICATIONS

Barrymore, Ethel. *Memories.* New York, Harper & Brothers, 1955.

Burke, Billie and Shipp Cameron. *With a Feather on My Nose.* New York, Appleton-Century-Crofts, 1949.

Chase, Ilka. *Free Admission*. Garden City, New York, Doubleday & Company, 1948.

Chase, Mary Coyle. *Harvey*. New York, Oxford University Press, 1953.

Gresham, W. L. "Comedienne from Radcliffe," *Theatre Arts*, June, 1945, 346–52.

Harding, Alfred. *The Revolt of the Actors*. New York, William Morrow & Company, 1929.

Kaufman, George, and Moss Hart. *You Can't Take It With You*. New York, Farrar, Scott, & Cudahy, 1937.

Kaufman, George, and Howard Teichmann. *The Solid Gold Cadillac*. New York, Random House, 1954.

Kelly, George E. *Craig's Wife*. New York, Samuel French, 1926.

Kesselring, Joseph. *Arsenic and Old Lace*. New York, Random House, 1941.

Kinne, Wisner Payne: *George Pierce Baker and the American Theatre*. Harvard University Press, 1954.

Index

INDEX

Pleasant Valley, Conn.: 104, 107, 125, 168, 177

Plohn, Mr.: 52

Pollard, F.: 73

Pollock, Allan: 167

Pons, Helene: 238

Poor Jo: 125

Portland, Me.: 9, 24, 53, 60–61, 107, 182, 212, 260, 278

Portland, Ore.: 128

Post, Guy Bates: 85–86, 88, 92–94, 106, 154, 162

Powers, Francis: 54

Powers, James T.: 174

Powers, Tom: 172

Prince, Dr.: 176

Prince of Pilsen, The: 42, 48

Princess Perfection, The: 23–24

Princeton, N. J.: 225

Prisoner of Zenda, The: 16

Producing Managers' Association: 155, 157

Providence, R. I.: 84, 87, 189, 192

Pulitzer Prize: 136, 179, 182, 229, 259

Queen of Chinatown, The: 61

Queen Victoria: 174

Quinteros Brothers: 172

Radcliffe College: 7, 10–14, 17, 19, 22–26, 29–30, 33, 36, 40, 52, 112, 120, 133, 192

Radcliffe College Glee Club: 17, 23

Radcliffe Magazine: 11

Radcliffe Sesqui-Centennial: 194

Radio Guild: 207, 222

Rainbow, The: 124

Rain Maker, The: 289

Red Bank, N. J.: 96

Reignolds, Catherine M.: *see* Mrs. Erving Winslow

Reik, Dr. H. O.: 132

Reiland, the Reverend Dr. Karl: 144–45

Repton, Leila: 93

Revolt of the Actors, The: 155

Rhodes, Harrison: 133

Rice, Adams: 162

Richmond, Va.: 127, 249

Riley, Lawrence: 272

Rittenberg, Henry: 269

Rivals, The: 173–74

Road to Yesterday, The: 82–83

Roberts, Florence: 118

Rochester, N. Y.: 83, 93, 183, 192

Rodgers, Richard: 282

Roger Bloomer: 173

Rolfe, Charles J.: 19–22, 112

Rolfe, William J.: 20

Rolling Stones: 130

Rollins, Leighton: 218, 220–21, 258

Rollins Theater School: 258

Romancers, The: 31–32

Roosevelt, Mrs. Franklin D.: 258

Roosevelt, Mrs. Theodore, Jr.: 258

Rosmersholm: 176

Ross, Elizabeth: 265

Ross, Tony: 246, 259

Rostland, Edmond: 31–32

Rowan, Frank: 154, 180, 183, 185

Roycroft Inn: 83, 204

Runaway, The: 124

Sacramento, Calif.: 248

Safford, Tom: 145

St. Agatha's Protestant Episcopal School for Girls: 134, 159, 182, 196, 207

St. Barnabas Hospital for Chronic Diseases: 293

St. John's Protestant Episcopal Church (Newtonville): 30, 146

St. Louis, Mo.: 72–73, 75, 79, 116, 125–26, 173, 248–49, 250, 292

St. Paul's Chapel (Chicago): 98, 100, 103, 196

309

Dear Josephine has been cast on the Linotype in 11½-point Caslon Old Face. It is an exact and faithful reproduction of the original Caslon letter designed by William Caslon in the eighteenth century. Because of its enduring character and simplicity, Caslon Old Face has been selected for this volume.

UNIVERSITY OF OKLAHOMA PRESS

NORMAN

22436

THE AUTHOR

WILLIAM G. B. CARSON took two degrees from Washington University, St. Louis, where he later taught English and dramatics. Now professor emeritus, he lives in St. Louis and continues his research and writing. He is the author of three one-act plays, as well as three books and many articles on the theater. A personal acquaintance with Mrs. Hull led him to write this lively account of her career.

UNIVERISTY OF OKLAHOMA PRESS

NORMAN